-THE-
BLEEDING
TREE

A Pathway Through Grief Guided by Forests, Folk Tales and the Ritual Year

HOLLIE STARLING

RIDER

1

Rider, an imprint of Ebury Publishing
20 Vauxhall Bridge Road
London SW1V 2SA

Rider is part of the Penguin Random House group of companies
whose addresses can be found at global.penguinrandomhouse.com

Penguin
Random House
UK

Illustrations by Sindre Petterson

First published by Rider in 2023

www.penguin.co.uk

A CIP catalogue record for this book is available from the British Library

ISBN 9781846047411

Typeset in 12/15pt Bembo Book MT Pro by Jouve (UK), Milton Keynes
Printed and bound in Great Britain by Clays Ltd, Elcograf S.p.A.

The authorised representative in the EEA is Penguin Random House Ireland,
Morrison Chambers, 32 Nassau Street, Dublin D02 YH68

Penguin Random House is committed to a
sustainable future for our business, our readers
and our planet. This book is made from Forest
Stewardship Council® certified paper.

MIX
Paper from
responsible sources
FSC
www.fsc.org FSC® C018179

AUTHOR'S NOTE

The five folk-inspired fictional passages in this book – 'Burial Tree', 'Devouring Tree', 'Tree of Ghosts', 'Bleeding Tree' and 'Shrine Tree' – are presented in the spirit of kinship and connectedness. I have, however, been careful to preserve the essence and specificity of narratives and motifs that come from cultures other than my own, using, where possible, the nomenclature that would be recognisable to people of that heritage.

While it is comforting to perceive the universality of human experience, it is important to resist the appropriation of stories. Stories are cultural artifacts as any other. All of them belong somewhere and still belong to descendants living today, with each possessing intricacies that are themselves meaningful and sacred. It is the differences in the interpretation of death, bereavement and mourning that we celebrate as much as the similitude.

Any parallels drawn between such stories and my own experiences are presented with this intention.

This book contains cultural depictions of suicide, and discussions of suicidal ideation and the act of suicide.

CONTENTS

-WHEEL *of the* YEAR-

YULE	December 20*th*-23*st*	Winter Solstice
IMBOLC	February 1*st*	Spring Begins
OSTARA	March 19*th*-22*nd*	Spring Equinox
BELTANE	May 1*st*	May Day
LITHA	June 19*th*-23*rd*	Summer Solstice
LUGHNASADH	August 1*st*	First Harvest
MABON	September 21*st*-24*th*	Autumn Equinox
SAMHAIN	November *1st*	New Year

INTRODUCTION

Ghost at the Feast

'You don't pick october in the Yorkshire Dales if you're worried about the weather!' I'd breezily told everyone, a tone I'd tried to calibrate between homespun congeniality and a circumspect wisdom of the countryside, neither of which I remotely possess. But after several days of watching grey mist spooling into the ancient Wharfedale valleys I'd abandoned the pretence. It was difficult to maintain a veil of airy unconcern when the twitch above my left eye had once or twice in the last few days bounced the glasses clear off my face. I'd made up prayers and pacts in my head, offered tithes (to whom I couldn't tell you – the Met Office?). So sudden was my total belief in the power of arcane gods to control the coming of the rains that I'll need to stay away from any charismatic leaders of death cults for the rest of my life. So, when I opened the curtains on the morning of my wedding, you'll appreciate that about 300 volumetric pressures of scalding anxiety dispersed like unlidding a boiling pan.

Blistering autumn sunshine. A smell of dull earth steeped in the wetness of deep virile roots, delicious and woodsy. The desiccated starfish of sycamores and horse chestnuts idling in the benign breath of the morning wind. The sort of day that feels stolen from summer, turning up later in the back of a drawer, an unexpected and soon-to-diminish bounty.

Perhaps this is where any other chronic catastrophists

reading this might jump ship. 'We were with you with the fretting and the bargaining,' they'll say (the catastrophists), 'and yes, okay, wrt the sunny day, but what about all the other things that can still go wrong? Nah, looks iffy to us.'

It was a compelling point and one that was tempting to spend 45 minutes in the shower contemplating, but for once I didn't want to hear it. Here's why. Natural catastrophists will instinctively register the change in intonation, but anyone else must pay close attention to the following two sentences. As I saw the honeyed day I'd prayed and cajoled for laid out at my feet on the morning of my wedding, for once I didn't think: *Everything will be okay?* Instead, I thought: *Everything will be okay.* Subtle, yes, but the difference is the security of certainty. A promise on a Post-it versus cold granite.

But now look at me! Chastened, out of breath and wheezing, banging on the sports hall door on the second Tuesday of the month, pleading to be readmitted. Catastrophists, I'm one of you! Take me back! It was hubris! I read too many magazines! I did my best but it got me in the end: the dreaded bridal palsy! It messed with my mind! And maybe they'll consider flicking the light switch and ducking down below the trestle tables for a minute but of course they'll relent in the end, they're a pretty tractable bunch ('Okay, then, don't let me back in the club – what's the worst that can happen?') To them and you all I can offer in my defence is this: weddings do weird things to a person and should probably be banned.

Richelle had run to the main building of the old coaching inn we were staying in to fetch sausage sandwiches and a round of tea for me and Mum. Shimmering Richelle; a work friend from both of our first years in London, a companionship forged in clinging on to an identity-crumbling service job all day and trashing the management in a Sam Smith's right after. She liked *Seinfeld*, traditional English steamed puddings, and the type of really rancid thrash metal that the CIA use at their rendition black sites. We came to depend on one another. Keeping up the friendship had been the easiest thing in the world and she was here temporarily from her relocation to Melbourne to be my best woman. At the time Richelle was a hospital educator working with seriously and terminally ill kids, so an actual angel inexplicably walking the earth just for my big stupid party. I kept looking at her; the entire day she took on the quality of a mirage, a not-quite-real figure that floated about the place serenely, as if on castors.

When Mum's mother-of-the-bride nerves were about to reach flashover Richelle grabbed her hands and started painting her nails so she couldn't flap about anymore. Just before we piled in the taxi Richelle ran back to the room when she realised I wasn't wearing the earrings I'd tediously deliberated over for many weeks on WhatsApp. Basically: she's *my* Australian and you can't have her, but try and find someone as alike as possible and don't let them go. I want to say that now in case I forget with the tonal downshift this introduction will soon take.

We were all on our way to a little pub with its own little barn in a revoltingly perfect little village named Appletreewick. So tiny it didn't even have a shop. Impending doom allayed, it was all now going to my head rather quickly. My guests were being bussed in from the only town in the area. I was already tipsy on the delirious vanity of holding 60 people captive in the middle of nowhere, knowing they were there to give me compliments for 12 hours straight. I pictured walking in and breaking the hearts of half the congregation as they shook their heads in the direction of my patient groom – *lucky, lucky man*. All this effort and expense just so I could behave like some sort of child emperor. Weddings! Ban them!

I had a fair-to-middling practice run at humility when on the way inside the venue a little girl on a walking holiday with her parents made me kneel down so she could whisper in my ear that I looked 'very beautiful, like a princess'. Moments later, when Dad first saw me in my wedding dress he very quietly said the same thing. This time though I stopped being a conceited dick and just thanked him. It wasn't really something he'd say normally and I knew he'd have pepped himself up to get over the discomfort.

'Very proud ... very proud of you ...'

His display of vulnerability brought me back from the fantasy land I'd been in all morning. It hurt me a little. It made me feel complicated emotions that I'd usually try hard to bat away. This isn't nice to admit, and I'm well aware how egotistical and bratty it sounds but I had a little sting of irritation: *Could I please just have a period of time* on my wedding day *when I just feel uncomplicated happiness? Just feel what it's like to be a bride?* Not also the uneasiness of being a party in a father–daughter relationship I'd spent 31 years trying to understand and wasn't any closer to that day. Not also the fretful uncertainty of whether 'all this' would be 'too much for Dad'. I wanted the day off.

He seemed stressed and when the celebrant came to give us the instructions of when to enter, on which side we needed to sit, etc., he paid very close attention. I could see he wanted dearly to do a good job for me, and I felt guilty. I took his arm and found it tensed up and hard as rigor mortis.

And then the music started and it was all about me again.

> There are places I'll remember
> All my life, though some have changed.

I take Dad down the aisle; now the sun is streaming through the barn windows, and he's smiling and I'm smiling.

> Some are dead, and some are living,
> In my life, I've loved them all.

I walk him to the front, make sure he knows where to sit and then I go and get married.

Michael, my now husband, is an empiricist. He acquires information through modelling outcomes based on evidence and probability. Even now I don't think he quite realises the extent to which I differ from him. On the surface I can and do convey logic, but at the heart of it all my stock is in signs, impulse and premonition. My decisions are predicated on emotion. I am not casual; there isn't anything I've brought into being about which I haven't first concocted lengthy and exquisite fantasies. The guiding principle is always: what does this *mean* for me? I find value in the story I can tell myself about it later.

Michael and I have been together since we were 18. Which I know in some people prompts the same unspecified disquiet as those cats that have thumbs or pictures of bottomless bodies of water. I'm bewildered too, to some extent. But somehow, we'd been given the lightning-strike implausibility that as we grew up we only grew closer. Not least because of his understanding of some of the difficulties within my family. Our longevity also meant ambivalence about the ritual of getting married. There was the obvious: marriage was a construct of conservative orthodoxy, little of which appealed to us. But also, we were a formidable battalion of two and incoherently happy. Who really cared about getting it in writing?

All hesitancy I'd had about marriage, however, melted away once I realised it was the ultimate opportunity to win at meaning. By which I mean everything on our wedding day was practically convulsive with significance. My earrings? Two white starlings in art-nouveau drop pearls, for the surname I was soon to have. You want more bird symbolism? See the cords we used for the pagan handfasting part of the ceremony – yes, handmade, each ribbon chosen to represent a different grandparent, obviously – and look closely, there is a pair of appliqué birds running throughout. And then of course we had to go all in and hire a barn owl as ring-bearer, who announced himself in a mid-ceremony conflagration of wings burning a flight path towards the best man's out-stretched glove to gasps of wonder. The date? Halloween, of course: 13 years to the very day we'd had our first kiss. In gratifying synchronicity we were both aged 31 and this longform love spell, as I'd taken to calling it, was about to reach its conclusion on the 31st day of October, *Samhain*. The very night that pagan societies in the Celtic and druidic traditions believed the boundary between the worlds of the living and the dead to be at its thinnest. A playful space reverberating with liminal potential. If ever there was a night ripe for the transition of two untethered souls into what I hoped would be the corporeality of enduring union, this was it.

Dad's tie was mustard yellow, to complement the dahlias (grace, commitment) in my autumnal bouquet. I'd had it made by hand and screen-printed with the Strawberry Thief, a Wil-liam Morris design that mirrored the place settings and the yards of bunting that hung from the beams of the cruck barn for our wedding breakfast. Michael wore a rust-coloured tie in the same print, Fintan, the best man, an olive-green one. If you'd asked me then why I'd chosen those colours I would have said that autumn itself was about transformation, that the leaves, ranging from light to dark, symbolised the passage of a woman from one family into the heart and hearth of another; from bride to wife. But really these colours, particu-larly the warm honey of Dad's tie in the crucial first look my guests would get of me, looked very flattering set against the cool oyster of my wedding dress.

Ten months later I would have the same thought as I looked

down at Dad wearing the same tie. It was pretty picked out against the white satin interior of his coffin.

Tomorrow will be my first wedding anniversary. For most of the world the year has been dominated by Covid-19, so I knew my hopes for a little weekend break in Budapest or Bordeaux were dead on arrival. Currently London is in lockdown, so no restaurants either. So then, Michael suggested, we would curl up, open the last bottle of wedding Malbec and look through the photos together, make a night of it. Which would have been more than satisfactory except that I can't look at them anymore. The prints are in the box they came in and I still haven't backed up the files. What am I supposed to do with the pictures of Dad walking me down the aisle? Dancing to the festively dressed skeleton jazz band I'd hired, swinging me round by my arms for the first time in living memory? Even in the ones without him, all I can think is, *Look at this stupid happy bitch, she didn't know what was coming*.

I said I wouldn't get drunk at my wedding or at Dad's funeral because it's not very elegant, is it? Turns out I'm not very elegant. At the wedding I clocked my friend Tom was wearing a baker-boy flat cap and demanded he swing me round in circles like Jack and Rose in *Titanic*, an amateur choreography that ended with me slammed into a small pile of broken glass, cackling, my backside in a puddle of red wine that cost £135 plus VAT to only partially remedy. At the funeral it was a hip flask and, at the wake, a somewhat illegal lock-in at Dad's local, many half measures of white wine, misplaced on several tables while I cut about, deranged with hostess energy, making sure everyone was topped up and demanding stories off schoolfriends I'd just met. I retain little.

A wake is a strange thing. Wakes are ritual spaces for

collaborative morbidity that to the British is hardly ever permitted. They are speakeasies for mortality contemplation. No parenthesis is required, the stories that are shared at wakes are not expected to have happy endings. The audience is impeccable: rapt, captive, tending towards the sentimental, craven for the words that offer impossible substance to the one soul conspicuously absent. At a wake we take our turn to tell our stories, dispatching the details generously. All death, any death, becomes relevant to the discussion. To the bewildered and grieving it is satisfyingly masochistic.

I was perched on an upturned barrel in the saloon bar of the beachfront pub when my Auntie Ros, Dad's eldest sister, casually threw out a detail that made my chest feel suddenly empty of all its contents.

'Emma, your great-*great*-grandmother on my – your dad's – side, had *nineteen* children. She died in labour with her twentieth baby! At *thirty-eight*.'

It was a little past 10.30 in the morning, the pocket that held my hip flask wasn't as heavy as it had been earlier, and a kind someone had just returned my most recently abandoned wine glass from a windowsill. Even allowing for that I was slow with the calculations.

A couple of pairs of twins? More than, even. Or it'd have to be something insane like quintuplets. Emma must have been pregnant for two decades. My creeping nausea wouldn't allow me to contemplate the physical implications so I thought instead of the logistical: 20 winter coats, 20 inoculation schedules. Until I realised, of course. Those 20 children didn't all make it to adulthood. This was a time when infant mortality was factored into the head count, an unremarkable bit of estate planning. 'An heir and a spare' is for bluebloods; an Irish immigrant fishing family in Grimsby, Lincolnshire, abided by their own domestic economics. Emma's abbreviated life would have borne a lot of heartbreak.

How did she process such unyielding loss? I was in a mid-morning lock-in on the north-east coast of England doing what we do after a funeral: drink heavily and exchange stories. I was probably going to go back home to London and google 'bereavement counselling near me', download an app on mindfulness, get really into running for a bit, get drunk again, 'detox' with another app. Before such things, before the extreme introspection that is commercially available to us now, how did people find the space for grief?

Whatever it was, I longed for it. These people at my dad's wake would disperse as quickly as they had gathered; this sublime, wretched, alcohol-enabled forum of remembering, a couple of hours with the sum total of the social fabric of Dad's entire life – was that it? Was that all I got? Wasn't there anything more I could do, *perform*, wasn't there anything else required of me? *Am I no longer required by you, Dad?*

To continue to have more children after losing a child is the very definition of hope. To be at the pit of what a human can endure yet first to imagine, then to ignite, to kindle and finally to fan into being the belief that things can get better. It said: *Though I may not know what will happen in the future, I do know that there is one.* Right then I didn't. My own father had opted out of mine. At some point, I don't know when (God, I wish I knew when), he too had ceased to see a future. In the early hours of one overcast August morning, during a global pandemic in which I had pleaded with fate for him to survive, he had taken his own life. And with it my timeline, the timeline in which I had a dad.

Something along the way had broken in him. I suspect it was when he failed to contemplate his own early trauma and loss. Maybe the same could be said for the societal abandonment of ritualised mourning. By trying not to think about death perhaps we have lost the tools we need to live. I sensed there was a pathway that had become grown over, and in writing this book that it might be cultivated for others who find themselves deep in the woods. I began to feel that by looking back through my family and the rituals of other families I might find a way to grieve better. My present had stalled utterly, but maybe the past could help realign the track.

These were thoughts that would stay with me for the next year.

As the news seeped out that first morning I'd taken calls with family, but the first person I personally told was Richelle.

11.27 My dad died
11.27 Last night or early this morning
11.27 I'm on my way up to mum now
11.28 He did it himself we think
11.29 I'm sorry

When it's suicide you are always sorry. You are the tax collector of sorries and the federal reserve of sorries, issuing enough sorries to flood the market, hyper-inflating and consequently devaluing both the hard currency and the commodity share price of a sorry, requiring ever more sorries to meet demand, life-savings-in-a-wheelbarrow volumes of sorries. Sorry because you are going to feel compelled to answer this message and not just pretend you haven't seen it on the lock screen whether it is a convenient time for you or not. Sorry because it's going to ruin your lunch. Sorry because everyone dies and – remember! – so will you. Sorry because you will not know what to say to me and this will make you feel alienated and guilty for immediately thinking, *Fuck, fuck, what if my dad killed himself? No, he wouldn't, would he? He's fine, he's fine, thank God,* thank God *this isn't happening to me.*

You picked up my book so you are partly culpable for engaging with the topic, but I'm still sorry. A few weeks after it happened, I was suddenly struck by the thought that I would never again make a new friend. I'm a contentedly antisocial woman in her thirties with a bunch of solitary and unappealing hobbies such as amateur taxidermy, reading plane-crash black-box transcripts and eating in the bath; I've also already found a band of perfect darlings, six or so optimal selections to be my close friends, to whom I adhere limpet-like and actively loathe when they try to expand my circle by introducing me to their other friends, so maybe the spasm of pain that accompanied the thought was a bit ridiculous. But I could just see how it would go. The otherwise pleasant progress of a developing friendship would arrest at a certain point. When I would have to tell them about Dad, in order that my authentic self could be substantiated, or fail to disclose it and curtail forever the promise of truly being known. What humiliating melodrama! And in the same way, as much as I'd like to kick the can down the road, this introduction couldn't have gone any further without acknowledging it. That thing being suicide. The thing that reveals the shape of my bereavement is not flat – shock on the x-axis, sorrow on the y- – but with at least a hidden third dimension, possibly more! The unicycling elephant on the margins of the page. Yes, that's what that noise was. Sorry.

So yes, this is a story whose ending is preordained. But I don't believe Dad's ending always was. You aren't supposed to say this, but I can't escape the thought that I didn't try hard enough to understand and for that failure I bear some responsibility for what happened. I feel the guilt sit heavy within me, even while intellectually I concede the illogic of it. Whenever I'm surrounded by a large group of people, in a big train station or a packed cinema, I have the dizzying thought that all these other biological forms walking about have their own interior lives that are just as rich and dynamic as mine, and it makes me feel sick. It's too much. As much as we may want to with those we love, especially those who are hurting, we cannot see beyond the opaque veil of another person's mind. That's why humans have stories. The stories that last longest, that are passed down through communities and that become animate in ritual, are the more successful in permeating this membrane.

Over his long career the folklorist D.L. Ashliman compiled an expansive library of folk tales called *Folktexts*, many of which he recorded for the first time outside the oral tradition that had kept them alive through many generations. In the introduction, he notes, 'There is probably more folklore emanating from mortals' response to dying and death than any other human experience.' The examples from folklore that he recounts, of portents of mortality, of deathbed revelations, of restless ghosts and unresolved souls, and of the festivals, ritual practice and observances performed by those left behind, show the universality of the human need to share stories about death. For death is a concept equally repellent and tantalising, with a magnetism that draws us all.

Some of these stories are thousands of years old. In these last months of endless, edgeless, ink-black grief I have cast my net towards anything that might help me understand. I have sought folk stories containing cautions that, to my shame, I had barely considered. What it means to be a man, a father and a provider, each wrapped up in deeply rooted notions of male strength, martyrdom and exceptionalism: masculinity itself as a performance of suffering. Fables about dead bodies, 'remains'. So hazy and jet-propulsive were those early days of fresh loss that I never stopped to comprehend what it is I actually feel around burial, or bodily display, disposal and lasting memorial, even as I was being called to make decisions about them. Why are these concepts never discussed until the moment in which you are least equipped? I mean, I come from a long line of dead people: where was the ancestral handbook to this stuff?

Mostly I searched for any inkling that what I was feeling was normal, that I wasn't the first person in history to feel so completely undone. What does it mean that some days I function much like I did before and others I spend incapacitated and shrinking from the world? Or why some days a flicker of sun on my face can thaw my icebound chest enough to breathe a little, but the same sun beginning to bring out the yellow climbing roses Dad planted just weeks before he died, with no one to stake them against the shed, no one simply to see them exist, can send me back to day one? I need to reconsider stories that before I would have found fun but inconsequential yarns: those about dreams, visitations and echoes from the world after this one. I need to comprehend how on earth people came to live with this pain, and continued to live with it year after year after year after year.

But many of the contexts around the conditions of my dad's death and my experience grieving it are contemporary. After all, all folklore that exists emanates from the interpretations by ordinary people of the realities of their lives. Dwindling mental health provision, exploitative labour models, the aggravation of economic disparity, the ambient dread of the pandemic and its interruption to so many cultural and social functions. All these inform the story of a life.

As I sit on this precipice of seasonal change it is that last point I am thinking about. The 2020 pandemic threw so much of our lives into disarray. From the removal of the everyday customs which inform our identities to the suppression of the few ritual gatherings we do still have and hold dear, notably weddings and funerals, everything that gave people meaning was disrupted in some way or another. Meanwhile, the world stopped for everyone at the same time. With old yardsticks of time, labour and productivity abandoned, many people spent a lot of their days just watching, noting the change of seasons and experiencing nature together in a way we never had before. Pagans have a name for this group observance based on the festivals of ancient Celtic and pre-Celtic societies: the Wheel of the Year. Now we are once more paying attention, maybe there are lessons in nature to be relearnt.

Tonight is Halloween, *Samhain*, one year since I was married. The urgent wind outside is whipping up vortex-like in the courtyard of my apartment block, the plant pots on my balcony are rattling like bones, and I am reminded that this night of all nights the curtain between the worlds of the living and the dead is at its most fragile. We need only to reach across.

BURIAL TREE

14°14'07.0"N 120°38'53.2"E
Philippines

THE FOREST EATS DEATH SO that it may live. It was there in the stale breath of the morning heat, bated and braced for the sparkling lash of the overdue rains. It was there in the brown dead-fall of the jungle floor given kinesis by unseen legs, busy and legion. In the perfume of the sweet yellow ilang-ilang spiking the rot with bitter spice and honey. In the footfall of scavengers circling the shell of some magnificent former thing. In the dotted graveyard voids of the canopy's shadow.

'He who does not look back to his origins will not reach his destination' is a Tagalog saying conjured in this autophagous landscape long ago, coined by people who had sustained full lives in the cradle of its vibrations. The woodland had given them food, shelter and protection from intruders, and generation after generation had given their bodies back in kind. Pillars of archives stored in concentric rings.

They went together to choose the tree. His toes were rigid with arthritis but he picked his way through the forest with surprising tenacity. A lifetime's learnt caution gave him a light step even now, barely disturbing the dirt track. The path was freckled with the remaining banaba petals that hadn't been picked for tea while indigo, now brown. She thought he must be in great pain but she hoped in body only. Overnight an owl had roosted high on the roof; they'd woken to find it snoozing incuriously and still as a monk.

Surely they'd gone further than they needed to, she thought, but the words were thick on her tongue. Since the owl had confirmed it there was little point in trying to alter what had been set in motion. And from the murmured yet cogent directions it was clear her father had only one tree in mind. In any case it was time for a break: she fashioned a seat from an overgrown jackfruit and, as she lowered him down by the crook of a trembling elbow, he told her about it.

He'd roamed around these trees as a boy, he said, him and his *kuya* – big brother. Once they had spent a long day foraging for mangoes. Sluggish with sun-sleep he had tried to hop across the crevasse between the roots of a great narra tree and had lost his footing; in breaking his fall had sunk a hand into a furious nest of red ants. Immobile with dumb panic, he had felt himself suddenly lift off the ground. *Kuya* had yanked him up into the narra with one hand, while the other took a palm frond and wiped the writhing glove of ants clean away. Together they climbed to the uppermost branch and threw down chunks of mango to divert the path of the angry mob.

This narra, he said, was one of the oldest, and it peeked out above its neighbours. From the top they could see all the way to the bay; he thought it must have been his first ever glimpse of Manila. The Chinese junks with their white sails like bobbing water birds had been dwarfed by the Spanish galleons, he remembered. Up in their den his brother had shown him a divot where the branches met, a hollow packed with moss to conceal his treasures; two silver dice *kuya* said grandfather had told him to look after, and together they'd taken a nap in the warm milk of the afternoon sun.

They began again but as the day slipped by their pace inched to a crawl, though in the end the narra wasn't all that far from home. She watched as her father's glaucous eyes became wide and wet. This, then, was the tree. The decades had made it a monster, with a bark of crocodile skin that burled outward in a paunch; a fat egg in a serpentine gullet. Being this deep in the wood it had escaped notice. There were trees in the north wider than a man is tall, trees the Spanish chopped down for their boats.

Together the eight of them assembled a hut from the materials they had brought. He sat inside the shelter placidly as the workers turned their attention to the narra. Every time they thought the old man might be asleep he poked his head out and gave them directions.

'A little longer, but not so wide!' he chided. 'I've lost weight, can't you see how handsome I am!'

'You'd have to walk over the mountains to find a man more handsome,' said her mother, who had approached through the forest soft-footed as a lemur.

Two sets of eyes reconciled, encircled both by the wrinkles they had made together. She sat down at his bedside, smiling widely. With his hands in hers he felt able to lay down and rest.

Through the evening they all sang together. With sidelong glances she watched her parents lie in contented silence, her robust *nanay*, her ebbing *tatay*, two halves of a heart, and tried not to be sad. Everyone was in good spirits and that helped. They played games to take their minds off what was coming. Of course none of the food could be taken back to the village, so they ate without prudence and drank deeply. There were jokes. The family – the *sakop* in Tagalog – never leaves alone a person who is about to die.

They used a chisel to make a door and scrapers to hollow it out, but not so hollow that the tree would die. They knew how from the ones who had done it before. There were new religions now and this way was dying, but this was the end her father had always imagined, the sunset of his long day, and she would complete this for him. She had heard of the mountain people who suspended their square coffins from the cliff-face in the clouds. Curled up like a baby once more, a comma in a sentence to the next world. She thought eternity with the view from up there would be nice.

It happened while they paused for water.

Tears trilled from her mother's chin onto the dry soil. She washed her husband's body and smoothed scented resin from the benzoin's bark over skin familiar as her own. They wrapped him in white and recited the prayers.

The shrouded figure was slight but it took all of them to get him on his feet.

The last of the light embered as they moved him into position.

They took off his shoes to prevent the haunting of relatives.

Bound his feet to stop the spirit from roaming.

Positioned him vertically inside the cavity of the tree.

Entombed him there.

She affixed the door. She wanted the last face he saw of this world to be one that he had made.

They didn't leave him alone even then. Death is borne as one. Death creates *sakop*. Every player and part helps the spirit ascend to *Maca*, the village of rest.

They each took a vigil – *paglalamay*. They spent the night there with him. Incantations, songs, stories and thanks.

In the morning they took a meandering route through the forest so as not to bring the spirit with them. They would take visitors for many days, after 40 return here to remember, after one year to collect the bones. And as they began the trail out of the forest there came a tremendous clap as the monsoon shook open the sky with acoustic precision, for the forest was as grand as the cathedrals they were building down on the bay, and now it drank, for it was being reborn.

AUTUMN

M Y FIRST CONCRETE MEMORY IS Saturday, 15 September 1990. I know this because it was the morning after my little brother Lewis had been born. I was three. I'd had some sort of stomach bug so Nanna was with Mum for the birth while Dad stayed home with me. We were on the bus to Grimsby hospital when I tasted the sudden metal flood of hot saliva, turned open-mouthed to Dad to remark upon this novel turn of events, then threw up all over myself and everywhere else.

'Ohhhhhh. Noooooo,' he said.

A kind woman passed Dad a green glass bottle of water for me, and I enjoyed the intrigue of this unfamiliar object and of everyone on the bus being very interested in me. I don't remember what impression meeting my new brother had, if any.

This is the sort of crystalline scene of high drama that often ends up becoming a child's first memory. But my first fuzzy memory is of the night before. It is a sense memory, I don't see it in pictures but in feeling. It is my sticky skin adhering in patches to clammy cotton sheets as I roll deliriously about on a soft surface, graceless as a beached seal pup. It is the air so hot as to be seemingly on fire, oven-roasting in the orange streetlight pulsing in from outside. It is the delirium not just of fever but of smugness, in the big bed with Dad, gleeful at the rare happenstance of having him all to myself, uninterested for the moment in where my other parent might be. A vile wet-sheened grinning little piglet.

23

I don't know this but I also do: if I'd been keeping any-thing down I'd probably been fed that night on fish and chips from Ernie Beckett's in the marketplace. Dad wouldn't have cooked, didn't. There was another time later on, Mum again absent for some reason, Dad having to provide for his disgust-ing kid off school with a bunged-up nose, being handed a big bag of newspaper-swaddled warmness with the words, 'You don't need a plate, do you?' I didn't, Dad, no. Battered had-dock with the scraps, golden buttery chips with so much malt vinegar there was a half-inch sloshing about at the bottom of the tray, peas on the side, doorstep bread thickly buttered, hoovered up with blue plastic forks even though there was cutlery in a drawer within arm's reach. It felt clandestine. I have the feeling Mum wasn't supposed to know because the evidence was taken to the outside bin straight after. Fish and chips leave a pretty distinctive smell though, and I'm sure she returned from wherever she'd been to find her small child's face saturated in chip grease and proclaimed the jig to be up. Nevertheless: chippie tea! Better than that: chippie tea for *din-ner*! Chippie tea for dinner off school in secret just me and Dad! As I grew up we would come to have a complex and often difficult relationship, but when I was really little he was wonderful.

You eat a lot of fish and chips when you have a house full of grieving people. That said, my parents lived in Cleethor-pes, a quintessential seaside resort town of arcades and donkey rides in the crook of where the Humber estuary meets the North Lincolnshire coast, so we always ate a lot of fish and chips. As Lewis and I got older it was no longer a special treat. We could even eat fish and chips for dinner if we wanted (din-ner was what lunch was called in 1995), though, unthinkably to child-me, I wouldn't choose to now if I hope to get any-thing else done for the rest of the day. Me and Michael up from London, Lewis and his girlfriend, Isabella, nipping over from Sheffield for the weekend; even the briefest reunion had to be baptised in dark vinegar and table salt.

It's what we ate on that first night. Obviously, no one was cooking anything that evening, and fish and chips is the quickest and cheapest way to get calories into faces red raw from crying.

I was grateful for a reason to get out of the house. The weather had turned and it was tipping it down as Michael and I walked to the marketplace. I didn't consciously choose Beckett's. Cleethorpes sustains what should be a greatly oversaturated market for chip shops, but in a crowded field Beckett's was Dad's clear preference. Wrapped and bagged, I hugged the hot parcel against my chest and, as Michael popped to Sainsbury's for something for afters, I walked on ahead. I hadn't eaten anything in about 16 hours and, unsupervised and suddenly crazed with hunger, I weedled my finger in through the wrapper which encased a thin cardboard box to extract a single fat chip. All at once I was hit in the face by a vapour cloud of hot vinegar on brown paper mingled with the smell of the rain dropping in torrents around me. By the time Michael had caught up I was already bent at the knees sobbing in a puddle. He picked me up and I emptied great gasping heaves into his coat.

It wasn't just the smell. You see, I'd had change from a 20. *That's cheap,* I'd thought vaguely as we left the shop. But, of course, there had been one less on the order.

Ritual food and funerary feasting

Dad was dead and when you are dead you never get to eat fish and chips again. That was the thing that distressed me most that first night. I wasn't thinking about how he would miss seeing Lewis get married or how he would never meet any grandchildren he might have had; in that moment I was inconsolable that he had left without one last time having this simple pleasure. The uncomplicated joy of a hot meal eaten with family. I was dumbstruck that we would never share one again.

Almost everyone I've spoken to in the Dead Parent Community has some specific attachment to a food item or meal that has the power to briefly bring their absent person back into being. Pink Panther biscuits with a cup of tea, chicken matzo ball soup, Wetherspoon's Curry Thursday tikka masala, a bucket of shucked oysters eaten fresh and still beating on a beach in Brittany. It is the alchemy of seeing some ingredients turn into a tangible essence of a lost person, one that you can hold in your hands and savour when everything else is made of air.

Marking a death with food and feasting takes place in nearly every culture. For reasons of social distancing we didn't have a buffet at the wake, which at the time was a huge relief. Wake buffets are gross and absurd, I thought, the oddest combinations of food thrown together and left to sweat under cling-film by a person enduring the worst days of their life. I couldn't think of anything less appetising. Having thought more on it, I've softened. I realise it's not what the food is that matters but the conditions of its presence. Preparing food is a practical task. More than anything in those first few weeks I had been unmoored by the turbulence of death-shock and all I wanted was practical tasks. Feeding people, providing things that can be portioned, shared, is also a loving reminder that we do not bear loss alone. 'Eat your feelings' indeed or, if you're not quite up to that yet, butter and cut your feelings into crustless triangles.

In the Oaxaca region of Mexico the immediate aftermath of a death sees a ritual gathering lasting nine days, called the *novenario*. Together the whole community eats tamales and mole, hot and comforting reminders of family dinners. Jamaican memorials also last nine nights, during which singing, dancing and the consumption of a strong aphrodisiac goat offal soup known as 'mannish water' is said to encourage the deceased spirit, called a 'duppy', to depart peaceably. The Jewish seven-day mourning period known as sitting shiva involves bringing food to the family of the dead person, customarily crowd-pleasing breads, sweets and cakes that take little preparation and can be picked at while reminiscing. Bagels, lentils and eggs are common potluck items at shiva. They are favoured for their shape; round foods not just to denote the cycle of life but to encourage resilience in the face of tragedy.

Bread is comforting in every culture that makes it but in Italy its gifting between Catholic mourners also reminds the receiver of a spiritual link between life and death. In cultures where the personification of death is a hooded figure that carries a scythe for the 'reaping' of souls, most enduringly in Western Europe from the Middle Ages onwards, the harvesting of wheat for bread has an obvious allusive proximity to bereavement. In medieval Germany, a storybook time before fast-action yeast and hygiene codes, dough was left to rise on a corpse's chest. It was then baked and distributed among mourners, in history's most unappealing example of the doggy bag. Though that is only an entrée to the ancient cultures that practised endocannibalism, the custom of consuming parts of the dead themselves so as to have the essence and traits of the person live on in their descendants. It is believed that some South American indigenous peoples ritually roasted the flesh of their deceased and turned the ashes and ground bone into a sort of porridge to be taken ceremonially.

But while a wake is often the one and only occasion for ritual eating, some cultures hold space for annual recurrence. All Souls' Day, or *Ognissanti*, between 1 and 2 November, is a time to remember all of the souls that have passed on, whether stranger or kin. Across Italy, families prepare offerings for their dead to welcome them temporarily back to the home. In Sicily these offerings popularly take the form of beautiful painted marzipan fruits, while in the mainland *ossi dei morti* ('bones of the dead'), long almond or spiced cookies, are doled out and dipped in sweet wine. Similarly *Día de los Muertos*, the famed Mexican day of the dead festival, a riotous celebration in technicolour, evokes the dead in the sharing of food and tequila. Common choices for the feast are bread rolls shaped with a skull and crossbones, tortillas baked with edible marigold flowers, and cups of dark hot chocolate spiked with chillies, but also specific favourites a loved one enjoyed in life. In this way the festival and any active grieving the participants might be experiencing is both communal and personal.

That food brings consolation feels like a universal truth. In a sea of flowers that we appreciated, my cousin Jane stopping round with a homemade lasagne as big as a kiddie paddling pool was what we needed; it fed us for days. Isabella brought fondant-stuffed pastries and mountains of tiny exquisite Italian biscuits so that there was always an artificial high in convenient reach of hands that didn't know what to do with themselves. Seeing that Mum and I had recently taken to opening the fridge and staring motionlessly into it for several minutes, Michael bought nine different types of cheese to keep the scenery interesting.

The Vietnamese bring food offerings to the shrines of their recently dead up to three times a day every day for 49 days, and then after 100 days a big feast is held to mark the *tot khoc*, the 'end of tears'. Though memorials then continue every anniversary and may involve a ritual exhumation of the bones to be interred into final rest, the end of tears is supposed to mark the family beginning to move on from their loss and re-emerge back into life. This makes me wince as much as it makes me envious. To put a time stamp on 'moving on'?

Inconceivable. Yet the social permission to spend 100 days in the mire but with the certainty, established through an ancestral plumb line leading all the way to you, of knowing the end had a date? What a thought.

I wrote my Dad's eulogy in my childhood bed as I munched my way through the rock-hard coconut candy I'd bought Mum and Dad during our February honeymoon in Vietnam. It was by then long out of date since lockdown, the week we returned, meant I never got to give them it. I was doing it wrong, though. All these examples of food-based folk customs had something in common: company. I didn't realise I was sabotaging any chance I might have at reaching the end of tears. I ate it all alone.

The day before the day that changed everything, I'd been lazing around, quite a few months into what, despite the context, had been the blissful gift of being furloughed from work. I'd used the time away to build a small social media following around 'folk horror', a fusion of all the weird shit I loved. Rural festivals and temples of the occult, local myths and urban weird, sorcery, straw dolls and outsider fears, where the very landscape seems haunted by ancient darkness, all bound up in *Wicker Man* aesthetics. I'd even taught myself small mammal taxidermy and had sold a fair few pieces to other folk horror fans around the world. I think I was investigating why a Morris dancer mouse had got stuck in American Customs when Mum rang.

She said that Dad wanted to talk to me. I didn't understand why there needed to be this preface, but okay. She passed the phone over and I had to turn the volume up to hear him. This was novel; Dad's customary telephone voice was how you might address an unfamiliar bear who had just short-changed you in front of your wife. As usual I'd expected a series of declarative statements about the Conservative government followed by five to seven minutes of questions about my life and finances. But he didn't say anything.

'What is it, Dad?'

He just had a lot on his mind, he said.

In different times that *just* might have been enough. I thought about hopping on a train, but it was 2020 and who could tell when their travel really was absolutely necessary? Lincolnshire's infection numbers had been very low, and I didn't want to be the one to change it.

'Like what? Can you tell me? Is it work, or your back problems? Is it money?'

I knew it wasn't anything with a word though. It hadn't been last time, or the time before.

For the last day, really no more than 24 hours, Dad had been bad again. Mum had taken him to the GP that morning, who'd prescribed Sertraline. He'd taken one dose.

Very gently I reminded him that whenever this had happened before he had taken the pills and they had, given time, made things better. Give it ten days, please, and you will look back and not recognise quite what you are feeling now. It'll be hard but you have done it before, haven't you? It's about taking one day at a time, and Lewis and I are both coming to visit really soon.

He said yes, okay.

It was the voice of a little boy. I gave Mum the helpline of a male mental health charity that was open until 6pm and the Samaritans one for overnight. I don't think he rang either.

Instinctively I'd understood that that 'just' was a plea. However, I didn't quite follow the thought through to its conclusion.

Just don't hate me for this.

I just need it to stop.

Hours later I woke up to Michael on the phone with Mum. He'd noticed my phone flashing repeatedly in the dark. I couldn't believe I'd left it on silent.

In a crisis Michael is the calmest and most reassuring person I've ever known, but I could tell his composed words were tinged with agitation.

'Have you rung the police, Caroline?'

I leapt out of bed.

'Yes,' she was saying, 'they've already gone out looking in all the places he might have gone, they know he is vulnerable.'

I spoke to her and she was ragged, my beautiful mother; how outraged I was by the vocal cords straining her voice out of recognition.

'We're booking a train for the morning, okay?' I told her. 'So we'll be there when he gets in and we can decide what to do then. Remember he's done this before, hasn't he, and he just walks and walks, forgets himself. It drives me fucking nuts that he puts you through this every time, Mum, but he does always turn up.'

When it had happened before, one of Dad's long night-time walks, the catastrophist in me had always pictured him walking into the sea. But I had been recently cured, hadn't I, finally believed that doom-mongering got me nowhere. So I really did believe he'd turn up. Once he went missing for three days. He'd been sick this time for a day and a half. People don't— I mean, not after a day and a half!

I went back to bed. I was almost too mad at him to sleep but I think I got another two hours.

In the morning I packed a bag and, with Mum reporting no update, the two of us decided we should tell Lewis. Lewis was in Italy with Isabella's family, in that little slice of time between lockdowns when you could travel. I woke him up with the news but said there was nothing to worry about, don't change your flight, the police will find him or he'll just walk through

31

the door, bold as brass, wanting to know why everyone was in his kitchen. Lewis chuckled.

About 30 seconds elapsed between that conversation and Mum ringing back. You know when people say, 'I just knew'? Well, I didn't. I really, really, really didn't.

'Oh, Hollie. They've found a body.'

For the irreligious there is no equivalent and yet it feels entirely appropriate. It was like hearing her blaspheme, desecrate. Not just: how can she be saying these words? But: how could she know those words?

'They think it's Rod's ... they think it's your dad.'

Roderick Heenan. Rod. That's his name. I hadn't told you that yet, which may seem like a bit of an oversight in something that has passed under the eyes of multiple publishing professionals before getting near yours, but it's also completely reasonable. Kids are solipsists. Even grown-up kids, for the most part. It's entire years before a child entertains the concept of a parent having an actual name, let alone a whole life before they existed. He was just Dad. Pre-dating all language, to me he was a person that provided.

Even if I only knew him as a father, I think provider was a foundational part of his identity. It began with a shock, when he was just 14.

Family trees and heavy inheritance

Dad was born in 1956, the second child of Marie Todd and John Heenan. Photographs of him as a little boy look to me like pages from the *Ladybird Book of Working-Class Vim and Vigour*, the type of rosy-cheeked cow-licked Boy Scout robustness that might be dispatched by advertisers to cajole a homemaker to buy a tin of Horlicks. The family's bungalow in Humberston, a tidy suburb just up the coast from the penny arcades, was a stable home, though provided as it was by my grandfather John's profession on board a trawler, it came with the ever-present threat of peril. Not to mention stretches of lone parenting for my grandmother, Marie, at home with Rod and the three girls.

I've often wondered if he'd been lonely as the only boy. I know playing football with his dad when he was home was a cherished treat. From talking to my aunties it is clear that for little Rod temper and boredom seem to have been absent an outlet. They recall balls stroppily hurled at the towering conifers that ringed the back yard, and family lore tells of an arrow crashing through the bathroom window when Marie was on the toilet, the curtain of shattered glass parting to reveal the blur of a small boy high-tailing it with a wooden bow under his arm. That these stories of mishap and destructive wantonness hold such appeal is probably because I am reminded of all the times Dad discovered that Lewis and I had settled on a game between us little more complex than 'smashing things', and yelling at the patron saint of children-sent-to-test-us why couldn't us 'bloody kids!' instead find 'something constructive!' to do.

A sporadically present father makes for an excellent disciplinarian, and I'm sure Marie invoked the spectre often, but she herself was certainly no pushover. Being surrounded by women, I think, gave Dad an innate appreciation of their reserves of strength and legitimacy of opinion that can be rare in men of his generation. Certainly throughout his life he spoke to women as equals, so long as they had the attributes he respected (common sense, shrewdness, no airs and graces). As an adult he had female friends, sought his eldest sister Ros's judgement before any major decision or significant purchase and never made me feel like I couldn't do anything I wanted in life. The only time I've ever heard him use a female-specific invective was in reference to Margaret Thatcher (but really, whomst among us?).

His schooling was the belt-and-braces style of English male provincial education in the 1960s: metalwork, woodwork, electronics. He excelled in these, nimble with his hands and understanding by doing. Mathematics and the rivers of the British Isles by rote, hymns every day, a bottle of milk at first break. Never once did he receive a rap on the knuckles for lateness or talking back. Dragged to church on Sundays, his shoes were shined by his own hand, a code of respectability that lasted the rest of his life (and would come to blight my school mornings). At weekends he liked films that had a timely John Wayne turn up on horseback to save the town from a pack of dubiously cast banditos, but mostly he preferred to be outside, exploring the sand dunes during long summer evenings or kicking a ball around with the boys on his road. He was quieter, more timid than his mates but part of the pack, loyal to the end and quick to join in with their exploits. The sixties were drawing to a close, a new decade was dawning, and all being well Rod would develop into a perfectly well-adjusted young man.

Parents are the picture frame of a family. A harmonious exhibit, tastefully flaunting yet load-bearing, structurally integral so as to be apparent only when compromised or missing. On a bitterly cold December night in 1970 Marie was rushed off her feet making Christmas happen in the way women do, trimming the fir with timeworn heirloom baubles, soaking her fruit cake in one last glug of rum before it could be tucked up in a blanket of marzipan and royal icing. Soon she would have a houseful. Meanwhile, 1,200 miles north-west, John left the safety of the galley to walk the deck of the *Northern Queen*, which had a few hours earlier left the port of Ísafjörður and sailed into the fishing grounds off the western coast of Iceland. During the later inquiry no-one could say why he did this. Out there the conditions were treacherous – 'heavy snow squalls' wrote the skipper James Gordon in his log – and the arctic wind pierced John's gloves like a curtain of needles. Visibility was minimal, and as he spun on his heels to find the rest of the crew had vanished he saw nothing but a bravura of whites, greys and then black black black as he was thrown overboard into the chokehold of the North Atlantic. His absence wasn't noticed for several hours. Death by hypothermia in water temperatures just either side of 0°C takes less than 15 minutes.

I'd never been brave enough to ask Dad how he found out. Did he return home fizzing from the last school day of the term, a games day no less, to find his mother's cinematic weeping filling the hallway, her impotent fingers grasping at air, becoming tangled in the telephone cord? Maybe they didn't have a landline; a Navy telegram then? A letter wouldn't have got there, post being what is it just before Christmas. Ludicrously I always pictured two solemn men at the door, downturned faces all black and white angles, weighty with occasion, like the opening page of a hard-boiled comic strip. Did they hesitate before tapping the knocker: '*Four* kids you say? Just before Christmas too, a terrible thing.'

Fourteen is no age to have your picture frame smashed, the portrait it contains warped out of shape. Fourteen is a child who needs his dad not dead, his mum not widowed. Fourteen is also round about ripe for absolute maniacs to start saying things like, 'You're the man of the house now,' and, 'You have to be strong for your mam.' Whether the invitation to become the young family's sole income generator was explicit or implicit, Dad didn't return to school in the new term. Instead, he left to apprentice as a TV repair engineer. Looking into the maw of grief he turned away from despair and towards responsibility, resilience and steadfast dedication to providing for his family. Over the next 50 years he'd do this again and again.

I was 32 when a loss of comparable magnitude happened to me. It's November now, I'm barely three months removed and I go through the motions of my silly little life fairly equably, but from time to time a 16lb bowling ball materialises from the great beyond and is hoofed into my lower abdomen at such a force I have to stop all motion instantly if I'm to remain upright. I'll be at the tills in Superdrug and have to wait for it to pass: the sickening vertigo of having nothing now between me and oblivion. I've no remaining grandparents, Dad's generation was and is the final bulwark in the eventual and inevitable collision with my own mortality.

But however fatalistic and introspective she may be, a half-orphan at 32 will live. A barely teenage boy, though? To suffer the slings and arrows of outrageous fortune and then the universe has the temerity to insist that you don't cower and keen like a pained animal but pack up and ride out for your similarly heartbroken loved ones? It's so very unfair. And it was that way because, what? Because boys don't cry? Because in England in 1970 the superlative in male value was a reductive combination of chest hair, a sober forbearance at the scene of colliery disasters and gamely having your skull caved in by billy clubs at picket lines? Because Marlon Brando gave such a romantic blueprint for young male submerged vulnerability as insolent grit and silent rage? Because grief counselling for children back then was unnecessary, even morbid? Our places reversed, I believe I simply couldn't have coped. My sorrow for him is almost too much to bear.

Heenan is of course an Irish name, an echo from quite a few generations past. Emanating from the emerald pasturelands of County Tipperary in the thirteenth century, the name's Gaelic derivative is likely: *éan* ('bird'); the original clan chief may have been a hawker or bird trainer. After the famine it became a rare surname in Ireland, rarer still in England, though a healthy population made it to North America and Australia where there was more labouring work and, purportedly at least, less overt anti-Irish sentiment. On the UK mainland the name Heenan is still clustered around shipping ports and heavy industrial towns: Motherwell, Sunderland, South Wales, Humberside.

Among this fairly homogenous Celtic diaspora of sharecroppers and stevedores I was impressed to learn of a Cardinal Heenan in our ranks. Supposing we couldn't be related to such an exalted station I googled the name and fell about laughing: the very counterfeit of Dad, uncannily so, sat on an opulent throne in a cassock and mitre and swaddled in a shawl of white ermine, looking like he was about to pop his solid gold crosier down next to the TV remote and ask whether I had got a seat on the train, the price of my ticket, and just exactly in what joke of a first-world country should one have to stand from Doncaster.

The Heenan tree's diffuse branches are heavy with rugby players, wrestlers and bishops; men with a predisposition for scrapping, whether over your immortal soul or in the name of manly sportsmanship. Most vaunted is the prize-fighting bare-knuckle boxer (and part-time rigged-election enforcer) John Carmel Heenan. Heenan's 1860 bout with Tom Sayers, the first to be termed 'the fight of the century' and witnessed by the Prince of Wales, the Prime Minister Lord Palmerston and Charles Dickens, was so bloody, so depraved in its savagery that a whole tranche of regulations (the 'Queensberry rules') was created directly because of it. Imagine being the youngest male descendant of a man who once brained a guy so hard that *all* boxers now have to wear gloves. So much piping-hot masculinity coursing through that bloodline that injured members might be expected to bleed single malt and barbecue propane.

When my father's mother, Marie, died after a stroke in

1993 I struck upon the question that turns every five-year-old kid into an investigative journalist who has just discovered an original and hitherto unexplored angle on what is surely the scoop of a lifetime:

'Dad, what happens when you die?'

'When you die you are just dead in the ground, and that's it, I think. Worm food.'

I remember how his face looked, like I'd never seen it before. Exhausted. It frightened me.

For the second time his world was upended and he had never developed the language to describe it. He had loved his mam so much; he was a boy again. The remainder of his picture frame had been collapsed. I didn't want to test my own for weaknesses.

I didn't ask again.

Legends of fatherhood and the threefold death

For most of us our first dip into our own ancestral well of folk-lore is through the fairy tale. Unlike legends, whose heroics usually demand some grain of confidence in their veracity, fairy stories more often than not encourage suspension of disbelief and contain those elements most appealing to children: monsters, magic and moral certainty. Using stock characters and situations familiar to everyday life, the function of these fables is to instruct: keep to the path, don't trust strangers, always tell the truth. Usually some disaster would befall the protagonist who fails to heed the caution. So it is telling just how often doom is heralded by a family that is fractured in some way.

Bad things especially betide those deficient in the father department. These sorry cases tend to fall into three categories. Tyrannical or oppressive fathers who pit their sons against one another or sabotage their daughter's marriage prospects;

such as the Brothers Grimm's 1857 version of 'Cinderella', wherein the father − you know how catty he gets whenever he's on the gin − makes small talk at a party with the eligible young prince, referring to the object of the boy's blossoming love as 'my dead wife's daughter, who's deformed'. Weak or subservient fathers are the second type, such as those in 'Rapunzel' or 'Hansel and Gretel', who are happy to go along with the diabolical wishes of some hot smokeshow of a step-mother and lock his only offspring up in a tower or banish the kids to starve in the woods. This guy is pretty much the ur-failure in masculine defender (though ultimately the blame lies with the bewitching ways of devilish women, corrupters of good men − truly a tale as old as time).

Finally we have the very worst of the bunch, the absentee father, whether the position is vacant through some short-coming in virility or just by virtue of being dead. The poor wretch Snow White of Giambattista Basile's 1634 version has no father at all, her mother having been impregnated by a rose leaf. Removed of men, I'm sorry to report these are unchecked households utterly amok with women. Abandon hope, all ye who enter. If by some miracle a daughter raised by a lone widow grows up to be good and chaste, unfortunately she is likely also to be defenceless and destitute. Alternative options include hag or slut.

As one folk tale from Italy shows, paraphrased here for brevity, the love of some dads can come at a premium. Yet, happily, even when Pop makes a truly zany parenting call all is well in the end:

Once there was a king who wished to know which of his three daughters loved him most.

'I love you as I do bread,' declared the first.

'I love you as I do wine,' followed the second.

'I love you as I do salt,' said the third.

Salt! Salt is cheap, as common a substance as dirt! Insulted, he ordered his third daughter to be executed. Her sisters arranged for her to merely be banished to a remote cave, bringing their father instead the tongue of a dog to prove his edict had been carried out.

The youngest daughter wandered alone, suffering much hunger and cold, protected by the fairies of the land. One day a prince rode by and, enraptured by the girl's beauty, took her home to be married. A great banquet was prepared to which all the nobles were invited.

At the wish of the bride, salt could be used in every guest's meal except one man's. This man was the king, her father who had ordered her death.

'Give me salt! Without salt my meat is tasteless!' cried the king. 'I see now that my youngest daughter loved me most of all, and I killed her for it! Now I will never see her face again!'

The bride took off her veil and revealed herself to be that same daughter.

The king begged forgiveness but the girl wouldn't hear of it, telling him to let bygones be bygones.

I'm sure this high-stakes psychodrama, entirely avoidable with a very brief exchange of words by way of clarification, is supposed to be a teachable moment in navigating the entanglements of father–daughter relationships, but whatever moral instruction it's supposed to decree I'm certain it's one for which a dog absolutely did not have to be maimed.

Fortunately, some folk stories have a simpler way to demonstrate the value of the male role model.

In the *Shahnameh*, the Persian book of kings, a warrior general named Zāl is everything one could want in a patriarch, including being a silver fox. When his wife is delivering their son and about to die in childbirth Zāl avows to the universe:

'My father abandoned me once; I am not giving up on you.' He summons a giant mythical bird who teaches him to perform the first caesarean section with a magical feather, saving both wife and baby. Most fascinating to me is the depiction of his refusal to repeat the cycle of abuse that so often masquerades as character-building 'tough love' through the male line in such stories. Zāl's sense of responsibility never wanes; he follows the child's entire mythic life, offering fatherly guidance at every point and standing back when required.

Greek mythology, meanwhile, recounts the actions of Peleus, a slightly hapless figure who is always accidentally killing people and then having to flee various kingdoms in ignominy. After what turns out to be quite an ill-matched marriage to the sea nymph Thetis, Peleus (sort of) redeems himself when he returns home to find his amphibious goth wife toasting their newborn son Achilles over a fire pit. Freaking out, the young father rushes over and dropkicks the baby out of harm's way. Unfortunately, Peleus' interruption of the ritual means his mother's spell of immortality is incomplete, and Achilles will have to live with a human weakness after all: his heel. 'Don't you think you're being a tad dramatic, love – over a *heel*? I can foresee absolutely no repercussions to this very specific vulnerability!' says Peleus, but Thetis is already out the door leaving in her wake a single dad, an infant demigod and a premise worthy of a heart-warming two-star nineties dramedy.

Finally, a short addendum for that undersung hero, the stepfather. Aslög is the beautiful queen who appears throughout the Norse sagas, yet she would not have survived infancy had it not been for the ingenuity of her mother's foster father, Heimer, who steps in after the untimely death of the girl's parents. Heimer hides the baby in his lute, and travels from town to town pretending to be a lowly minstrel and playing sweet music to soothe her to sleep.

One commonality to the constructions of folklore fatherhood

is the way in which children must impress or otherwise earn his love in some challenge or trial or simply by being the fairest in the land. A mother's love, meanwhile, is always unconditional. Twentieth-century advertising used this deeply meshed cultural belief to great effect: Dad stepping through the door and hanging up his hat is the high point of the day, kids tripping over themselves to greet the returning workaday champion, all made possible by Pears Carbolic Tooth Powder or Batchelors Whipped Egg Paste or whatever. Dad's love is hard won, thus its prize is more valuable.

Such is the universality of this motif that it was established by Carl Jung as one of his 12 archetypes. To Jungians these are universal primal symbols that unconsciously dwell in the human psyche and are shared by us all in a sort of collective wellspring of memory. Your mind, when casting characters to populate your dreams, may pick from this shared stable of figures. The father symbol, to which all humans instinctively respond, may take the form of king, judge, doctor, leader, holy man, wise elder or, indeed, God. He can be aligned with various tools of penetration (for our primordial reptile brains are not subtle) – the knife, the spear, the ray of sunlight – the latter also a potent image of fertilising power central to this father template. The positive aspect of the father principle suggests law, order, discipline, rationality, intelligence and the spark of inspiration. When our inner authority figure is supportive and benevolent our ambitions are realised and our essential being is empowered.

But with every archetype lies both light and dark aspects, giving rise to the concept of the shadow father or 'devouring father' type. This figure finds expression in many examples from folk tradition; for example, the giant, the tyrant, the executioner or the Devil. Here the father's guidance and protection has degraded to an abuse of power, and his grandiosity, selfishness and hubris becomes a danger.

Nowadays Jung's ideas are not considered a serious thera-peutic tool by most modern psychiatrists, but they undeniably persist in the stories humans have made up and retold and, in the case of our male stock figures, I suggest, they reflect deep cross-cultural truths about masculinity and sacrifice.

Male exceptionality even comes with its own death. The 'threefold death' is the death suffered by kings, heroes and gods across early Indo-European mythologies. It is a literary device which, when invoked, conveys greatness and evidence of prophecies coming true, or else as punishment for insulting the gods in threefold ways. But, as some archaeologists have suggested, the threefold death could also have been a real sac-rificial ritual carried out among the peoples of Western and Central Europe. Supposedly a great honour, if selected you might find it the sort of gift you pretend to be grateful for, being as it is one that saddles you with a quite embarrassingly extravagant death.

In ritual threefold death a person dies simultaneously in three ways. First by hanging, then by wounding or burning, and finally by drowning (or poison, depending on the trad-ition). The French mythographer Georges Dumézil suggests this punishment was for an offence against what he saw as the three functions, the *idéologie tripartite*, across southern Russian, early Germanic, Old Norse, Ancient Greek and Indic soci-eties: the sacral, the martial and the economic, corresponding in turn to the three classes of priests, soldiers and commoners respectively. This manner of death is, quite literally, overkill. King Agamemnon was slain in the bath by his wife after being ensnared in a net with which he was asphyxiated, and then stabbed for good measure.

Evidence for the presence of this ritual in Celtic societies comes from a fascinating copy of Lucan's epic poem *Pharsalia* upon which a tenth-century reader scribbled notes in the mar-gin. Alongside Lucan's description of the druidic human sacrifice to Teutates (Mercury), Esus (Mars) and Taranis (Jupiter) our doodling scholar writes: 'Taranis was propitiated by burning, Teutates by drowning, and Esus by means of suspending his victims from trees and ritually wounding them.' The Romans were famously appalled by what they saw as the barbarity of the Celts and Britons (Diodorus Siculus wrote that the Gauls 'kill a man by a knife-stab in the region above the midriff, and after his fall they foretell the future by the convulsions of his limbs and the pouring of his blood'), so this later addition might be distanced enough from the propaganda to ring true. In any case the Celts were mad for the number 3, and indeed three of their gods were said to be appeased by the sacrificial methods of hanging, burning and drowning. Logic follows that a sacrifice rite covering all bases would surely avoid incurring the wrath of one particular deity.

Curiously, what to the Irish Celts and others seems a severe punishment of a deserving scoundrel, the threefold death feels much more deific and ceremonial in the poetry of the medieval Welsh. The prophet–poet and wild man Myrddin Wyllt (a prototype of Merlin), who Jung would consider another father-template of the 'sage' or 'magician' type, has many stories of the practice associated with him. In one he astounds the court of Arthur by making the outlandish claim that a boy, presented to the mystic three times in different disguises, will die in three different ways. During a hunt the youth trips and hits his head, and falls, unconscious, into a tree that hangs him head-down into a lake, drowning him. Myrddin Wyllt later foretells his own death in the same manner, the auspicious end to a man who spanned the three functions, with an implied self-sacrifice lending credence to his otherworldly mantic wisdom.

I spent my first year in London patrolling the galleries of the British Museum. Whenever I was posted to the Iron Age

Britain galleries on the third floor I'd spend most of my time hovering around the tucked-away corner that was the home of Lindow Man. No other object in the collection captivated me more. This is the male body found in the peat bogs of Lindow Moss in Cheshire in 1984 that was so well preserved on discovery a murder investigation was initially opened up. Due to the weight of the peat upon him for centuries, Lindow Man has a distinctly deflated quality, and an unfortunate shredding incident at some point sliced him clean in half, but his face is unmistakably mortal and to look upon it is humbling. He reminds me of the stretched skull, the anamorphic projection in the foreground of *The Ambassadors* by Hans Holbein, whose distortion evaporates out as you walk around it.

Lindow Man was around 25 when he died, which radio-carbon dating suggests was around the time the Roman conquest reached north-west England in the early 60s AD. Though it is true he could have been the victim of a violent crime, or perhaps even have been executed for criminal misdeeds, compelling evidence suggests otherwise.

On death his beard was well groomed, his fingernails manicured, and his belly was full making him likely a man of means. Perhaps, some have suggested, even a high-ranking druid. But a noble birth did not shield him from a death that was very violent: his body bears many wounds including a vicious blow to the top of the head powerful enough to crack a molar, multiple stab wounds and a broken rib. A garotte of animal sinew was ligatured around his neck and poisonous mistletoe pollen was found in his stomach. After death he was placed face-down in the bog. Some Iron Age experts claim Lindow Man may have in fact suffered the apocryphal three-fold death as a human sacrifice – throat cut, strangled and submerged in the wetlands – and this would have been a powerful offering to several gods. Considering the suggested time stamp, such a drastic and valuable offering may have been an effort to call upon the aid of the three Celtic gods to stop the advancing Roman offensive.

Learning of these rituals brought up a question that I hadn't much considered. Many of these stories may be mythical but Lindow Man isn't; he was a once-walking, -laughing, -dreaming, sentient being whose tangible remains lie for all to see in Bloomsbury. Lindow Man left behind family who had to process and live with not only the reality but the manner of his death. It may be grandiosity but I feel a connection to them. I find myself wondering if this manner, whether it was voluntary or involuntary, likely as it was to have been for a purpose – be it holy appeasement, invocation of prosperity or moral instruction to the community (i.e. a greater good) – made the loss more palatable? Wanted, even. With death so commonplace to Iron Age society, did this auspicious and masculine-coded death give a mortal man a rare proximity to divine greatness? It goes against all instincts to find greatness in my dad's death, but perhaps there is something to interrogate in such a perspective shift that may help to usher my grief into a manageable size.

Jung didn't deny that history, culture and personal context shape these manifest representations of the father archetype, and that all sorts of sources would assist in giving them their specific content. Which is to say I didn't read the Greek classicists as a kid, or even some of the slimmer Norse sagas. I didn't even really like much of the Disney canon, so I'm not sure my notions of father–daughter relationships were particularly influenced by the classic fairy story adaptations beloved of most little girls. (My politics, on the other hand, undoubtedly were; *Robin Hood* and *The Sword and The Stone* stamped into my plastic grey matter a partiality towards wealth redistribution and scrappy little rank-and-file proles under-mining hereditary systems of absolute rule of the sort that would make the too-online flag crowd sputter 'cultural marx-ism' and that a single google of 'Walt Disney personal views' would undo.) No, what gave form to my particular corner of the collective unconscious came from upwards of a thousand hours sitting cross-legged in front of *The Simpsons*.

There is no meditation on the human condition that hasn't been tenderly, and with an irreverence that is surely a necessity in that particular contemplation, encapsulated *par excellence* by *The Simpsons*. Talk about archetypes. Smart, prideful, neurotic and with a tendency towards being an affected little shit: I would say as a kid I was a prototypical Lisa Simpson, but to be honest I've never really outgrown these traits.

I think I can identify when it began. In the mid-nineties pri-mary schools were just introducing 'the issues' to the classroom. My class had been learning for the first time all about the perils of drugs. Finding I didn't have the patience to get all the details straight – who can sit idly by when this social evil was in my own house, nay, my own fridge! – I had elided the menace of lager with that of heroin. Rushing home, I primly trotted into the kitchen and while his back was turned, tipped Dad's half-finished can of Boddingtons down the sink with a self-righteous flourish. In justification, the curriculum apparently hadn't been given a look-over since the sixties, as I vividly remember colouring in a series of thought-bubbles around the subject of mescaline. I mean, I was a nine-year-old in an insular coastal town, not Wil-liam Burroughs about to hit the Mojave. I don't even think ayahuasca has a street value on a Grimsby housing estate.

'That bloody crap they teach you in that school!' Dad yelled when he became aware of my sudden embrace of public health.

I was bamboozled. Dad being negative about anything connected to school? I thought they were all on the same side.

I treated everything either told me as gospel. Now it seems such a minor event to have forced me on the side of what he considered sanctimony and I enlightenment, forever pitting us against one another. Which is why one *Simpsons* episode remains particularly painful for me to watch.

One day Lisa arrives to class to find her usual schoolteacher absent and in her place a supply tutor, Mr Bergstrom, with whom she has a brief, intense and identity-defining emotional affair. He is everything her actual dad isn't: educated, cultured, witty, debonair. At a dinner party the duelling of her two father figures is given explicit reckoning when Mr Bergstrom takes Homer aside to encourage him to be a better role model for his daughter. When Mr Bergstrom leaves Springfield Elementary for another teaching post Lisa has her first experience of grief. Hurting badly she lashes out at hapless Homer, calling him a 'baboon!' and retreating to her room to cry.

At the time I found a kindred affinity in Lisa's experience that wasn't entirely comfortable. I too felt a claustrophobia at what I perceived were the limits on my potential placed by my small town and ordinary life. It was also deeply romantic, especially Mr Bergstrom's parting gift to Lisa on the train platform. That scene filled me with a vague embarrassment I didn't understand, being that I was a very studious kid and 'a pleasure to have in class' yet already sensing the egoism that label invoked in me was unattractive. I didn't know it at the time but I also shared Lisa's vulnerability and the bottomless capacity of little girls to experience trials of the heart so acutely. Her wrangling with abandonment is heartbreaking.

But today this episode produces different yet equally intense feelings in me. I hate how much I see of myself in Lisa's snobbery. I recoil at the presumptuousness of a man who has known his student mere days to *go round to her family home* and *lecture her blue-collar father* on his negligence towards his daughter's spiritual growth, as though such a thing should be gatekept by the professional-managerial class for everyone's benefit. In fact I detest the suggestion that any male role model must be in contest with the biological father, that the hearts-and-minds of little girls is a question of asset ownership, the spoils of the one true hero.

Lisa's myopia is what I can hardly stand. It brings back images of my wretchedness, my pretension, my self-righteousness towards my own father. I hate the thought that I ever lorded my education over him, when all the privilege I have in that area is because of his many sacrifices.

When Marge hears Lisa sobbing upstairs she urges Homer to go and cheer her up. Homer enters his daughter's bedroom all sheepish and awkward, admitting he's never lost anyone and that he can't understand how she feels.

> Now, you'll have lots of special people in your life, Lisa. There's probably someplace where they all get together, and the food is real good and guys like me are serving drinks. Oh well, maybe I can't explain all this, but I can fix your doll-house for you. At least I'm good at monkey work.

He strikes upon a method of defusing the tension, making monkey noises to make her laugh.

Everything I ever broke could be fixed by my dad too. Homer, pitted against his intellectual and social 'better', doesn't resort to the flexing of masculine influence or prowess, but shows Lisa that even if he doesn't understand he'll always be there to mend her when the jagged and uncompromising world injures her tender heart. His is a father type I take more and more stock in, because it was mine too: the fixer, the repairer, the carpenter. The Mender of Things.

It bears repeating that a child is a terrible biographer. As far as I was concerned, at the beginning of the universe my mum and dad were somehow already 30 and 31 respectively. I don't know what Dad was like in his twenties, though I've enjoyed tracing the decade through photos of his preference for hairstyles that could only reach their full aesthetic promise by the wearer sliding over the bonnet of a turmeric-coloured Austin Allegro. I only know the bones of how he courted Mum: buttering up her old man by mowing the lawn for him in exchange for being able to take his daughter out on long bike rides. On Friday nights he took her dancing at the Flamingo in Humberston, gallantly paying the 20p admission for them both. But I can't know what he was *like* back then, his affectations, his verbal tics, his attitude to life. They married and bought their house, a shell of an Edwardian terrace without a boiler, for £13,000 when she was working part-time in a betting shop, he on the dole; what did that feel like? The pride and the exuberance of pulling yourself up on that first celestial rung of adulthood, building a home and life from twigs and hope?

For most of my life Dad had work, but how he felt about it, whether he experienced any disconnection or challenges to his self-worth when the engineering trade for which he trained became all but obsolete by the early 1990s, I don't know. I don't know because I didn't ask.

His unfathomability wasn't limited to great unanswered questions of existential being, but in hundreds of maddening everyday ways. I can only assume his training manual on how one might best baffle his children included the following pointers:

1. Use mysterious phrases but never explain their meanings: e.g. testily entreat children to stop being 'cloth-eared', yet through intonation establish 'buggerlugs' as a term of endearment. Threatening to have their 'guts for garters',

while sounding like a threat of violence, should be delivered with ironic amusement. For fun, sometimes describe your child's new school friend thus: 'Oh yeah, nothing gets past him. Knows which side his bread is buttered alright,' and then enigmatically walk away.

2. Maintain complex algorithms of acceptable ice lolly requests – but it is *essential* to always keep the exact rubric a secret: e.g. children may think all they are permitted is Mini Milk strata or under (25p) but then at random upturn their entire objective reality and offer a Calippo (65p) or even a Twister (80p!). Magnums, inviolably, 'are bad for kids' and strictly for *dads only*.

3. Ordinary dads arrive several hours early for anything, but you – *you* – are destined for a far grander mission: have every clock in the house be up to 45 minutes fast but, and we cannot stress this enough, no two should ever be wrong *by the same amount*.

4. *Never* throw away receipts – even for Woolworths, which went into administration in 2008: that's exactly what they want you to do.

Lewis and I had an upbringing that felt full at the seams, so much so that I was only peripherally aware that we weren't well off. Living at the beach is the most bountiful free playground you could want and Dad was always up for what is its unquestionable best use: digging a big hole, burying a small child up the neck in it, and pretending to leave as the tide comes in.

Activities that were free were always favoured. Dad would often take us to pick brambles on building sites by jimmying the lock or yeeting us one by one over the wall. We'd spend a happy hour scurrying between blocks of concrete like busy field mice and wiping sticky purple jam down our shorts, returning with any blackberries we hadn't hoovered up in an ice-cream tub for Mum to make a crumble. During my circus period Dad welded me a trapeze from bits of old scaffold and painted it the colours of a big top with house paint. Never mind your John Lewis Wendy houses, our dens were built from railway sleepers. And not in deference to an Instagram trend for reclaimed timber; Dad's fashion-forward skipcore aesthetic came from the code that anything deposited on the street for council collection was fair game. Likewise when I complained about my frumpy white school sandals he painted them cherry red with Dulux undercoat, like placating the whims of a primary-school-age Queen of Hearts. Recycle and reuse, make do and mend. There is no more creative ingenuity than one that arises through need.

These are the sorts of details that make up a person. Not what they did for work, not even necessarily their familial station ('father, husband, brother'); all these particulars are the sort of nominative labelling you'd use to describe a person to a stranger. And yet when Dad died we still had to put them in the local newspaper notice, for really no other reason than it's what is done. It strikes me that a neutral list of a person's idiosyncrasies, neither strength nor flaw, would be so much more appropriate for conveying the interrupted patterns and negative space that declare themselves the loudest during the earliest days after a loss.

It was the last point of order in what had been two hours of softly expressed questions in an airless lavender room at the funeral director's, and Mum, Lewis and I just wanted to go home. We were grateful to be presented with a laminated sheet of suggested wording, selecting the option with least adornment. Nothing could be enough of course, but if I were to have a proper stab at it the notice would have read something like this:

The Heenan family wish to announce the death of Rod on 26 August 2020, aged 64 years. He could mend anything his ungrateful hooligan kids broke. He would interrupt games of Trivial Pursuit by shouting out the answers when it wasn't his go, doggedly maintaining that he should get a cheese anyway for a correct one. His garden was the best in the town; every summer his hanging baskets would be overspilling with colour. Everything he ate was smothered in Colman's English mustard. He trusted exactly one cash machine. He always referred deferentially to his team by its full name: 'Manchester United' rather than the coarse 'Man U'. He hadn't wanted us to get another cat but when we did he secretly grew to adore it. His one infuriating vanity was not getting the varifocals he desperately needed. He could simultaneously read the paper and watch the news and if anyone tried to change the channel when he wasn't even watching he'd drone, 'Change it back,' without missing a beat. He believed that quality could only be assured by the following brands: Cadbury's chocolate, John Smith's Extra Smooth, Zanussi washing machines, Warburtons Extra Thick Sliced White, Sony audio products, Arm & Hammer toothpaste, a specific fishmonger on the market known to us only as 'matey who does the fish'. His slippers always had the backs trampled down and his final pair are still in the hall. A funeral will take place at Grimsby Crematorium at 9.45am on Monday, 5 October. All are welcome to attend.

It was only when collating stories for the eulogy that I could fully indulge in genuflection to his many venerable qualities and acts of humanity. The time he sacrificed his trainers to the forceful suck of wet quicksand in order to rescue a toddler Lewis, who was standing there dumbstruck and boggling at the space his feet used to occupy with the aplomb of a haggard New York comic imploring, 'Well, ain't life just a bitch, huh?' and making no attempt whatsoever to help himself or the sinking man flapping profanely around him, while up on the dry safety of the beach I sat, howling. The fact that over the years he saved many children from drowning while working at our local leisure centre; that it is not at all fatuous to say that there are people walking around today only because of him. How he never turned down overtime, working double shifts to keep us afloat. The way he always volunteered to come along on my school trips; my pride at my classmates clamouring to be in his group as he was the most fun of the dads on offer and would do keepie-uppie contests with the boys. How during the wedding the celebrant asked everyone to turn round and introduce themself to someone they didn't know, and Dad was having such a diverting chat with my uni mates he had to be urged to sit back down so we could get on with the ceremony.

That he had a love of tradition that was sentimental rather than jingoistic: taking me to see the Morris dancers on May Day; getting into the local folk scene when Lewis and his friends were old enough to start playing pubs; becoming misty-eyed at Salvation Army brass bands; surprising us by expressing admiration for random dreary landscape watercolours; loathing the dyed-black teenage hair that temporarily replaced my 'bonny' natural copper; and persisting in a refusal to wish anyone a happy birthday, instead issuing a bizarrely formal, 'Many happy returns of the day.' Each and every year that made me laugh out loud, and he'd say, 'What?' warmly, pretending not to understand how weird it was. It was a cute bit we had. It's nearly my 33rd and no one will ever say that to me again.

His reluctance around displays of emotion wasn't unusual for his generation of men. I suspect I'm just one in an undeclared caucus of millennial daughters who can pinpoint a eureka moment of realising their father's love for them wasn't missing but merely expressed in alternative ways.

During the weeks leading up to my going away to study I

felt all sorts of tension radiate from him. This anxiety was apparently channelled into stockpiling boxes and boxes of Weetabix and powdered milk, as though I were about to depart to an end-of-times bunker rather than the University of York. When it came to dropping me off it turned out his impassivity was exactly what I needed (if Mum had been there too I would have sobbed like the sappy fresher I was pretending not to be), and it meant his leaving gift, the perfectly bonkers combination of a shoe-polishing kit, 50 pounds cash and a rape alarm, had me in stitches rather than tears.

At the end of the year I moved off campus into my first student house. An important developmental milestone: baby's first slum landlord. All my housemates had already left for the summer break, the derelict terrace was damp and cold, and there were slugs all over the kitchen floor. I stopped pretending to be brave and rang Dad, who came on the very next train to get me. That day I let myself be looked after by him in a way I hadn't for years. He could be pensive, quiet and hard to read, and his illnesses further complicated my understanding of him, but even then I can truly say that there's never been a point in my life when I ever doubted that my dad would show up when I needed him. Dependable as a port in a storm. That's really the most a daughter could want.

Speaking about the recently dead comes with the temptation to tip towards hagiography. And this is that and it isn't. He was these things. My father performed remarkable acts of self-sacrifice. Time and again he exhibited so much kindness without expectation of acknowledgement or reward. He could be jovial, good-humoured, irreverent, playful. He was intellectually curious; he had considered viewpoints on current affairs and I respected that his political opinions, though broadly socialist, were melded from first-hand realities, not wholesale or prescriptive ones like many of my own and those of my lefty friends.

But he was another person too. There was an animus in him that I didn't understand. Between us it widened into a gulf of difference of which I never stopped being afraid. At the funeral colleagues and friends described a man full of warmth and affability. Over and over again I was given the report that he never stopped talking about his pride in me and my brother; showing everyone pictures from the wedding until they couldn't take any more. This was a bittersweet comfort. The truth is I was jealous. I was jealous that these people were so unaccustomed to his vacillating moods that they found his suicide incomprehensible. Apparently he'd pulled off a very convincing job.

That night I didn't sleep. All I could do was recount a story of a man who slips into a defensive persona in every aspect of his life except for when he is with his closest kin. Then the mask slips. An unforgivably childish part of me wanted to know why he couldn't have kept it up for me.

It feels like a betrayal but a memorial isn't a memorial if it commemorates only half a thing. Lovely words on a page are decorative dross unless their truth is unvarnished. Some elements of Dad were his illness, some his childhood ordeal, but some were just his personality. All of the things above are true but so are all the things below.

Even as an adult I was often uncomfortable alone with my father. Sometimes I had to remind myself to stay in the room. There are times I actively put energy into forcing a comfortable silence with him, a veneer of tranquillity that is simply instinctive with the other people in my life. At any time it was impossible to be unaware if he was home. If he was in a bad mood his anger seemed to seethe throughout the house like carbon monoxide; if he wasn't, his heavy footfall indicated his presence in a way that could extinguish everyone's else's serenity anyway.

Diligent in matters of his kids' health, his conscientiousness could be submerged in a sort of medical paranoia. Admittedly this is not unlike my own catastrophising, but his fretfulness made me feel not only like I was minutes from death but worse than that would be how much trouble I'd be in if I were to die. Once, aged about seven and briefly unsupervised, I was rummaging through Dad's tool box enraptured by all the medieval devices inside, when a penknife cut a deep smile into the side of my thumb. Pain and panic sunflowered from my throbbing hand but rather than alarm at the blood pooling around my wrists what I remember most was being terrified of his reaction.

When we were little, 'Dad's home!' wasn't a phrase of transactional information but an entreaty to stop playing, put all evidence of games away and be quiet now, preferably in your room. Of course I didn't understand the huge amount of stress he was under, the brutal overtime hours he put in, or appreciate that coming home to a messy house could trigger such exasperation. I just thought he didn't like kids. He could also be extraordinarily miserly. This I understood to be anxiety from periods of unemployment and us having very little, but it meant that even in times of relative security I was always aware of exactly how much my existence cost him.

My mother is fun, creative, a gifted artist and enterprising in all sorts of crafts. The three of us, Mum, Lewis and I, would write nonsense poems together, make up silly stories for one another, make sketches, scrapbooks and shoebox dioramas, create creatures from rags and felt, bake rock cakes, draw our dreams, paint, plant, potter, play. These activities felt illicit. The mess they created had to disappear as soon as we heard the latch on the back gate. I remember the dissonance upon realising other kids didn't associate the word 'dad' with a vague sense of fear. For some of my friends their dad was the parent they 'liked best'.

I loathed his habit of reading the paper while talking to me without looking up, blurting out non-sequiturs with agitation that I hadn't followed his untraceable line of thought. When he was giving me a lesson on some careless error of judgement of mine he'd often absentmindedly call me by the wrong name.

'What you want to do, right, Ju—'

Judith is his youngest sister, 12 years between them, and though it drove me crazy that he routinely forgot his eldest child's name, it did give me a sympathetic glimpse into the lecturing she must have endured.

He didn't understand leisure time and took none for himself; a denial far exceeding self-sacrifice and into the realm of personal neglect, damage that simply radiates out to those closest. If we were going out for a meal and he had let us all know the table was booked for half-six, he'd be clattering around in a cyclone of impatience at 5.45pm, demanding to know why no one was ready yet. I'd be upstairs, home from uni and catching up with Mum, borrowing her perfume, discussing if we needed tights or would we be okay, and he'd be downstairs loudly cursing.

In my heavy, guilty heart I know he felt fundamentally estranged from us and I wish I'd worked on including him more. But also I know that he could make it so hard to want to.

Taken together, all the inconsistencies, all the prismatic hues of a complex identity twinkling in the sun of preposterous mortality, what I'm left with is this: he was a man who took up so much space. His absence feels very acute. And the most surprising thing is realising that just as much as those rose-tinted remembrances stored away in the verdant uplands of sun-drenched childhood, it is the loss of many of his aggravations that give me the most anguish.

Unsubtle in all things, Dad would do the washing-up with strong bleach. This would turn my stomach, not to mention make a sloppily rinsed cup of tea a violent assault. Recently

I've found myself opening a bottle of Domestos just to inhale it, breathing deeply into the fumes, whatever loss to my upper respiratory system and blood-brain barrier a gain to momentarily tamping my free-falling sorrow.

Dad was the only person who ever called me on the landline. We only kept it for him. Knowing I was about to be harangued about something or asked to drop what I was doing and research a kitchen appliance online, hearing the ringtone was often accompanied by irritation. Now I ring it from my mobile just so I can hear it again.

Mere weeks after he died the boiler packed in. I was really beginning to lose it with the apparent campaign of karmic retribution the universe had for the Heenan family but I was most forlorn thinking about how Dad would have dealt with it: fuming at this outrageous and targeted misfortune, not trusting anyone except the Which? catalogue and some note in his little black address book under 'Steve Boiler Man' with whom he played five-a-side in 1986, and maintaining an equilibrium of silent hard-done-by fury for the next three to four weeks. All these things that would have driven me mad I would now relish spending 90 minutes discussing. Hang on, let me get a tea, Dad, and let's really get into it. Combi boilers are a false economy in the long run? Tell me more!

Anna Karenina opens with the line: 'Happy families are all alike; every unhappy family is unhappy in its own way.' I don't know about Tolstoy's relationship with his father, whose death when the author was nine might have contributed to this fatalism, but I have reason to believe that a state of collective unhappiness can always be altered. After his mental tumult came to a head in a nervous breakdown in 2010, Dad changed altogether. These changes must have been very frightening and he suffered a great deal. But one side effect is the anger that I had assumed was part of his genetic makeup almost completely dissipated. And when he got better, we too, as a family, functioned better. We all exhaled. He was a lot easier to talk to. Gentler. He started telling me he loved me. Barring a wooden ornament for my bedroom that said I ♥ U that he made in the shed from a chunk of a pine bedpost one summer, I couldn't remember him ever saying he loved me. He just hadn't been that sort of parent. Now what started as a drip at first, just testing the waters, became a reliable trickle, so that eventually he said he loved me at the end of most phone calls and when he dropped me at the train station. In the last few years it made me very happy.

The problem with parents is how much they adore you. It's a bit of an evolutionary weak spot, really. The deal is you give a kid the spark of existence, your DNA, hand over all of your income, right to privacy and prerogative to leisure, and sometimes forfeit your marriage, identity and sanity too. And they have the audacity to take it all, greedily shovelling from the trough of your good grace like animals. They seize the territories you have built with patience and love and put up settlements of stroppiness, they annex your mid-life respite to hormonal righteous indignation. When adulthood is close enough to taste they drop you without hesitation to seek their own lives. They accept money and support. They roll their eyes when the landline rings. Write books about you with nasty little details that'll make people wince. And still you love them without condition.

You see, I am, as the books say, classically 'acting out'. It's all very tedious. How pleased I am with myself. Performatively deconstructing the archetype of the hero, the warrior, provider, king. And then following it by puncturing the armour of the man in whose image they are made? Groundbreaking. Really it all comes down to self-pity. Because while I do believe strongly that dismantling the pernicious tropes of masculinity is a matter of public health, I'm also a little girl who had a champion who is no more.

The number of people who love me unconditionally has reduced by half. My stocks have never been lower.

Bodies disposed and bodies eternal

I saw two dead bodies in 2020. My dad's and Hồ Chí Minh's.

During his life the revolutionary and beloved president of Vietnam expressed his wish to be cremated on his death, common practice among atheist communists and fundamental to the country's ancient Buddhist traditions, and so befitting a champion of class solidarity. When it came to his death in 1969, however, such was the collective grief of the Vietnamese people that it was felt he should be honoured on a commensurate scale. Since then, Hồ Chí Minh's embalmed body has lain in a glass coffin in a purpose-built mausoleum in Ba Dinh Square, on the spot where on 2 September 1945 he had read the Proclamation of Independence that formally established the Democratic Republic of Vietnam.

Visiting is very formalised. Obviously no cameras are permitted. The queue, which is enormous every day of the year, is managed by an armed honour guard who will tap you sharply on the shoulder if you divert an inch from the given path. Visitors are not allowed to stop in the presence of the Chairman, and so my look at him was fleeting. The light is soft and flattering. There is good reason; even embalmed bodies break down eventually and he's 50 years into eternity.

'He looks well!' said Michael impishly, when we'd been escorted out and corralled so far away from the great man that we'd have to take a taxi back to downtown Hanoi.

A few months later in what I came to call my Dead Dad Diary, with whether or not to view Dad's body on my mind, this memory made the con list: 'What if he looks like HCM did? i.e. Babybel.'

Throughout human history the occurrence of a death has given rise to two immediate concerns: what to do with the body and how to contemplate the other bit. Considerations of the former fall into two camps: those traditions where bodily disposal is the primary concern (though it may be highly ritualised, the aim is ultimately to get rid), and those which retain the physical form in some way, where the 'disposal' is really just of the unsanitary bits, sometimes with elements kept as relics.

For many ancient traditions seeking complete or near-complete removal of a body, cremation was the favoured method. Cremation was practised by the Romans, the Greeks and some Mayan societies, and it continues to have deeply rooted importance among Hindus, Jains, Sikhs and some sects of Buddhism. This is particularly true in Shinto-majority Japan, which has one of the highest national cremation rates in the world, with over 95 per cent of Japanese people choosing cremation. In the UK the number hovers around 75 per cent; a quick survey of my friends found that only one or two had ever been to a graveside burial funeral.

When my family and I were asked for our preference by the funeral director we briefly deliberated and then chose cremation sort of by default. In the UK there are really only two options. Dad had never expressed an opinion, and I didn't want to be thinking about what to do with his body at all, let alone have a strong viewpoint in either direction. It must be how a lot of cremations happen.

Our lack of intention couldn't be further away from that of the Balinese cremation ritual. The Ngaben is performed in the ancient tradition to release the soul so that it may be reborn in another form. Bali is unusual for its enduring Hinduism among a majority-Islamic Indonesia, and additional Buddhist and Catholic influences ensure that the island's funeral rites are quite removed from the type of Hindu funeral you might see in India. A fiery spectacle ensures that the soul can transcend and not be claimed instead by the evils of the lower realm. Families save up their money and save up their dead so that many deceased, sometimes dozens, can be cremated at the same time in a great community-wide and elaborately choreographed pantomime of pyrotechnics. Each body is placed inside a brightly coloured coffin shaped like a bull, which is made of bamboo and paper and covered with intricate gilding and beadwork. This fantastic vessel is carried high on a long procession of floats and costumed gamelan musicians and eventually installed onto a shelf within a towering decorated pagoda. Anything flammable is then immolated to rapturous applause.

The festival atmosphere isn't just for show; the Balinese eschew any negative emotions at their funerals, believing any weeping or lamenting to hamper the journey of the soul they are attempting to send off. I love this. In the weeks after Dad died any instances of laughter or joy, vanishingly scarce a commodity as they were, felt to me like an indiscretion. Not really if observed in other people, just a wicked transgression in myself. To think instead these could be feelings that are permitted, or even necessary, freeing up earthly bonds and bringing about a new beginning through the external performance of happiness and excitement for what is to come, a true gift of love, seems far more restorative and quite beautiful.

On a similar scale of beauty and symbolism is the Viking ship cremation. What could be more poignant than a boat pyre set adrift while the clan of the deceased watches on the shore, drumming a dirge, and sending flaming arrows to set it alight as it sails valiantly to Valhalla? This was the legendary end of the Norse god Baldr, whose death began the series of cataclysmic events that led to the ultimate destruction of the gods known as Ragnarök. Unfortunately this custom was not as widespread as you might have thought from cultural depictions of the Vikings, and if the rite was ever performed, more likely the boat would sink before it could burn out.

There is only one historical written record of a Viking longboat being burnt in a funeral pyre. This was chronicled by Aḥmad ibn Faḍlān, a tenth-century Arabic diplomat, in his colourful travel journal, *risāla*, which has an elastic association with credibility but is nevertheless quite fun. Ibn Faḍlān is travelling in the Volga River area, which links the Baltic trade routes to the Black Sea, when he encounters a funeral of a chieftain. He describes a highly ritualised ceremony, only some of which sounds like my idea of a good time:

> They make a little boat, which they lay him in and burn. If he is rich, they collect his goods and divide them into three parts, one for his family, another to pay for his clothing, and a third for making intoxicating drink, which they drink until the day when his female slave will kill herself and be burned with her master. They stupefy themselves by drinking this beer night and day; sometimes one of them dies cup in hand.

Spending a third of your lifetime's wealth on booze, you'd expect the final sesh to be a memorable one. Indeed our bemused envoy lists some of the highlights of the party: ritual sex, slave girls volunteering for sacrifice, the lucky winner getting to decapitate a chicken, an appointed crone to act as 'the angel of death', horses raced until they are exhausted then diced up and scattered about, a dog cut in two for good measure and finally the dear departed king laid to rest with his entire arsenal of weapons as well as all his earthly 'meat and onions', a garnish atop already so gargantuan a euphemism the whole thing is in danger of toppling over. With equivalent solemnity, the fire, tells Ibn Faḍlān, is then lit by the closest male relative of the dead man who must depart, naked, from the pyre walking backwards 'with one hand holding the kindled stick and the other covering his anus'.

Cremation in Europe, meanwhile, is a relatively new technology; or rather its modern comeback is more of a rediscovery. The Romans and Anglo-Saxons cremated their dead. The epic poem *Beowulf* ends with the scene of the hero's funeral pyre:

> The smoke-cloud ascended, the sad-roaring fire,
> Mingled with weeping (the wind-roar subsided)
> Till the building of bone it had broken to pieces,
> Hot in the heart.

Beowulf is set in the sixth century but the poem's only manuscript is eleventh-century, by which time Europe's fledgling Christianity had all but stamped out the pagan barbarism of burning the dead. The example of Christ's burial and belief in the resurrection of the literal flesh meant interment was the preferred method of disposal for the next several hundred years. Anthropologists can trace the advance of Christianity throughout Europe by mapping the spread of its cemeteries.

This status quo was challenged by the onslaught of the Black Death. Between 1346 and 1353 between 75 million and 200 million are estimated to have died by infection of *Yersinia pestis* across Eurasia. In just four months Florence lost 80 per cent of its citizens. 'As our city sunk into this affliction and misery,' wrote Florentine scholar Giovanni Boccaccio in 1348, 'the reverend authority of the law, both divine and human, sunk with it.' The desperate thrashing of city states as they were forced to stare annihilation in the face is documented, but the psychic desolation this must have caused on an individual level is unfathomable. Death was almost guaranteed mere days after infection. It was impossible for any surviving priests to issue last rites to all those who needed them.

Neither the doctors nor the folk healers could do anything for the afflicted, and since no one understood what caused the plague people became wary of tending the sick or touching the dead for fear of contracting it themselves. Miasma theory, the belief that the epidemic was spread by 'bad air' and smells, abounded, leading people to abandon their elderly parents and even their children to die. But those who did wish to honour their dead found the graveyards were full. Proper Christian burial demanded a grave, yet there was nothing Christian about the mass plague pits which had become the only option. Perhaps it didn't matter anyway; the God that had sent this pestilence had apparently forsaken them. Hopelessness reigned.

In Britain the case for cremation didn't really get going again until the beginning of mechanisation. The population explosion that accompanied the Industrial Revolution meant people flocked to cities and lived in close proximity. Communicable disease flourished once more. We think of the Victorians as the originators of the morbid, and indeed purpose-built funeral homes, coffin-making and gravedigging are all industries created by the tastes of the era. Not to mention an impassioned embrace of conspicuous mourning, a topic we will look at in depth later. What is interesting then is where previously a deceased person would have their body washed, prepared and laid out for visitors by their closest relatives, often on the family dining table, the nineteenth-century fashion for more and more ostentatious death services meant the furthering of the body itself from being the focus of the death.

Alongside this community outsourcing of death was the enthusiastic incorporation of science and technology in the public sphere. Overstuffed graveyards were tainting drinking water in the cities and once again the question was raised of what to do with all the excess dead. Perhaps this time there could be a more enlightened recourse.

Some progressives thought so. In 1874 Queen Victoria's

surgeon Sir Henry Thompson set up the Cremation Society of Great Britain and successfully cremated a horse. The clergy, ever measured and proportionate, denounced it as a heathen disavowal of resurrection and a prelude to individual immorality and societal collapse. Though we will never know if Thompson's experiment denied the world the messianic second coming of that specific horse, resulting in the biggest ecclesiastic schism since the Reformation, the results spoke for themselves: cremation was simple, clean and removed of unsightly images. Parliament passed the Cremation Act of 1902 and slowly the British public came round to the method.

Of course there are other types of complete body disposal. These usually involve another of the two elements – water and earth – with methods both traditional and contemporary. The Solomon Islanders, for example, leave bodies of the dead out on the beach to become a meal for sharks. And water cremation, resomation or alkaline hydrolysis, in which a body is liquidated using the same chemical process of natural decay only speedier, may soon become available to consumers.

There are many types of natural ground burial, utilising biodegradable 'eco-pods' or body suits implanted with mushroom spores, that ensure a body comes into immediate close contact with the worms, insects and microbes that have been efficiently chomping through human beings since our earliest arrival on the planet. Alternatively, a somewhat contradictory way to return to the earth is to first go into space. For a few thousand pounds an organisation will launch a capsule containing your remains into Earth's orbit, and after a few rotations the ashes will cascade gently over many months into the global winds encircling it, eventually falling as snowflakes.

Considering water, fire and earth are sacred to the Parsi people of Iran and India, the modern descendants of the ancient Zoroastrians, all these options are unavailable for means of disposing of bodies. That leaves only air. The use of *dakhma* or the 'tower of silence' dates from the early thirteenth century and removes a body by the process of excarnation. After a lengthy ritual of washing by the family and the tower attendants the remains are placed on a high circular brick amphitheatre, constructed with a concentric ring each for men, women and children. Here the corpses lie exposed, to be eaten by vultures and other carrion birds. After the bones are picked clean by scavengers they collect in a central well that forms an ossuary. To Parsis the ritual is seen as a final act of charity; gifting to nature what would otherwise be destroyed. I was pleased to find that the collective noun for feasting vultures is called a 'wake'.

Nature-assisted platform burials were also used by the Comanche Nation of the Southern Plains region and others. Leaving remains to the elements on top of a designated burial tree was the first step in a Choctaw ritual which then had a 'bone picker' remove and clean the bones of any remaining flesh for interment. Bodily disposal for indigenous Americans is a mix of the spiritual and the pragmatic: scaffold burials meant people wouldn't walk over the sacred ground mistakenly, wolves could not dig up the remains and burials could take place even when the ground was frozen.

These examples are to assure the physical form be completely removed. But what if you want to hold on to a souvenir?

Europe has many ossuaries, crypts and charnel houses. The beautiful town of Hallstatt in the Austrian Alps has one of the prettiest, if such a thing can be pretty. Behind the twelfth-century St Michael's Chapel there is a small cemetery which contains the Beinhaus, a charnel house tightly stacked with over 1,200 human skulls. The oldest has been there for three centuries. Short of space, beginning from the 1700s any bodies that had been buried for less than 15 years were exhumed to make room for newer residents. Remains were firstly bleached in the sun then stacked in the sepulchre next to their nearest relatives. With such numbers, however, it was difficult to keep track of who was who, so in 1720 a tradition began of painting the skulls with symbolic decorations, as well as dates of birth and death, like a tattooed graveyard. Growing up with the skulls, one local woman's last request was to be displayed in the Beinhaus on her death. Her painted skull was entered into the ossuary in 1995. You can tell it by the gold tooth.

In Bolivia, meanwhile, decay is held aloft and paraded through the streets. In the boisterous *Fiesta de las Ñatitas* respects are paid to the dead as personified by their very skulls or, in the case of infants, entire skeletons. These communities of the high Andes see no reason why the relationship with their kin must end because of the mere fact of death. Earthly remains are the conduit to the afterlife; during the rest of the year the relative's skull is displayed to ensure a tranquil home, offer guidance and even advise children in their schoolwork. Familial roles far exceed mortal life.

The Londa burial caves retain the whole body, not just the skulls. This is the practice of the Toraja community indigenous to South Sulawesi, Indonesia. The rituals before they even get close to the caves are some of the most elaborate in the world. Bodies may be kept in the family home for years, being periodically washed, redressed and exhibited in the local village. Cock fights, music and an enormous feast accompanies the eventual interment. Coffins are stacked up high in the caves, and as they decompose and collapse the remains of its occupant may go careening down the precipitous cliffs below. But that is alright, these goings-on are supervised by a council of elder sentinels, wooden effigies of the deceased called *tau tau* lined up like a town meeting, some uncannily human, some cartoonishly unblinking, all maybe a tad unsettling to outside eyes. To the families of the departed, however, they are reassured to know their loved ones are being looked over with love for eternity.

The last word in long-term corpse preservation is of course the mummy. Mummification can shield the body from decay for thousands of years. The word 'mummy' is lodged in the consciousness with the word 'Egyptian', yet a full 2,000 years earlier the Chinchorro people of Chile's Atacama Desert region had already been preserving their dead with the method. Mummification was also favoured by the Incas, the indigenous islanders of the Torres Strait and frequently by Capuchin orders of monks. The oldest deliberately mummified body ever discovered is the Spirit Cave mummy of the Paiute-Shoshone tribe, which lay undiscovered in the Stillwater Mountains of Nevada, USA, for 9,400 years.

The longevity of the 8,000 bodies, of which around 1,200 are mummies, that adorn the walls of the Capuchin Catacombs in Palermo vary. Here, rather than eviscerating the chest cavity, the organs were left intact and the bodies dipped in arsenic or lime, washed with vinegar, and left to desiccate in the town's favourably hot and dry microclimate. Some, it's fair to say, look a little worse for wear. However, the catacombs' star attraction is little Rosalia Lombardo, startlingly unchanged after succumbing to the Spanish flu pandemic in 1920, one week shy of her second birthday.

A beautiful corpse is not enough for some. What if you're nursing a hope of surviving the death process? Turn then to that curiously American industry, cryonics, and ask that you be positioned with your fingers crossed inside your −130°C chamber, with the wish that during the centuries spent in deep-freeze science might come up with a way to defrost you intact (and before your direct debit for continued storage runs out).

If you just hate the thought of missing out, consider human taxidermy. It's long been said that nowhere does funerals like New Orleans, and now that you can be propped up as a guest at your own wake, that couldn't be more true. After his death the family of Lionel Batiste, drummer in the famed Treme Brass Band, requested Charbonnet-Labat-Glapion Funeral Home display him decked out in his signature cream sports coat, elegant pocket square, sunglasses, drum and cane. He took in his funeral leaning against a Bourbon Street lamppost, with all the time in the world.

After Beethoven died there were reports that music could be heard coming from his grave. Intrigued, the local undertaker visited the gravesite and put his ear to the ground. He was astonished to find that yes, faint melodies were indeed rising from the great man's grave!

The undertaker fetched the priest and together they hunched over and listened. What they heard was the unmistakable opening of Beethoven's 9th Symphony. This was followed by his 8th, then his 7th, then his 6th, until what was happening was abundantly clear.

Beethoven was decomposing.

For most of us decay is unavoidable; without intervention a human body enters the process a mere four minutes after the last heartbeat. At any one time your body is just one standard pop song away from rotting. Not a happy contemplation. Of course we find it hard to let go, and the idea of a pause button can be irresistible.

Most likely if you're looking to preserve a corpse in the twenty-first century you are talking about standard American-style embalming.

Embalming is one of those modern technological advancements whose development accelerated through wartime need. The American Civil War produced 600,000 casualties between

1861 and 1865, mostly young men who were killed away from home and in a manner that didn't ensure a complete body would make it back for burial. A New York physician named Thomas Holmes commercialised what up until then had been a fringe science by embalming the body of Union officer General Ellsworth. The result attracted great acclaim and made Holmes a star. If you could afford it, the chance to have your son shipped home, his fatal injuries restored and his face made peaceful and at rest, must have been an enormous comfort. Once Abraham Lincoln's embalmed body had made a multi-stop tour, allowing hundreds of thousands of Americans to see their treasured and tragically slaughtered president in repose, the embalmer found himself wildly in demand.

One century later and the role of the mortician had become much inflated. Jessica Mitford, author, investigative journalist, and (to save you a Google) one of the good Mitford sisters, discussed embalming in her uproarious take-down of the funeral industrial machine, *The American Way of Death*, in 1963. She paid particular attention to the embalmer's process, describing in exquisite detail how each body is 'sprayed, sliced, pierced, pickled, trussed, trimmed, creamed, waxed, painted, rouged and neatly dressed – transformed from a common corpse into a Beautiful Memory Picture'. Much was traded on the implication that to forego such a thing would be skimping on the very best for your loved one. Enterprising funeral directors experimented with pseudo-psychology; not only was this how your grandmother would like to be remembered, they might say, but the optimising of your own grieving process rests on the perfection of this Beautiful Memory Picture.

As the sadmin of arranging the funeral gave me something to do, it also distracted me from an intrusive thought that had been droning like a low-level siren. It was especially loud when I was trying to sleep. Did I want to see Dad's dead body?

Lockdowns had meant I hadn't seen him since January, seven months before he died. Afterwards I moved in with Mum and I didn't end up leaving for several months. Every day it was true his absence felt inescapable, but it also felt like he could just be at work. Or away somewhere. His body was missing like it often was, but this time it was not coming back. I just couldn't seem to make my body understand that.

If the object was to get my brain to understand my dad was dead then embalming him seemed a terrible way to go about it. Of all the traditions around the world an American-style open-casket funeral of a highly manipulated corpse is the one I find most incomprehensible. Placed on a pillow as if merely at rest amid piped music and conspicuous expense. Even the terminology feels alien: 'a viewing'. We see a live person, but we view their dead body.

Embalming certainly wasn't something I'd planned on. I'm always up for a rewatch of *Six Feet Under* but that doesn't mean I didn't have a horror of the American funeral industry, which seemed to insist on the most costly and yet somehow the most impersonal wrangling of death, including the use of chemical compounds to postpone the fact of it for as long as possible.

There was also the cognitive dissonance: every other aspect of the modern funeral industry seems to be shutting death away from view and outsourcing it to various billable professionals, yet with embalming here the body is once more at the centre of the ritual. And its artificiality, the hollowness of the cosmetic, the placing inside a polished wooden coffin – all of it conspired to designate an object rather than the body of a former person. The British Museum has the death mask of Oliver Cromwell on display. I pictured embalming to produce this effect; waxen and ghoulish. It turns out UK funeral directors have a much less intensive method, the effect more temporary and less mannequin-like. But that's not the reason we chose to have Dad embalmed. Manifold delays meant I was too scared not to.

The manner in which he died meant the involvement of a great many bit parts: police, pathologists, the coroner's office, the undertakers. As if sudden loss wasn't disorientating enough, we didn't even know who had the body at any one time. And he got about; shipped from mortuary to funeral home and back again when the pathologist wanted to check something or take more X-rays. It was like being in an immersive theatre production of *As I Lay Dying*, William Faulkner's great Southern Gothic tale of a family's tribulations to bury their dead mother, if rather than dramatic predestination they were hampered instead by the labyrinth of local government and out-of-office replies.

It was over two weeks until the body was released for a funeral. A near-intolerable amount of time. But then when it actually came time to organise the funeral, another surprise. For cremation the earliest they could possibly do was six weeks' time, first thing on a Monday morning.

Now this was mid-way through the pandemic, so while upsetting I had prepared myself for a delay, even if this time-scale stretched my expectation a bit. I looked up and the funeral director was searching for words.

'No ... it's not because of Covid restrictions. Though of course there's been far more deaths than usual. The crematorium is down to fifty per cent human funerals at the moment ...'

'Sorry, did you say "fifty per cent human funerals"?'

'The council has ordered human cremations only take place in the morning for the next three months while they build a pet crematorium.'

To: bereavementservices@nelincs.gov.uk

Subject: Pet crematorium enquiry – multiple gerbil discount? Can provide own Pringles 'casket'

Good afternoon,

I recently had cause to become familiar with your decision to run a 50 per cent service in human cremations.

You might be aware there has been much discussion locally on whether the construction of this facility should take precedence over the continuation of funeral services funded by the public, such as, for example, my father, who worked for and paid into the local authority for much of his life and now requires one, having recently become dead. It's a real shame that these provincial hicks can't see beyond the end of their own ruddy muck-shod noses to what's important here: that an exciting new income stream is in the bag for the private contractor selected.

The astonishing entitlement of these people has them asking why an essential service should be cut when *they* should be asking *themselves* why they would delay a fledgling company in turning a profit. Now more than ever we should be supporting businesses!

I don't like to say it but comparatively it's the devastated widows who've had it easy, and really they should lighten up.

My family and I wouldn't wish to burden you during this delicate transitional period, but unfortunately the inconvenient timing of our circumstances, for which we can only apologise, means that we find ourselves in a bit of a bind. I am writing, therefore, with a request for advice, tips and tricks, etc., for a staycation cremation? If these unusual times have gifted us anything it's the exhilarating restoration of self-reliance! Yours is a timely reminder that to come cap-in-hand expecting one iota of commiseration anywhere on the scale from 'special treatment' to 'basic dignity' from your fellow man, even in death, is the opposite of the good honest caveat-riddled compassion this country was built on.

Please also enclose a quote for a Flemish giant rabbit and a copy of your pamphlet 'How to Tell Your Pet's Denomination' – I've always taken a great deal of comfort in 'Nearer My God to Thee' but what if Waffles was Sikh?

Yours warmly,
Hollie Starling

Listen. Michael's family's Jack Russell, the noble Billy, advanced in years and sausage negotiation, was sadly lost after a short period of infirmity at the end of an otherwise obscenely happy life. And on hearing the news I sobbed my eyes out. I am not about to suggest that a sentient being with whom you have shared every ebb and flow of daily life, who for perhaps multiple decades guilelessly bestowed unconditional love and companionship upon you with its entire tiny throbbing heart, is unworthy of a meaningful final chapter. But my dad was kept in various nondescript storage rooms for six entire weeks until he could be 'fitted in', and in that time I never once stopped picturing it. Mum wanted to see him wearing his wedding ring. His sisters wanted to say goodbye in person.

FIFTY PER CENT HUMAN SERVICE. In a pandemic!

So yeah, we got him embalmed.

I had been looking at the world through the gauze of derealisation.

Louise, our funeral director, was superb in all aspects of her profession. But as an eldest daughter I'm used to having a

handle on things. I'm used to insisting on my inclusion in matters of organisation. I am not used to bobbing around on the sea
of another's decisions. I'm ashamed how much I let that fall by
the wayside, letting the industry system commandeer my dad's
body without so much as a tracking number.

A suicide always requires a post-mortem. Yet, for various
reasons that I scribbled down in automatic writing in the Dead
Dad Diary (one of which appears to be, improbably, 'only one
pathologist in Lincolnshire and he's broken his leg skiing'),
what normally takes around two days took a full two weeks.
The 'big police computer was down' (?) or that he 'might have
been taken to Hull' (??) were other entries I made in an attempt
to capture a grain of information for use later when my higher
faculties had had a factory reset.

One morning I snapped out of it. I stomped into the
funeral home white hot with rage. It is a dance almost too
nuanced to describe, when a man of a certain aspect makes a
breezy determination of your female/other over-the-topness,
with open-palmed assurances of not to worry, he'll steer this
ship back to reasonable waters with his firm-hand-on-the-
tiller leadership, that for the sake of expediting the end of the
interaction you pretend to find satisfactory or even disarming.
I wasn't in the mood to pretend. I told the weaselly man on
the front desk that my mum wanted to see my dad's body and
I expected that to happen right now, making a fist at my side
so as not to push his teeth in when he tried to de-escalate me
with casual affect, chuckling that 'of course' he'd get 'the lads'
to bring him 'right round'.

I've been reading a book of traditional Irish lamentations,
verses for the bittersweet contemplation of the chapters in the
life of the deceased, to be sung at memorials. Indulge me.

> The lads'll bring him round, love,
> Oh, the lads they'll bring him round.

And he'll only have to go to Hull
If he has gone cracked his skull,
For the lads'll bring him round.

Why didn't you say, love?
It was only your delay, love.
Calm ye passions now, my dear,
Just thank the Lord I'm here.
I'll tell them bring him round in the van,
In the van,
Oh, the lads'll bring him round in the van.

Popping off at trifling men exerting superficial power over me is one of my great joys in life, and in times of adversity a radical act of self-care, but though I was pleased to get Mum what she wanted, internally I began to panic. Now I had to decide.

I'd spent two weeks vacillating on whether or not I wanted to see him. At first I checked my instinct to go against the tack I knew Michael would take to persuade me not to. Not to suggest Michael is in the habit of telling me what to do, or is given to claiming he knows best. But he has to view the aftermath of tragic circumstances on a regular basis and his instinct is to shield others from having to do so unnecessarily. Currently he works on a unit for violent crime within the Metropolitan Police, but his first few years were spent in first response, during the course of which he saw dead bodies, among them victims of suicide. One story was so harrowing I couldn't get the imagery out of my head for weeks and Michael was very sorry he'd told me about it. I know he doesn't tell me all of his work stories anymore.

So I knew my husband wouldn't think it was a good idea, but I also knew he was exactly the sort of person who wouldn't benefit from viewing a dead relative's body anyway. It was an empty container, he reasoned; what was the point of re-traumatising yourself for nothing?

One windy autumn day briefly back in London, Michael had urged me on another desultory walk during which he noticed me scanning around, eyes like an owl, and had asked me what I was looking at. Exhaustion had given me a lack of filter so I replied I was searching for Dad. From Michael's face it was clear it was about the bleakest thing he had ever heard. I was surprised. It didn't feel strange to me. What felt strange was accommodating the notion that the world no longer had Dad in it. Yes, I accepted it was unlikely that I'd spot him puttering down Camden High Street, but that didn't mean that I didn't eyeball every middle-aged man in a sensible waterproof just in case.

Without the conclusive proof of seeing his body forcing me to admit he was gone, what if I never really believed he was?

Yet what of the uncanny element? The potential for desta-bilisation from a recognition deep in the genome? Where Lewis and Mum have elegant tapered feet, the second toe longer than the third, I have Dad's little hooves, the paltry lit-tlest nail the size of half a grain of rice. I have his stumpy hands and high forehead. To see his dead body would be to pre-see my own.

No, then, I wouldn't do it. I had been through enough, hadn't I? I would protect my battered psyche from any more lasting damage. I would safeguard my fledgling marriage, not even a year in, from an unequal distribution of crisis manage-ment resources. Michael had been saddled with a Sad Wife and I was terrified about buyer's remorse.

Of course, in choosing to forego that final irrevocable image I had invited my imagination to fill in the blank. They came on like migraines. Fauvist brushstrokes of green and purple, bloated pudges of disgorged density, a paper-thin shroud teeming and undulating and promising to rupture. And that was far, far worse.

A 1990 study found the heavily cosmetised open-casket display of corpses favoured by Americans overwhelmingly to disturb rather than comfort the mourners surveyed. Meanwhile research carried out in 2010 by medical sociologist Alison Chapple found that in cases of traumatic death, of those family members who chose to view the body, only a single-digit percentage later said they regretted it. Many participants reported that while in the short term they were more distressed after seeing their deceased, the findings of the study bore out a more positive long-term mental health outcome. This, remarkably, was even true in instances of significant injuries such as road traffic accidents, shootings or house fires.

Did I want to see my father's body? I had seen his foot launch a football full into my face when I wasn't paying attention in the park. I had seen him turn his shoulders into a stepladder to heave Lewis over a wall as a shortcut to a swimming lesson, getting his entire front covered in anti-vandal paint. I had seen his back become a saddle on a wild horse, now tame enough for me to ride around the garden. I had seen his mouth gnaw the end of every biro into useless shards. I had seen his timorous fingers pin his father-of-the-bride buttonhole to his lapel.

I wanted to be alert that my decision was not simply down to the ticking clock – or worse, curiosity. For Lewis it was resolutely a no from the beginning. And if it hadn't been for the specific circumstance of the pandemic I think I would have reached the same conclusion. But I hadn't seen Dad since my cousin's wedding in January, after which three weeks' travelling returned Michael and I to a lockdowned country. That night we'd all been worse for wear; any memory that features me barefoot and carrying my shoes back to a B&B isn't going to sustain a lasting impression of an unexceptional parting conversation. It was a bleached, threadbare, unsatisfying memory and I couldn't even see his face in it. I hadn't seen him, his body, in nearly eight months. How could I not?

A couple of days after visiting Dad in the funeral home I was with Carly in a pub on the seafront. We were sharing a plate of halloumi fries as death-toll chevrons lurched past strato-spheric line graphs on multiple Sky Sports screens, which (in what surely has caused irretrievable psychic disrepair the full extent of which may not be apparent for decades) we had all got used to filtering out like traffic noise. Carly and I have been friends since we were four and she's where I go when I need to dispense with the niceties of preamble. Helpfully she also shares my anxiety-motored fascination with the morbid so she doesn't experience whiplash when I introduce a topic of, say, Dead Bodies We Have Seen.

I was hollowed out from lack of sleep and I still wasn't sure if I'd made the right decision. With anyone else I would have been embarrassed by my equivocation; admitting to reluc-tance or discomfort at going to see the person who raised you – what spinelessness, what ingratitude. I'd come prepared with my own stick for her to beat me with. Of course, Carly didn't see it that way.

She told me that when her grandma had died of complica-tions from surgery she had right away decided that she wanted to see her body. And as she approached her grandma's hospital bed Carly had had exactly the same thought as me: they do not, despite what everyone tells you, 'look like they are sleeping'.

'They look like a corpse,' said Carly, as a second bottle of white Zinfandel was delivered to our table by a young woman in full PPE.

'It's ... the hands,' we said in unison.

The nail bed on a dead body recedes quickly after death, so that the nails protrude garishly, like a full set of acrylics in a colour no one has ever asked for. In life Dad's nails were always bitten to the quick, so even though the mortician had neatly trimmed them they still looked too long. There is also little to be done about the wrinkling of the hands themselves. A body dries out quickly and these extremities empty first and begin to turn black, even if embalmed.

To look at a dead body is to look at an absence, and is therefore impossible to capture in words, like trying to imagine a new colour. The figure who had been laid out was indeed Dad, and so the viewing had served the purpose that I needed so badly: confirmation. But it would be more accurate to say he looked more like a model of him. Or even a model of a twin brother we hadn't known about. Unbidden from the depths of my long-term memory, my first instantaneous thought, as I approached from the foot of the room and the nose and eyebrows came into view, was that he looked just like Grandma. But of course, she died when I was five and, though I couldn't remember her voice or clearly picture her face, my most abiding impression of her was looking up from below, slouched at her feet as she made rum custard on the stove. What a revelation to have that Christmas-scented memory return wholesale just then.

He looked far taller in the coffin than seemed correct, his face wider somehow. The cosmetologist had done an expert job but I couldn't help but pick the effect apart; the lips set slightly too wide, the cheeks puffed up a little too much. Our faces fall to rest when we lie down, so an artificial fullness to mimic the upright appearance comes off as doll-like. From taxidermy I knew that brains without pumping blood quickly turn to liquid. In birds you need to swab out the inside of the skull with a cotton ball. In human post-mortems the brain is the only organ that can't be put back, so the liquid is collected in a plastic bag and placed in the chest cavity. I wished I didn't know this. I also couldn't unknow what I had spent several nights googling before bed: the plastic discs they used to fill out the eyelids, the cotton packing in the mouth and nasal cavities. Makeup, presumably. Though it couldn't disguise everything.

I'm not going to pretend it wasn't upsetting, or that it didn't make my pain much worse for quite a while. It's an image I can't expunge and one I willingly admitted into my vivid dream factory to fire at random like a toddler stumbling on an assault weapon. But that was the point: I was no longer burdened with a bunch of alternatives instead. I'd conjured up all sorts of grotesqueries, applied theatrical makeup, uplit the scene from below for maximum macabre – cavorting Goya nightmares, George A. Romero's deleted scenes, the baby from *Eraserhead* grown up. The realisation that a body is indeed just a shell is anticlimactic, but it is an anticlimax that, I think at least, needs to be experienced.

Autumn is on the turn now and winter paces on the porch, waiting to be let in. Yule, the midwinter of the Celtic wheel and the darkest of nights, is nearing and with it the 50th anniversary of that frigid December night when my grandfather John was lost to the sea. Only now do I comprehend how much this tragic event must have destabilised the people in his life. For in their loss there was one vital difference: his body was never recovered.

I'd been thinking that in times of suffering uncertainty is a luxury commodity. A priceless one, for its presence supports an alternative reality. Until they found the body. Until I 'viewed' it. I'd got that the wrong way round. The worst thing is not to have your uncertainty suddenly snatched away but to live with it forever.

Either way the discordance remains. I can recount looking

at him and finding, finally, the body to be only a vessel, and still even now type a sentence using both 'him' and 'the body' as object signifiers. The night after I saw Dad's body I ruminated on whether he had a pillow, fretted that he was lonely, or cold. I wondered if the last person to leave the funeral home that evening had turned the light off or left it on, and which was worse.

On his death in 2009 the philosopher H.J. Blackham was called the 'father of the international humanist movement'. A committed atheist, he took aim at what he saw as the nonsensical fripperies of religious funerals, in a seminar delivered to the Royal Society in 1965: 'Surely it is time to look critically at this ritual. Why this concentration upon disposal of the remains? It is a wrong focus. It turns the knife in the wound. It is gratuitous, even superstitious.' Blackham wasn't suggesting that ritual had no use, though his detractors didn't see it that way. He described the outcry to his statements, even among his scientist colleagues, as 'almost violent'.

It is likely Blackham's critics took umbrage with his dismissal of the body-focus for reasons of scripture on the topic of resurrection. But this aside, was he right to claim that funerary rituals that centre on the disposal of remains are so gratuitous as to turn 'the knife in the wound'?

The Muslim burial is quick and physical. Less than 24 hours after death the body is bound in a simple shroud and placed in the ground by the closest male relatives. It is a humbling act; the grief-stricken cannot shy away from the fact of death when they must get down into the grave to lay their loved one literally to rest. Grave markers are all identical, so in death every Muslim, rich or poor, is equal. Nothing about this feels gratuitous to me.

Meanwhile, historical examples where the body very much recedes from the funeral event might well tip into vulgarity, depending on your sense of humour. The ancient Greeks hired 'funeral clowns' to attend the ceremony and loudly heckle from the wings in order to ridicule the dead person being commemorated. The object was to diffuse anxiety in the mourners and focus attention instead on having a laugh, but I daresay some attendees wouldn't have got the joke.

Until recently I would have described myself as a humanist. Almost exactly a year ago our wedding ceremony was conducted by a humanist celebrant. But if superstition is antithetical to the principles of humanist thought then perhaps we need to part ways. Holding superstitious beliefs is an attempt at control, as reasonable a response to chaos as any other. There are few things more chaotic than the notion that death can befall any of us at any time.

Perhaps this is why I'm so taken with the wonderful individualism of Ghanaian coffin culture. These are the *abebu adekai*, or 'proverbial coffins', that ordinary people commission in life to be used after they die, from speciality carpenters clustered around the city of Accra. A cobbler might request to be buried in a giant moccasin. Members of high-status families might decide on a wooden effigy of their clan's totem, such as a leopard, crab or cockerel. Others choose a coffin based simply on something they like: a bottle of Lucozade or a packet of Marlboro Reds. Some, like Blackham, might find this custom garish, even tawdry. But that misses the point. Though the fantasy coffins of Ghana quite literally hold the dead person up for scrutiny, it is not the body that is centred, but a mirror of their personality and self-image. In their specificity and eccentricity lies something consoling, knowing that this coffin is the absolute fulfilment of how this person wanted to go out, and the possibility that if we spent some time considering our own death we might exert some control over this final event.

Blackham described a funeral as a personal event that takes place in public. So where do we place the phenomenon of the macro-scale event-funeral? Does the size of the crowd alter the dynamics of the funerary ritual?

One in six of the population of Iran, some 10 million, turned out to witness the coffin of Ayatollah Khomeini being carried through Tehran in 1989. Over 2 billion people around the world watched the funeral procession of Princess Diana in 1997, and the sea of flowers that were laid in person outside the gates of Kensington Palace in some places reached 8 foot deep. At such numbers the overwhelming majority of participants in these rituals do not personally know the dead, making their attendance something closer to pilgrimage. The parasocial bond to some public figures is so strong as to prompt behaviour that should be absurd: travelling the length of the country, camping out overnight, openly crying on national television. Shockingly in the week following Diana's death there was a 33.7 per cent rise in suicides among women in England and Wales.

Perhaps it's an illusion of intimacy co-mingled with the feeling of participating in history, but scenes of mass grieving can feel more representative of how each mourner's worldview and identity has ruptured than anything else. Not to suggest that such outpourings of devotion are always inauthentic, though some certainly are. Look at the performative mourning that accompanies state funerals in undemocratic regimes, such as the mass wailing and keening at the funeral for North Korean father-god Kim Il-sung, captured by television cameras for the world and invigilated for sincerity by armed guard. It's the perfect modern analogy for the emperor whose death demands the sacrifice of hundreds of servants to serve him in the afterlife. Now that's gratuitous.

These are a stark contrast to the shrines and vigils that commonly appear after tragedies and disasters. The local gatherings in the wake of the ethnonationalist-motivated terrorist attack in Norway in 2011, where the speaking of the perpetrator's name was forbidden, or the nightly vigils that united communities across the Indian Ocean after they shared the devastation of the 2004 tsunami, were spontaneously established and separate from official memorials. Time and again humans are moved to honour perfect strangers and have their anonymous body be counted as one of a multitude, a beautiful and sobering demonstration of community.

It didn't occur to me until I experienced my own close bereavement, but I wonder now about the families at the centre of large-scale funerals to which a great many others feel moved to be a part. Because to me, the loss of Dad was of that same monumental stature. When your missing person was a pillar of your life, so fundamental and as much a part of you as an organ, is it comforting to see your turmoil mirrored on a commensurate scale? Or disorientating and insincere?

What happens if that scale falls far beneath what feels appropriate? Before 2020 it was unthinkable to have limitations imposed on grief. However, that is what thousands of families were forced to experience during the Covid-19 pandemic. Restrictions on attendee numbers, a blanket ban on wakes, no hugging or hand-holding. Some were unfortunate enough to find out whether a personal event can be said to take place in public if the only 'public space' available is via Zoom. There is a grim irony that the most communally experienced phenomenon in a generation could result in a group observance of ancient tradition that was so utterly atomising.

For my family the bodily disposal didn't unfold along the expected schedule and the funeral itself was curtailed to just a few mourners sitting metres apart, unable to touch. Funerals can take many forms and have different elements as a focus, but at their most meaningful the grieving should find themselves among others, whether known to them or not, to whom they are bound by love and respect for the departed. They should feel the solace of intimacy but find the elevation of their loss to be exalted by the ceremonial. Sitting at the front of the chapel listening to the eulogy I'd written but was unable to deliver, I stared at the flowers we'd picked out for Dad, yellow roses and orange daylilies like his garden, sitting atop the shiny box around which the sparsely populated room was situated. And I thought how much it looked like a wedding cake and had the horrible urge to laugh. I wondered then how many other people, prompted by the similarities in our ceremonial customs, had had that same ludicrous thought. I saw then how ritual is a periscope that allows us to reach through time to touch the faces of our ancestors, to invoke commonality in thought, to feel their breath on our necks.

Autumn had quickened. It felt like days since I'd opened the curtains in my childhood bedroom to see Mum making the most of the last sunny day of September to hang Dad's work uniforms on the washing line, and wept at the exquisite kitchen-sink drama of it all. October went by in a flashy torrent of hail and tempest winds and skies of apocalyptic yellow. In November I slept with the windows open to watch the sheet lightning turn my room into Dr Caligari's cabinet. Now it was as though all the kinesis and colour had been extracted and all that remained before it got dark by mid-afternoon was a wet and tepid grey.

I found myself noticing churches. My walking routes had developed around them. St Pancras Old Church especially. As winter set in I observed the change in the iridescent lacquer of frost that coated the slate roof. The creaks of spartan branches where just a week before leaves had rustled. No birds, except for the fresh carcass of a pigeon that had hit a hoarding and become disembowelled.

Supposedly St Pancras Old Church is England's oldest site of Christian worship and the soil of its burial grounds holds many layers of history. In the fabric of the tower there are Roman tiles and an inscribed altar stone that pre-dates the Norman Conquest. Percy Bysshe Shelley proposed elopement to Mary, author of *Frankenstein*, as they crouched at her mother Mary Wollstonecraft's grave. The design of London's red telephone boxes was taken from the tomb of Sir John Soane. And then there's my favourite stop, the Hardy Tree.

Thomas Hardy wasn't always a Wessex mythologiser; his first vocation was as an architect's apprentice. In the 1860s Britain's rail system experienced immense growth and the Midland route expansion was planned directly through the graveyard at St Pancras. The grim job of exhuming 10,000 remains and reburying them elsewhere was assigned to young Hardy. Unfortunately, no one had instructed him on how to dispose of the headstones. Hardy took it upon himself to arrange the grave markers in a striking circular mound at the foot of an ancient ash tree in an undisturbed corner of the churchyard. Today they still nestle in tight under a blanket of moss.

Dad liked churches. His Christianity shifted between various levels of dormancy throughout his life, though all too memorably it intensified towards the end of it. He sent us to Sunday school as kids, not out of any sort of religious fervour but more, I think, to capture a mythic little England of virtuous simplicity that his notion of fatherhood had promised. The Sunday school people seemed nice. They told me to pray and I really did try.

I wonder if only now I'm experiencing the casualty of my

agnosticism. These absent rituals I've been pining for? The ancestral solace of deeply held belief? Why not the Church of England? A ready-made oral tradition of parables, stock characters and supernatural theatricality; an overflowing font of familiar superstitions and symbols right there!

I could gesture at my doctrinal quibbles or give a tinpot exegesis on human suffering, but plenty of sensitive and intelligent people can reconcile it all and I don't know why I can't. I wish I could. Because I do feel there is something about losing the convention of prayer that cannot be replaced with anything else. Its utility is the human need for attention. To be heard. There are few outlets for a person to ask for sympathy. And I do mean sympathy, rather than empathy. Pity me. I am in pain and I desire your pity. Imagine asking that of a friend, or even a therapist; it feels pathetic, indulgent. Praying, though, is an unvarnished expression of humility, a prostrating of the self that entreating your online friends to 'please send good vibes' simply lacks.

The number of church services I ever went to with Dad is probably in the low double figures, limited to the usual weddings, christenings and funerals, but what I remember of them is my embarrassment over *his* lack of embarrassment at singing hymns and reciting the Lord's Prayer at a volume that made his presence in the pews impossible to mistake. Why couldn't he mime or mumble to his shoes like the rest of us?

At his own funeral I spoke the Lord's Prayer, the loudest I ever had, not for Dad, but in provocation to a universal power that, if it does exist, inculcates many of its lessons by the vector of human pain and refuses to explain why. *Thy will be done.*

The doors of St Pancras Old Church had been flung open for pandemic ventilation on that frosty day and I heard that low tremulous hum of united voices. *Daily bread.* That lymphatic cadence trilling up and down. *Trespasses.* The words themselves melting into a murmur — *trespass against us* — but that didn't matter as I was already saying them out loud.

It was Hardy's wish to be buried at Stinsford, Dorset, his childhood parish. However, on his death in 1928 his wife, Florence, was instructed that such a titan of English literature should be interred in Poets' Corner at Westminster Abbey. As a compromise Florence decided that Hardy's heart would be buried in Dorset and that his ashes would go to the Abbey. Partway through the operation the doctor briefly stepped out, leaving Hardy's heart on the side, then re-entered the room to find his cat eating it. So the cat was killed too and buried with the remainder of the organ at Stinsford.

Hardy, an interpreter of the essentials of being, might have laughed at the episode. For both creatures were simply obeying their own nature: the cat its need for a meal, the human its compulsion towards sentimentality, and taken together it is the latter's that appears irrational. For every living thing except humans death is a gift, a means to continue to survive.

Over the years the Hardy Tree slowly began to absorb the headstones around it. It became a living monument that assimilated the load it had been made to bear, and by extending itself to reach the resources it needed, it continued to grow.

DEVOURING TREE

30°21'46.5"N 130°31'54.9"E
Japan

THE WATCHER HAD A CLEAR view. She was tall but hidden well, the spines of the cedars all around shawling her in an embroidery of dark greens. From a distance their spindly leaves were woodsmoke and she peered out as if atop a pyre. She mistook the man for a hunchback at first, for it had been a long while since this ancient spectacle had advanced along the velveteen moss of the forest path and she couldn't immediately place it. The cycle was a long one. When all was well few came up the mountain road and the seasons would pass, but in times of long winter or long war she had seen that funny two-headed monster do its strange lurching dance in the direction of her forest hideaway many times.

To live in the same place for a lifetime is to have its wonders become furniture. Perhaps it was the weight of what he was about to do that inflamed his senses so extraordinarily that morning, but for the first time in a long while he could smell the cacophony of the rain-soaked cedars acutely, needles of tart freshness spiked with resin and fallen stone fruit, a scent that he had long ago stopped noticing. Yet today it was as alive as the red-bottomed macaques in the rafters above, darting in from the rain as they searched for a dry spot.

The people of Yakushima liked to say it rains on the island for 35 days a month. The path through the woods runs along a trail of protruding stones laid centuries ago by travellers and plunderers of timber, a guyline through a sea of sodden peat and slimy tree roots. These men too would have struggled up and down the mud-slicked hills in their straw sandals with cords of bound wood strapped to their backs. Except his pack held a different load.

The family had said little as they saw *Obaachan* take less and less of the already small allotment of food they could share with her. Slowly she became lean, then more rapidly.

'Mother, please eat,' he urged once and she looked up at him with the relic of a smile.

Despite this he was surprised at her lightness and he moved her onto his back with great delicacy, his consignment an oversized and improbable goose egg. She wrapped her arms around her son's shoulders, her legs a bony belt resting on the ledge above his hips.

For many days the sky had been washed a baleful white but today of all days it had ruptured with sumptuous winter sun. The eddies of careening rainwater across the island's granite bedrock made bubbling waterfalls and *onsen* hot springs, and the ice crystals that dusted every visible ridge of rock burst with colour as the morning skittered across them. In the summer these pockets would fill with rhododendrons of fuchsia and coral. But for now everything was bearded with the same turquoise lichen that covered the trunks of the many *sugi* – the old men of the forest, some a thousand years or more – the largest of them garlanded with *shimenawa*, thick twisted ropes and dangling tassels, in the Shinto way.

A burst brook slowed their progress when his shoes stuck in the sludge. Forced to stop and reposition his mother, apprehension caught up. The preceding harvest had been smothered by rain. Last month he had seen his children eating bark.

It is what is to be done, she was saying. This is the only thing she could have wanted. Now that Yumiko had another on the way. This is how she could help. The man said nothing. He had listened to her say these things for many months.

He wanted to leave her water but to do so would only prolong it. That was the surest way; the winter had been mild and, though it was true she was very frail, exposure alone might have taken many days and nights. He held her quickly once but didn't linger or turn round as he walked away. Fortunately her tears were quiet.

The watcher had observed the old woman as she had been carried up the mountain. Clinging to the man's back she had stretched out her arms to grasp at passing branches. With no small effort she snapped off small twigs where she could and had dropped them carefully on the grass below.

It was a trail. Afterwards her son would be able to find his way home. The watcher had come to understand that it was part of it, this benevolent abandonment, this *ubasute*. But she wondered who this part of the ritual was for. As the woman dropped her twigs the watcher saw that the man pretended not to see.

Returning down the eastern face of Mount Miyanoura a weight far greater than his tiny bird mother had been lifted from his back. Though he hadn't yet stopped to rest he found he took bigger, easier strides. He thought of the village; the houses in which there had been four generations then one day only three. His calves had lost their tightness, his spine was unfurled.

In the closed circuitry of the island's climate the east was semitropical. Giant bromeliads pointing their vivid beaks into the sky, weeping dragonfruit trees awaiting their pink-spined fruit, branches budding with tiny unripe citrus nubs that would transform into a festival of orange ponkan, all beholden by the monster chusan palm and its windmill sails.

A great doorway lay ahead, two thick pillars topped by a black lintel. *Torii*; a gate between worlds. On the other side, the thousand-acre Shiratani Unsuikyo Ravine.

His mother's Shinto gave her trust in *kami*, spirit trees that attested to the divine essence and life of the forest. But here there was no birdsong. Not even the whistling green pigeons that are Yakushima's music.

One tree diverted the man.

He couldn't say why, except that he could feel it somehow. It was as though it was watching him.

A strain in the branches, a torsion about to uncoil. Its leaves were dark and molten, the colour of aubergine skin. As he got closer he realised what had stood out. All of its neighbours were desiccated and grey, whereas this one tree looked in the full flush of youth.

He bumped his foot on a swelling of bleached hardness protruding from the ground at his feet. What was that?

The watcher closed her eyes. She didn't need to watch anymore. He was close enough.

The moment his throat snapped shut he already knew it was too late but he spun and darted anyway, a silver minnow with nowhere to swim. As his sandal was tugged off by the projection from the soil, soil once saturated with the blood of thousands of felled warriors, he saw then what it was. An elbow. Two bones joined still by the merest of ligament.

A seismic whip past his ears and all at once lashed about the face and torso, hopeless legs pinwheeling, only to find he was pinioned by branches. Yet these didn't feel like green sapling branches. They were articulated, long. Fingers. Each one pierced his skin, and his mind turned inside out when he felt it. Sucking.

The branches were *sucking*!

She was Jubokko, the great tree *yōkai*. Having long ago drunk a battlefield of slain warriors she had forgotten the taste of rainwater and could no longer be quenched by it.

Both of the man's palms sloughed off onto the tree's rough bark as she hoisted him upwards. She opened herself and presented her centre point like the obsidian beak of a colossal squid. A terrible creak as she engulfed him. The dull monotone began behind his eyes and became a shriek as his skull caved inwards.

The Jubokko drained the man until sated. Knowing her part she returned the exsanguinated meat to the ground for the use of the birds and animals. Then only bones would remain to be bleached by the sun.

And on her knotted trunk another face. A distinctive O below centre. It looked like a scream.

But only if you got close.

WINTER

IN ITS HEYDAY IN THE mid-1990s Pleasure Island Family Theme Park, Cleethorpes, attracted thousands of visitors every day of the summer season. The decline was slow, and then fast, and soon after it shuttered in 2016 the site fell to dereliction. Mock-Tudor arcades were left haunted by the animatronic ghosts of Billy Bob Bear's Orchestra, metal smiles fixed and rusting. A static convoy of swan pedalos, now forced to share their lake oasis with migratory birds, sprouted a down of green algae and duckweed. Purple buddleia broke through the crumbling concrete where once fell the fizzing blue vomit of overstimulated children. Where consumers had consumed nature quickly and deftly reclaimed.

But not quite everything disappeared.

Sometime after the park's closure a local drone operator discovered a couple of after-hours stowaways. In the corner of the site that had housed the former sea park the aerial camera captured two sea lions circling the water of their tank. It is extraordinary footage. A pair of plump cigars performing balletic stunts to an empty amphitheatre. All for no applause, for they had no one to entertain except one another.

Pleasure Island is positioned on the curve of ancient marshland where the Humber estuary flows into the North Sea proper, and as the drone pulls out it reveals just how close the landlocked animals are to the coastline. Metres from the waterway that would take them to their ocean home.

The sea lions, who belonged to a separate franchise and

contractually had indefinite leave to remain, were looked after by a steward and were perfectly secure and healthy. Nonetheless, their rudderless circling is hard to watch. They were used to being left for the long winter off season, for better or worse awaiting the return of the warming temperature to resume their performances for the summer crowds. But what if that winter continued on and on? After being socialised to respond to humans and toiling for their entertainment, it would be nice to imagine for them a long and happy basking in the reward of retirement. Instead, abandonment and exile. It could be the mawkish anthropomorphising of someone who has recently become, shall we say, a little unhitched from scales of emotional proportionality, but to me it seems nothing short of a tragedy.

Growing up in a resort town is inescapably seasonal. As a little kid the diversions of the North Lincs riviera were miraculous: a sandy beach trimmed with amusement arcades, crazy golf, waterslides, pleasure boats, nature trails, a tropical aquarium, sports pitches, a weird little reptile house that no one but Lewis and I seems to remember and may have just been a guy who had some snakes, a whole bloody theme park. Every other weekend carnivals, air shows, kitesurfing tournaments, folk festivals, Bobby Roberts circus or the Radio 1 Roadshow rolling up at the showground, or my favourite: the towering municipal bonfire on the beach on Bommy Night. Doughnuts fried in chip fat, Mr. Whippy cones, pink-and-green spun candy floss, little punnets of cockles swimming in vinegar. The bright face of summer smiles on the young and easily pleased.

Then all at once, in a shift as imperceptible and transmutational as the release of hormones into the bloodstream, the winter of discontent pitches up.

As a teenager, when the sense of the future, however undefined, is vital, I regarded Cleethorpes as the most stagnant and deadlocked place on earth. End-of-the-pier and end-of-the-line. I felt just like those sea lions, circling from pillar to post to pass the years until escape, though in my case the pillar and post were the two nightclubs in Top Town (the agreed sobriquet for neighbouring Grimsby) that played alright music and didn't check ID too thoroughly.

Derision for your home town is far from unique and teenage hauteur wasn't invented by me. I thought I knew everything, thought I could categorise all places and things into good and bad based on criteria copied off others or the troubled young protagonists of great American novels. Fortunately, pretension of that sort is usually a temporary kind of blindness. Now I can see Cleethorpes for its many charms. I even love the ebbs and flows of its seasons, with the frenzy of the warmer months giving way to the eerie gloom of coastal winter. One of my favourite feelings is the one I get when I step out onto the seafront from the hug of a warm pub and the company of my very favourite people, collar turned up against the wild air, and look out across the estuary to the peninsula of Spurn Point, the slit of sun falling behind its black-and-white lighthouse and decommissioned sand forts, and the manned gas rigs standing in the coastal bed twinkling like low stars. However do I manage in London, on those nights one is the right sort of drunk to feel mighty and fulsome, with no sea to stare into and feel like a god?

After many years and many miles I can see now that my home county is truly beautiful. From North East Lincolnshire the coastline unfurls round to Donna Nook, 6 miles of salt-marsh where a colony of fat grey seals flop about on the shore, their pups born and raised over the winter months, sheltering in place while their first baby fur comes in. The miles of marshes, latticed by becks and irrigation routes known as drains, were for much of prehistory covered by sea, evidenced in the marine fossils that can still be found there. The North is fortified by roads and settlements left by the Romans, but in Lincolnshire and the east it is the Danes who left the most indelible mark, evident in the many place names ending in –by, –thorpe, –toft and –holme. The uplands, if such a thing can be said of a terminally flat county, is the Area of Outstanding Natural Beauty called the Wolds, a swathe of rolling chalk hills half concealed in low mists and turquoise mystery. Between the ancient wetlands of the Fens and the Carrs, Lincolnshire is a festival of green, an infinite baize whose agriculture provides a huge proportion of the country's food, as industrious now as it was five centuries ago.

In the Middle Ages Lincolnshire was a wild and desolate land, its bogs and marshes blanketed by unearthly fog that concealed what the locals knew all too well stalked the region but could name only in whispers. Countless were the tales of mischief wrought by the race of tiny fenland people known as the Tiddy Mun, all in the name of protecting their waters and wildlife against those who would cause them harm. Across the Fens magic abounded; here a man could attempt to transform himself into a psychic magician called a 'toadman', a process which involved pinning a toad to an anthill until its bones had been picked clean, then tossing the bones into a running stream on a full moon at midnight. Near Cranwell in North Kesteven you can still see the infernal hoofprints of Blind Byard, the preternaturally powerful horse that a champion witch-slayer sat astride when he assailed Old Meg, a sorceress who had allegedly terrorised the town with her hexing and conjurations, before fatally flinging her in the air by the might of his steed. And of course there's the well-known tale of the Lincoln Imp, an obnoxious little lout whose Satan-sponsored path of destruction caused him to be turned to stone. He still sits in Lincoln Cathedral stewing about it.

None of this remotely interested me as a kid. It's only

recently that I've come to find an appreciation of my home county's past and present, but with the caveat, true for me at least, that this is specifically because I've lived elsewhere. Absence makes the heart grow fonder. There is nothing to stop a person choosing to live their whole life where they were raised, but I can't say I will ever be able to relate to it. Dad spent his entire 64 years in the same town. Didn't the familiarity ever breed resentment? How long can you swim in the same tank without it eventually becoming a prison?

17:35 Do you mind if we walk to country park
       tomorrow? I know it's a bit weird but if I don't go
       soon I don't think I'll be able to go there ever again
17:36 I just need to see where he died

Cleethorpes Country Park is 160 acres of parkland adjoining a golf course through which Buck Beck flows out to the sea. A large lake supports the protected wetlands and reedbeds that are the home of many species of waterfowl and waders, sometimes visiting kingfishers. In the summer the wildflower meadow colours the open grasslands, two fields of which are used for respite by the seaside donkeys when off-shift. I used to have a grassy spot nearby where I'd go to read graphic novels and listen to the Pixies on my CD Walkman and find myself very interesting and complicated.

In Country Park the flat expanse of the land redoubles the wind chill. Taking a turn of the lake I said, 'That dog has a little coat on' to Carly every time we saw a dog with a little coat on. Ringed by ancient hedgerows, in the colder months the land has a sparse beauty, with pops of purple thistle, burnt-orange bittersweet and the twisted blackthorn with its deep sapphire fruit. In a small wood of lime, alder, ash and aspen, someone had hung fairy doors on many of the larger trunks.

Red rowan berries and the silver leaves of the white poplar cluttered the ground like an upended box of Christmas decorations.

Carly and I walked together, tossing about a favourite topic of ours – why the genre of true crime appeals to the clinically anxious – in a way that I was aware was being dispatched as a bauble of distraction but in its generosity made me, still makes me, love her. Yet all the while I was looking covertly for a certain tree in the same way Dad had not long before, checking each according to the same criteria (height, strength, access, seclusion) but for very different reasons, and I felt the sudden urge to scream. The hilarious horror of it. To be treading these same steps through wet grass, for him with August early-morning dew, for me the sodden crunch of first frost, felt perfectly demented. Because the place he had chosen was undeniably and outrageously lovely.

Why do people kill themselves in beauty?

It is a comfort and an obscenity. Blessed, thankful, that the last things that touched his body were grass tickling his ankles, the rough-shod hulk of bark on his palms, the salt air from the morning tide pulling at the opening of the day and settling on his lips.

But it also feels to me the most abject sadness. Like the atheist who proclaims a wish for nothing more than a quick torching and a cardboard box, but as the hour draws near speaks of his ashes finding their way to the feet of some lurching willow by the little church on the cliffs, a memory captured and coddled since childhood. At the threshold of death extremities of opinion often lose their conviction.

It is obscene to me that my father killed himself among natural beauty because it proclaims something still alive and throbbing and not done with this world. How could his preference for death over life win out when he still *had* preferences? For oak over birch, for smooth bark or crocodile hide, for sparse cover or full canopy, for the tree that huddles close to its neighbours or one that stands alone. He stood here and he chose.

> It was in the clove of seasons, summer was dead but autumn had not yet been born, that the ibis lit in the bleeding tree. The flower garden was stained with rotting brown magnolia petals and ironweeds grew rank amid the purple phlox. The five o'clocks by the chimney still marked time, but the oriole nest in the elm was untenanted and rocked back and forth like an empty cradle. The last graveyard flowers were blooming, and their smell drifted across the cotton field and through every room of our house, speaking softly the names of our dead.

So opens James Hurst's 1960 short story 'The Scarlet Ibis'. We're not doing an A level here so let me just briefly say I find it one of the most sensual opening paragraphs in the English language. It contains not just vivid colour but the degradation of it right before our eyes, in the petals turning 'rank', the nests vacated, the spectre of depreciating value and incessant tick of time between 'cradle' to 'graveyard', and the piquancy of death and rot already diffuse though the new season had 'not yet been born'. Here death predates creation; we are born dying.

Bleeding trees reveal injustice, in folk stories where a terrible crime has been covered by a shallow grave, only for the tree that grows atop it to bleed in accusation. Others tend the dead, like *Dracaena cinnabari*, the 'dragon's blood' trees found on the Socotra archipelago in Yemen, whose red sap was once used to embalm corpses. Tragic lovers cause trees to bleed in sorrow, as in the doomed Babylonian lovers Pyramus and Thisbe, who each stab themselves for love of the other, splattering their gore onto the mulberry tree whose fruit has remained blood-red ever since. In the Old English poem 'The Dream of the Rood', the 'rood' (cross) of the crucifixion recalls how it was once a tree but was cut down for a higher purpose and, pierced too with nails, it bleeds along with Jesus, their two bloods combined in sacrificial ecstasy.

A magpie was cawing from the tree line. One tree was a lot thicker than the others, with a trunk that you could feasibly scramble up. It had a fairy door with the number 9 painted on it. I took one of its leaves. A beautiful tree but it wouldn't stand out much in the dark. Nearby, a compact hawthorn where the canopy concealed the branches as if a marquee. All around the lake men loitered on their own, looking for a fishing pitch or having a quiet crisis.

'I think it's starting to rain,' said Carly.

The white sky signalled sleet as we rounded the petrol water and Carly guided me out of the park and towards somewhere upholstered and of the living. The day before the Met Office had issued an amber wind warning. We picked up the pace as the brittle wind started to fling the first drops of rain into our faces. Storms on the coast always seem to come out of nowhere.

Dad was born in February, the end of winter, the calendar cusp of warmth returning. The last few spokes of the wheel before the first chink of sunshine. This birthday would have been his 65th, his retirement day. I wish he could have observed the first hint of returning light and found that maybe it expanded the walls of the tank a little. No winter is perpetual.

By the end of 'The Scarlet Ibis' the magnificent red bird is dead, blown off its migratory course by a storm. So too is the character Doodle Armstrong, the earnest and enfeebled boy who is pushed past his capabilities by his brother, the unnamed narrator. Doodle's limp body is found lying face up with blood spooling out of his mouth, staining his chest a 'brilliant red'. The narrator cradles the lifeless body of his little brother, weeping and raging against his own selfish pride. It is clear now that it wasn't just the ibis, magnificent yet fragile, who died 'in the clove of seasons', but Doodle too.

Doodle is pushed beyond the limits of his fragile heart by the tempest winds of the world's uncompromising standards and ultimately, like the ibis, the indomitable forces of nature. As we are given to understand from the beginning, the Armstrong family tree is bleeding – it is losing sap and ailing – a process that can occur in a tree when stress or trauma is neglected and nourishment deficient. As with every element in the vivid picture the bleeding tree exists between the worlds of the living and the dead.

It was the last of the ebbing days, the brink of the new season. It was the murky hours, the clove between sunset and sunrise. It was a tall tree with deep roots and it had been bleeding for a long while.

Tree lore and the immortal yew

However increasingly the modern world seems to want to ignore it, humans share the planet with trees. They give us oxygen and nourish the land we call our home. They allowed us to build the first shelters and later the boats that would bring us together as a species. You might plant a sapling as a child and, when you are 80, see it grown into a giant. A tree's seasonal recession and revival may mirror how we interpret our own lives and generational cycles. Many folk tales exploit this sympathetic bond: a child survives sickness and the family tree replenishes, a hero is slain and back home a tree dies. There has always been a closeness between human life and the woodlands of the world.

In 'The Life Tree and the Death Tree' folklorist Claire Russell charts the transmission of trees as foundational folk symbols which, like dreams, can have many interpretations. She details how the fruit tree can be considered the oldest form of heritable fixed property: since they can be cared for over generations they became an important part of early kinship succession. Indeed, a stolen fruit tree could be a very serious crime. It is out of this, she argues, that the concept of the family tree arose, connecting together property, kinship and a type of generational 'eternal life'.

The Celts had their own 'tree alphabet', an early medieval form of cipher for early spoken Irish, known as ogham. According to a few surviving manuscripts such as the Book of Ballymote, names of various trees can be ascribed to individual letters. Some scholars have suggested that ogham was first created as a cryptic means of communication between communities opposing the authorities of Roman Britain, with short messages written on sticks.

People have always assigned power to the trees around them. A sick child could be passed through a hole in the trunk of the ash tree and have his face washed in its morning dew to be cured of his ailment. 'Money trees' – felled tree trunks into which coins are driven through the bark for good luck – tend to be hawthorn for reasons of prosperity. The same is true of banyan trees in Hong Kong, where wishes are written on paper and tossed high into the tree's branches; if the tree 'keeps' it the wish will be granted. Cedar is important to many First Nations groups including the Salish, who use this sacred tree of plenty ceremonially in sweat lodges, and some indigenous groups place the placenta in a cedar stump to promote prosperity for a newborn. Oaks have been considered oracular trees that could speak to individuals gifted in divination, and are particularly associated with the druids. The bright-berried rowan, meanwhile, could be used as a pocket charm or protection amulet against witchcraft. In Argentina Charles Darwin encountered a tree known as *Walleechu*, around which local people laid meat, cigars, threads from their clothing and 'the bleached bones of horses that had been slaughtered as sacrifices', not in belief in the tree as a conduit, but as a veritable god itself.

Trees have been a vessel for cultures all over the world to ponder the exegesis of creation. They have been imbued with shamanic power, sought as an answer to questions of the stature of life and death. The seductive fruit of the biblical tree of the knowledge of good and evil is the reason humans were condemned to suffer pain. But trees can also bring about life, in the many rituals around fertility. Trees have been regarded as a sort of open-air church in some cultures; in Serbian tradition special *zapis* trees are cross-marked to form a village's protective boundary. Tacitus describes Germanic peoples consecrating copses to particular gods as altars; and the *Landnámabók*, which described the Norse settlement of Iceland in the ninth century, also depicts a sacred ring of trees that became a sacrificial grove. Some trees have a direct role in death. The Moriori people of the Chatham Islands (Rēkohu) placed their dead in a sitting position in the sand dunes looking out to sea; others were strapped to young trees in the forest. In time, the tree grew into and through the bones, making them one.

The weeping willow, native to China and brought to the West with colonialism, immediately evokes grief and loss and is often to be found in graveyards 'crying' over the deceased. India's 'tree of sorrow' meanwhile is the *parijat*, a night-blooming jasmine of sweet white stars that open with the moon and 'die' by sunrise. Long ago Princess Parijataka was in love with the sun god Surya and killed herself when her love was not returned. The tree that grew from her remains could only bear to blossom out of the sight of the sun; the petals that fall every morning at dawn are said to be the princess's grief-stricken tears.

Trees reflect back our desires and fears, and are bound up with what makes us human.

But there is one tree whose spiny leaves drip a stronger intoxicant. A majesty of age, diameter and multivalent meaning, 'of vast circumference and gloom profound', writes William Wordsworth of the uncontested Tree of Death: the yew. Its American cousin, the 'stinking yew', emits a disagreeable, fetid odour when any part of it is bruised or crushed, but the perfume of the British yew is softly sweet and balsamic. One of Britain's few native evergreens, the wood's tensile strength made it superbly suited for the longbow, yet its exceptionally languorous pace towards maturity meant the yew bow was the preserve of only the very best archers. The yielding red berries are the Japanese blowfish of the forest; as candied in taste as they look, yet requiring a faultless preparation. Mistakes are deadly; ingesting the berries' amniotic goop or the yellow seed it encases, as well as any part of the bark or the needles, can result in convulsions and agonising stomach cramps, followed by death by cardiogenic shock in two to five hours. There is no effective antidote. Yews are highly toxic to curious livestock. So why have humans tolerated, even encouraged, these totems of death to share our terrain for so long?

From the inscrutable Sphinx to the siren on the rocks there is a certain irresistible glamour to the outstretched hand of beauty that leads us inexorably towards the grave. The poison yew makes this explicit; it is of course the species of tree most associated with graveyards, the figures that loom spectrally over Robert Blair's 1743 meditation on mortality, 'The Grave':

Cheerless, unsocial plant! that loves to dwell
'Midst skulls and coffins, epitaphs and worms:
Where light-heel'd ghosts, and visionary shades,

Beneath the wan cold Moon (as fame reports)
Embodied, thick, perform their mystic rounds:
No other merriment, dull tree! is thine.

Yews and churchyards have a fellowship so ancient that its origins are uncertain. Julius Caesar wrote of the druids meeting beneath yews as their sacred tree, and their shamanic staffs and wands were made from its wood. (Caesar also records what is perhaps the first documented case of poisoning by yew when Cativolcus, king of the Eburones, died from drinking its sap.) Pliny and Ovid both wrote of the Roman symbolic tradition of yews marking the entrance to the underworld. Corpses would be rubbed with yew leaves to send them on their way. In Anglo-Saxon England churches were likely built on pre-existing sites of yews deliberately, as Christianisation often adopted the trappings of the so-called heathen religions, absorbing them into its own traditions and liturgy so as to encourage conversions.

It was once widely believed that falling asleep under a yew on a warm day would bring on terrifying hallucinations, madness and death. This belief can be traced back to Robert Turner, a seventeenth-century physician who believed that the roots of a yew planted in a cemetery could take up the constituents of decaying bodies and exhale the noxious vapour through its leaves and branches. Even dreaming of one could be dangerous. Indeed, there are many folk examples in which yews are connected with the allusive 'long sleep'. In Brittany the roots of the yew tree are said to grow up through the eye sockets of a corpse, keeping the dead pinioned in the ground and preventing them from rising from their everlasting slumber.

Given these preternatural powers stories of yews often have a proximity to magic and necromancy, and they were especially likely to undergo monstrous changes in moonlight.

In the Fens witches were said to use yews as meeting places; it was commonly held as bad luck to cut one down unless you wanted the whole coven after you.

So why put up with such a sinister and threatening presence as a neighbour? Ancient communities understood the flip side to the symbol of death: the reminder of life and its precariousness that could at any moment tip us into the next one. The yew has an incredibly long lifespan due to its phenomenal ability to 'resurrect' itself. Nearing the end the yew can produce new roots from its centre that plunge into the ground beneath to stabilise and prolong the ageing tree. From this new branches can grow up through the dying hollow, appearing as if the yew has risen from the dead. If you are ever in a yew woodland, look out for 'walking trees'. Here the lower branches of the tree hang so low that they take root in the soil, producing a child yew a few metres from the parent. Both of these processes can continue for centuries, sealing the yew as a potent symbol of rebirth and immortality.

You can see how irresistible I found all of this. Not only did this bank of folklore deliver a magic meeting place for ritual, the solace of communal practice and belief and the macro *memento mori* of nature, it also offered a reminder of the natural and humbling cycle of the parent organism keeping and feeding its child even as it must perish. The yew is a beautiful symbol of post-traumatic growth, for it literally adjusts around its scars and finds ingenious ways to withstand and carry on.

What a shame this image has become unhitched from our cultural imagination, I thought, congratulating myself on reaching a shrewd realisation on parent loss. No doubt my bereavement pathway was reaching an end! How fortunate that I could game grief better than my ancestors could. Simply by googling 'forests within 30 minutes of St Pancras', I could help myself to the pacifying tonic of nature.

Sydenham Hill Wood is the largest remaining tract of South London's ancient Great North Wood, where medieval kings hunted wild boar and where meticulous coppicing for centuries provided timber for Deptford's shipbuilders and charcoal for the city's forges and kilns. Now curtailed to all of ten hectares Sydenham Hill still feels like a sanctum of wildness, silent and still among the wider conurbation of busy Crystal Palace. Once the site of several sprawling Victorian villas, today the veteran beeches and muscular hornbeams hustle between ornamental garden plants that went rogue; rhododendrons, monkey puzzles and one enormous cedar of Lebanon keeping periscopic watch over Southwark.

For days my mind had been a rotted peach stone circled by fruit flies, skittish with morbid activity yet with no clear plan of action, and so I gave in to Michael's attempts to get me out the house. On the Overground train south my heart began softly thumping on the off beats, my vision ever so slightly liquefying round the edges, but I didn't say anything. There is a converse to the contemporary encouragement to verbalise everything: sometimes to speak a feeling is to materialise it, like invoking the name of Bloody Mary three times into the mirror in order to have the apparition appear in your bedroom. At least that is what I felt about my growing anxiety, that a full-blown panic attack that I didn't check in time was 'my fault' and undeserving of sympathy or even tolerance by anyone who happened to be in its fallout zone. Anyway, I'd feel better when I got to the forest – that's why we were coming here, after all.

From the station at Sydenham Hill there is a reasonable incline past a pretty church and into a tree-lined passage that takes you to the heart of the woods. Ahead the silver coin of the morning sun promised serene pleasures waiting at the climb's end. We were about halfway up the hill when I dropped my gloved hand out of Michael's. The disconnection from my surroundings was now too strident to ignore. What was happening to me? Everything: too bright, too loud, the mild altitude suddenly Andean, the tepid London murk suddenly tropical. Why was I wearing a hundred layers? Previously unresolved questions rematerialised. How could my heart be pumping this hard when all the blood had apparently drained from my head, feeling like a useless balloon that any second could disengage and sputter directionlessly until empty? Am I actually, improbably, drowning? The compass pointed to 'yes': the sea-salt taste of nausea, lungs encircled by octopus suckers, vision from the wrong end of a telescope, inner ears the pressure of twenty thousand leagues, the silent tears falling between heaves of useless gasping, drowning breath.

Michael inch-wormed me to a pub beer garden and stuck me in a lovely pastel summer house while I cried myself out and munched through as many propranolol as I had in my bag. He held my hand as I settled down into the familiar enveloping fatigue that succeeds every panic attack, with the draining of the flood of cortisol that had been issued as though I'd just fight-or-flighted a pack of wolves rather than trusted the promise of a nice day out.

It was my first true panic attack in several years. I was as humiliated to have had one in public as I had ever been, but there was something else. I'd failed. Fucking idiot. How could I possibly think I could beat the grief process? Like his death was 100 and all I had to do was count down to zero and it would be done. That wasn't the deal, you didn't get to decide the pace or the order of service.

I'd grown oyster mushrooms on my dining table from a grow-at-home box, and the way the mycelium spun a cloud of white spores that settled on our unopened post and miscellaneous scatterings of pens and loose change was like the unseen dust that settled on my days, suffusing everything. Each day was a fresh loss, each unremarked-upon news story, each time I battered away a happy memory for being too painful. I hadn't 'dealt with' grief. I was tipping it out in pails while the half-submerged boat was still filling with water. Bloodletting while every day more and more was produced in my marrow.

Still exhausted and unable to write about the miserable return of my panic attacks, the Dead Dad Diary entry for that day simply reads: 'I'm his little girl, how could he do this to me?'

How was I ever going to go back to work when a quiet woodland walk was too great a stimulus? That was what made the thought so unbearable. Nature hadn't consoled me, couldn't. I had put my unravelling mind in among the horrific figures that I now realised I had dreamt of over and over, encircling, sneering, swaying like teetering carnival floats. They weren't benevolent or neutral keepers of beauty and magic. And on the walk up Sydenham Hill I had been surrounded by them. *They* had forced my breakdown. It had been the trees. Trees from which rope could be tied.

I didn't want to be a yew growing up from his hollow.

I needed help.

The light half and the dark half

'You're planning on wearing those, are you?'

'You just watched me lace them up, Michael.'

'...'

'What's wrong with them?'

'No, they're ... nothing. Nothing.'

Going out with someone from the countryside means you will never, ever be granted parity of opinion on shoes. 'Perhaps we could get you something a bit sturdier?' they'll say. 'Perhaps,' you'll rejoin, 'we could get you a nice ruddy farmer's daughter for a wife, who can slaughter a pig with one arm and toss a tractor tyre into a hayloft with the other and always has a cagoule in the car, but instead you married me, a sophisticate.' It isn't clear whether you are joking and the walk is ruined.

Fresh off the regional line at Burley-in-Wharfedale station, bungling the making of a good impression on some parents by turning up to walk the dog through a public bridleway in ballet pumps (it was 2007). Ill-prepared. This is how I imagine the Oak King feels at this time of year.

In the throes of high summer the Oak King rules. In his cloak of tender green leaves he is the Lord of the Forest, a prancing Green Man, filling long light days with warmth, fecundity, abundance, Bank Holidays, lawn tennis and Aperol Spritzes. But immediately following his Midsummer peak his eternal nemesis, the Holly King, begins to stir. Temperatures teeter and darkness shortens the days; by degrees the Holly King rises, fortified in strength by hearty stews and Fair Isle jumpers. The Holly King has a cloak of evergreen prickles and red berries draped about his polar bear heft. His whole being: mulled somehow; his whole deal: darkness, decay, hibernation and death. He is Ded Moroz, the Slavic Father Frost; he is St Nicholas and Santa Claus. And he is ready to fight.

Our sweet, dumb summer child the Oak King has learnt nothing from last year: he's turned up in open-toed sandals! His crown of fruits has been picked clean by wintering animals, his coat of leaves turning to umber and withering, shedding acorns all about him as a coterie of squirrels trail after the providence.

It is an easy defeat, and at the strike of Yule the Holly King is back on his throne for the dark half of the year. But when we start to see buds and green shoots the Oak King will be preparing for a rematch, and so the cycle continues, as year after year one king is dethroned as the other succeeds.

A perpetual battle between light and dark is seen in a great many folk traditions. Mummers' plays, a ritual form of folk performance in England and Wales, typically include a battle of paired figures in some form, and Arthurian legend has Sir Gawain and the Green Knight locked in an infinite game of combative beheading. Sir James Frazer wrote of ascendant and descendant combatants in his milestone of comparative mythology *The Golden Bough* (1890), describing vegetation goddesses who journey to the underworld, bringing darkness to the earth, such as Persephone in Greek mythology and Ishtar the Mesopotamian goddess. Robert Graves finessed it into the battle between the Oak and Holly Kings, the God of the Waxing Year and his 'blood-brother' the God of the Waning Year, in his treatise on poetic myth-making *The White Goddess* (1948).

This is closer to the cycle schematic employed by ancient communities across the Celtic world. Pre-modern groups in Ireland and Britain seemed particularly given to explaining the vacillations of their year with this light/dark analogy. The transformation of the natural world would have perturbed such communities as much as it fascinated them. Seasonal change governed everything from how people lived and worked, how they thought and felt and whether they had enough to eat, whether they survived. In the scarcity of winter it could seem like summer was never going to return. And that's why what may initially sound surprising was actually necessary: the winter had to be given equal symbolic importance. The Holly King isn't the villain. At the very darkest point of winter his presence always promises the opposite is coming. Death is a beginning; renewal is always assured. There is comfort in this inevitability.

So the Wheel of the Year turns on its axis, and around every six weeks we celebrate a festival and are reminded that life is a cycle. The Celtic Wheel of the Year is a composite schematic brought together by neo-pagans interested in the festivals described in old Gaelic and druid languages. It consists of eight festivals linked to the seasons in the Northern Hemisphere. Four of these correspond to the solstices and equinoxes: *Yule* and *Litha* (winter and summer solstices), *Ostara* and *Mabon* (spring and autumn equinoxes). These are the high points of each season, indicated by the sun and stars, and revered by the Celts. The other four festivals, known as the cross-quarter days, meanwhile, are the 'doorways' to each approaching season, and these were particularly honoured by pre-Celtic societies as fire festivals. *Imbolc* is at the beginning of February, the first stirrings of spring, *Beltane* (May Day) ushers in summer, *Lughnasadh* prepares us for harvest and *Samhain* (Halloween) is the transition of the dead. These are doorways. They are the clove of seasons.

It is close to Yule. I am not a Christmas person, but that can't have always been the case. Once there had been that fizzing excitement on Christmas Eve that was almost excruciating, ahead of the explosive release of throwing off the sweating covers and scrunching over the end of the bed to retrieve that most extraordinary of things, the Christmas stocking. To have been at tantalisingly close contact with magic yet so frustratingly separated through sleep.

I intuited that Father Christmas was a treat for the faithful so I barricaded up my belief in him longer than was genuine, pushing aside any incongruous details that might reveal the truth. My developing understanding of air flight and the survivable altitude temperature of the cloven-hooved was uninterrogated. The clementine in the toe of my stocking having a Kwik Save sticker on the peel was a dissonance I would deal with simply by placing it back in the fruit bowl on Christmas morning before breakfast.

As was the brattish hunting for the present stash Lewis and I conducted one year. They were merely being stored on top of Dad's wardrobe before 'being sent to the North Pole for wrapping' said Mum, visibly upset in a way that a little voice in my head noted was perhaps too sensitive, and maybe how you might react if you'd saved months of Child Benefit to provide a bountiful Christmas and it had all been ruined by the obnoxious entitlement of a pair of little shits unaware they were stealing their own childhood memories.

I rang Mum recently to ask what my first real Christmas would have been, what would be the first 'big present' that I'd remember. Everything she listed frustrated my memory. I suspect any familiarity with specific gifts was probably through family photos. Because Christmas Day is really more of an essence, concentrated through annual repetition, than a specific memory. When families gather each member tends to slot into his or her defined role to create a shared ritual experience. Each Christmas the effect is strengthened.

At ours there would be the common dad stuff of hovering with a bin liner, frantic that no paper should be strewn across the living room carpet for even ten seconds. Notes taken and affixed on every present so that each thank-you card could be properly personalised ('Thank you so much, [NANNA] for the [STATIONERY SET] and [MINT MATCHMAKERS]. It/They was/were the best present(s) I got!')

But there were some tensions that seemed specific to us. On Christmas Dad preferred dinner to be ready at midday, which would have been merely a ludicrous quirk had it not meant Mum having to start on it while we should have been watching *The Snowman* together over breakfast forming cosy family memories. Of course, he wouldn't help with it. Later Lewis and I liked helping with Christmas dinner, and the three of us chopping vegetables together, sipping red wine and bopping about to the radio was for me the highlight of the day. As soon as he'd finished eating Dad would simply get up rather than wait for the rest of us, until one year I told him to sit back down and thank Mum for once. That year was a tense one.

I struggled to have kindness in my heart for my dad at Christmas; he seemed so remote and hardened. One year I suspected (correctly) that Michael was going to propose on my birthday, the 27th, which gave me an excuse to spend Christmas away from my family for the first time. The following year Michael couldn't get out of a late shift on Christmas Eve: well, I couldn't leave him alone, could I? So again I stayed away. But when it became a pattern I had to admit it to Mum: I found Christmas in Cleethorpes so stressful that I'd spend all of December fretting about it and by January fall into a profound depression. It was too much pressure to be happy, mixed with the increasingly obvious understanding that Dad loathed Christmas and wasn't prepared to make an effort, leading to the inevitability of the two of us arguing at some point during the holiday. She understood, of course she did. The whole thing made me acutely unwell and a valve-loosening visit a weekend either side instead was agreed to be a reasonable compromise.

One of the most popular pastimes among the suicide-bereaved is to nail down the stats on exactly how much of a revolting and self-centred wretch you are. I'll start: I chose not to spend Christmas Day with Dad on what turned out to be his final five of them. Even if everyone to whom you disclose your tally of shame insists that your decision was the right one for you under the circumstances, that the linear nature of time unfortunately precluded you from perceiving the true stakes, and that there is no way to know if your presence on any occasion would have had any bearing whatsoever on the ultimate outcome, you can never quite get the tune out of your head. Join in on the chorus if you know it: but – if only I'd known!

At Christmastime in 1970 my grandfather John had only very recently gone back to sea, having worked at the Mother's Pride bread factory in Grimsby for several years until being made redundant. He went back to what he knew. Talking to Mum about it recently she said that time ashore meant he would have 'lost his sea legs'. I laughed, I thought she was joking. But she was right; her own father had been in the Royal Navy, and losing one's sea legs, the phenomenon of 'vection', that is illusions of motion and disruptions to the balance-monitoring vestibular system, was in sailors and fishermen a real and disastrous malady. After rejoining the trade John had been on only two voyages until the one from which he didn't return. And he might have done so if he hadn't been such a loving father.

Auntie Sarah remembers it like this. The Heenans weren't well off and who got the 'big present' each year had to alternate between the four children. That year it was two-year-old Judith's turn. However, the redundancy pay hadn't quite stretched far enough. Marie said it didn't matter, that Judith was so young that she wouldn't notice or remember anyway. But it bothered John. So the evening after an early-morning return from the last posting, with barely a few hours to sleep, he set off to the shipping port again. One more voyage before the big day. He wanted Judith to have a rocking horse to open on Christmas morning.

A story like this is gilded with potential to become the folklore of a family. Whether the tale has gathered embellishments or not it hardly matters. We are dealing in heroics here; of duty, of questing, of valiance and poetic sacrifice. The masculine vocation to provide literally come hell or high water, and the almost implausibly dramatic conceit of the one single chance a year to fulfil the promise: Christmas Day.

No wonder Christmas was fraught with tension for Dad. I had been an empty-headed kid, a self-interested teenager and a busy and vaguely embarrassed adult. He never spoke about it so I gave little thought to the pain and introspection that time of year must have brought him. A marconigram, the radio-telegraphy used by ships, that John issued on 9 December with the intention it be sent out just ahead of his arrival home, was cancelled by the operator a few hours after the first report of a man overboard, presumably to spare the family further pain. It said: 'Merry Christmas to all – Love Dad.'

He had lost everything at Christmas aged about the same as I was the first time I stood up to him over Christmas dinner. For Dad all Christmas hope has been trapped in aspic long ago. That's the problem with cycles. Festivals can be a comfort but they can also be a clockwork reminder of what you are missing.

Christmas 2020, peak pandemic and just months after Dad had died, was never going to be a normal one. Still, the plan had been to transport Mum away from the house and the deafening symbolism of an empty chair at the table, to my brother's bright and inviting houseplant-filled home in Sheffield, a real change of tempo and one for which I was very grateful. Then with five days to go the government announced London had been designated 'Tier 4', thoughtfully evoking a fruitcake to give this surprise dystopian argot a little festive zest. Basically it meant I couldn't join them. Instantly Christmas was transformed from something to be endured to a meaningful and yearned-for festival snatched away from me.

'It's okay,' said Lewis, a humour to his resignation, 'I think we've all become used to bad news lately.'

I'm not claiming our circumstances were even that remarkable. Probably every family in the country had had miserable news in 2020 they had hoped to process together with the balm of tradition and familiarity at the year's end. But the eleventh-hour cancelling of Christmas was, of the whole sorry year, one of my lowest points.

Michael was grounded too and with the shops cleared out we rejected Christmas altogether to make tacos and spend the day watching horror films. We denied even the season and drank zingy summer beers to support the pretence we were elsewhere, perhaps on sand and in view of the sea. While Michael was making guacamole I rifled through the post I'd put aside and forgotten to open.

A Christmas card signed 'love Mum' and the howl of the sleet wind outside blew over my flimsy fantasy. The unassailable fact of winter brought back and with it the screaming absence of the words 'and Dad'.

The cycle rolls on whether you believe yourself to be participating or not. You are fighting a futile battle with the Holly King. You are turning up in the wrong shoes over and over again and expecting different outcomes. I wish Dad hadn't resisted the confrontation of his pain and found a way to experience the grief of Christmas by reframing the season's emotional intensity as proof of his love for his father. I wish I'd shown him how.

But through craven and self-interested administrative mishandling that I will never forgive, to have this ritual suppressed completely took away something far more important from the struggling and the downcast. The aspect of Christmas I had never credited until then. It took away the reminder that the Holly King isn't the enemy, and that the very darkest point of winter always promises the return of the light.

Grief after a bereavement is metastatic. It can start off in the realm of the physical and cognitive, then radiate out to the social and behavioural, and further circle the spiritual and philosophical, with the potential to warp every element of identity and test every tether to the world.

Sigmund Freud conceived of a process whereby the grieving person has to accept and disengage from the object of their loss and be 'cured' by reinvesting in new relationships. Child psychologist John Bowlby built on this with his notion of attachment; whether an individual has a 'healthy or problematic pattern of grief following separation depends on the way his or her attachment system has become organised over the course of development [in childhood]'. In 1969 the famous 'five stages' concept of Elisabeth Kübler-Ross brought grief theory into the public domain like never before. However, the many peer-reviewed studies by George A. Bonanno and others have revealed the limitations of the five stages theory, and support that the vast majority of people recovering from a loss do so in multiple trajectories and without necessarily ever arriving at a sense of completion.

In the 1990s psychologists Margaret Stroebe and Henk Schut proposed a model of grief which they called the dual process model of coping. It describes the human mourning process as occurring along two streams, 'loss-oriented' and 'restoration-oriented', and, crucially, finds that people switch back and forth between the two as they grieve. Loss-oriented stimuli are things that put the pain and shock of your bereavement front and centre, leaving you distressed, immobilised and in physical turmoil. Restoration-oriented actions are those that let you get on with daily life and distract you from your grief for a while. For its own survival the brain will not permit round-the-clock incapacity; you would simply die. So, Stroebe and Schut argue, grief shouldn't be considered a distinct state to be 'worked through' or 'faced head-on', but rather a naturally self-regulating process in which intense emotions are portioned out between periods of relative placidity. Eventually it is reconciled.

I decided to synthesise all the research and simply become the best at grief. Now that I knew they were coming I could smash through the loss-oriented days, six months tops. In between I would perform the requisite rites; I was executor of the estate, I compiled a chronology for the police, I even cancelled Dad's library card. Yes, it's sad, but there was so much to do! My loss-oriented valve would come at a prearranged time every week with David, a kind yet robust counsellor I'd found of exactly the right disposition to wail at. *But, God, how boring for him*, I thought. So between squawks of hysteria I used all the right words – secondary loss, the ripple effect, anticipatory grief – so that he understood I wasn't just any dullard with a dead dad – I'd shelled out for the premium fast-tracked experience and he could go ahead and skip the entry-level lesson plans. I would have *insights*. He might even learn a thing or two.

Meanwhile, I wasn't prepared for what an adventure grief would be physically. The first inkling was on the train up after hearing the news; my left arm went completely numb and I wondered idly if I might be having one of those quietly cataclysmic heart attacks you hear about. Later, for the first time in my life I threw my back out. I'd wandered to Pets at Home for want of something to do, bent over the enclosure to look at some degus and it took an hour for me to stagger home in tears of hot pain. One day my jaw did a gruesome sideways click and the terrible fibrous ache lasted for days. Sinus swelling, shooting interstitial rib pain, an old knee injury sparking back to life. My poppet must have looked like a hedgehog for all its pins.

No one talks about the compromised executive functioning of grieving. My brain fog, the inability to locate things or grasp a word, lasted months. I threw teabags in the sink and teaspoons in the bin. It wasn't just dottiness; I felt slower, stupider, unable to articulate myself at all, and that made me violently frustrated as well as quite lonely. 'There is a sort of invisible blanket between the world and me. I find it hard to take in what anyone says,' writes C.S. Lewis in *A Grief Observed*. 'Yet ... I dread the moments when the house is empty. If only they would talk to one another and not to me.'

Then there was the weird stuff. My eyesight got suddenly, precipitously worse. I couldn't hear properly; I was always asking people to repeat themselves and studying their lips to help me parse what sounded like nonsense. I either binged or forgot to eat completely. Sometimes things tasted like metal, other times ash. When I drank hot tea the end of my nose went numb and tingly. For a single day I had a crimson rash on my upper back that burned severely then vanished. I've always bruised like a summer peach but I'd wake to find dalmatian patches on my thighs whose origin I couldn't place. I went from a B cup to a double D. Troubled, I typed 'access to additional support' into the NHS website and then the M&S one.

But more than anything the months that followed were typified by exhaustion. You'd think the sheer John Carpenter of it all would have kept me up, but I never had a problem sleeping; I slept for ten hours every night, longer if allowed. Thick crusty sleep that washed me up on the shore every morning still sapped from treading water all night.

The problem was my nerves were shot. If I'd been a 1950s Richard Yates housewife I'd have been given a warm bath of benzodiazepine to lie face down in, my worldly concerns economised to brisket and vulcanised rubber diaphragms. Instead, my default became hypervigilance, convinced the world would somehow end on my watch. I had proven I could endure the big stuff. But now my endocrine system thought everything was the big stuff. When I smashed a Pyrex jug on the kitchen floor I had to spend the day in bed.

'Rabbit heart,' Michael's new name for me, his head lying on my fitful chest.

Feeble catalepsy gave way to a sort of brittleness that also meant my face now just leaked unpredictably. With no small satisfaction my Spotify end-of-year round-up placed me in the global top 0.5 per cent of Lana Del Rey listeners, making

me officially one of 2020's foremost Sad Girls. These are some
of the things that I cried about in winter 2020:

When my really quite substandard short story got
   rejected by a literary magazine
Thinking about 'how the girls will cope' when Jesy
   Nelson announced she was leaving Little Mix
One of my tweets going viral and one (1) stranger
   saying something mean about it
The out-of-season bloom of a fuchsia bush at my
   taxidermy teacher's house reminding me of Dad's
   hanging baskets
Unchecked climate change responsible for the above/
   anthropocene hubris in general
'I thought there was a glass of wine left in the bottle,
   Michael – did you throw it out?'
Extended Child's Pose
The death of Diego Maradona
Sylvain Chomet's *L'Illusionniste* (2010)
An illustration of a frog in a frock coat that I thought
   looked like Dad
Laundry
An email from Thames Water to 'Miss Heenan' and
   being triggered by my own name
The bravery of search-and-rescue dogs
'Death of a House Plant', a radical immersive
   reworking of the play by Arthur Miller
Not understanding pensions
The quiet dignity of a duck on the cover of a
   bereavement book for children
Getting to Tesco and Michael declaring he 'didn't
   really feel like stir-fry' after all and not being able
   to come up with a single other meal that exists

Though of course I was only ever crying about the same thing. I'll only ever be crying about that one thing forever.

Unfortunately, a certain amount of the grieving process (even calling it a 'grieving process') is received wisdom, a sort of cultural blob of circumspect bromides outfitted in millennial pastels. A webinar on suicide bereavement told me I might feel like I was contagious, tainted, persona non grata. Did I feel this? I understood suicide was too bleak a topic that most people might not spend long pondering it, but my solitariness was about my disinterest in the world, not my shame separating me from it. Some of the Dead Parent Community resources struck a chord. Like that of being a kid again, yet at the same time delirious with responsibility, feeling suddenly in charge of your remaining parent's prospects. Many of my experiences were represented nowhere: the sense of invincibility, powered by fearsome energy and resolve, almost exhilaration with all the occupation of my time, an unimagined reality about to dawn and the creativity that inspired. The boredom when it ended. Grief is so boring.

I'd contacted David when I had finally seen the value of a disinterested ear. Michael had lost his remaining grandparents during lockdown. He was spending the height of the pandemic ducking the airborne droplets of frothing anti-vaxxers to come to the aid of women trapped indoors with their abusers. Adding me to the list of people he had to look out for seemed too much. I was basically fine! (Obviously now that seems preposterous.)

'I am being very responsible,' I informed David sagely. 'Just because I'm fine now doesn't mean I will always be, so I'm getting out ahead of it.'

I also thought I'd got to the root of why I had become so preoccupied with bereavement rituals. Many funerary practices fulfilled exactly the restorative function Stroebe and Schut described. A ceremony was performed, followed by an allotted annual festival or rite of memorial. The continuing relationship between the dead and the still-living was honoured in a discrete portion of time and place. This left both psychic space and moral permission to spend the rest of the year on the practical tasks – the tilling of fields, the raising of livestock – on which survival depended. Today, in our much-diminished observance of bereavement, we are missing the tangible comfort of this social and cultural function.

Hmm, David would get a kick out of this insight, I bet. At least I'd stand out among all the other sad sacks he had to listen to every day.

I'd been reading about the Sagada people of the Philippines, I told him on our next call, who practised sky burial by suspending their coffins from mountain cliffs. On the way up the mourners jostle one another so that the corpse might drip some fluid or another on them, a sign of good luck.

'That's lovely, Hollie, thank you for sharing that.'

'But before that – you'll love this – the body of the dead relative is strapped to a chair and left out front for several days. This is so any neighbours can stop by, bid them a final farewell and deal with any unfinished business. You can vent any pent-up anger at the corpse, it's even encouraged.'

'You didn't get to do that, though, did you.'

Woah, buddy, don't start with all that head-shrinking stuff – I was regaling you.

'No.'

'Do you think that is what you are struggling with right now, the lack of final exchange?'

'It was like we were having a conversation and he just ... got up and left in the middle of it. I wasn't done talking yet.'

For all my prattle, for once I couldn't think of anything more to say. We finished the hour early.

The only solid thing I have learnt is to try to trust in the two phases, the loss and the restoration. Here's one plucked from the griefgeist that does hold up: you will probably laugh sooner than you expected but you will be in pain for much longer than you could have imagined. Everything you feel in whatever order you feel it is legitimate. Disorder is going to be your shadow for a good while but it's worth not taking him *too* seriously.

Some days it can seem like only the grand sweeping macro tides of life now bear any significance. In the morning you can make all the decisions: I will quit my stupid job, I will write a book, I will travel the world with my great love. And in the afternoon you can break down and cry because your great love was slightly late home because he was picking up pierogies and you had a very vivid fantasy that he had fallen under the tracks between Hornsey and Finsbury Park. And you didn't want pierogies anyway, you wanted pizza.

On mourning, mortality and memorial

To assume that humans are the only species to grieve their dead would be a grave mistake.

Pack animals like wolves and goats have been shown to become agitated, stop eating and isolate themselves after the loss of a mate. When an infant chimpanzee dies its mother may carry around the body for several days. Elephants have been observed returning periodically to the site of dead relatives purely to stand around. The BBC documentary *Life on Earth* captured a herd gathering to carefully touch the bones of a long-dead member in turn, before covering them with vegetation.

These are signs of the internal maelstrom let loose by grief: pain, disbelief, loneliness, panic, fear, yearning and emptiness, just as humans experience it.

But as the outward expression of this emotional and psychological tumult, the phenomenon of mourning is exceptional.

Mourning is an intriguing combination of how we feel and how we wish to be seen to feel.

Neanderthals are known to have intentionally buried their dead around 130,000 years ago. Whether this was merely for reasons of preventing scavenging was unclear, until excavations of the Shanidar burial cave in Kurdistan revealed the remains of ten Neanderthal men, women and children scattered with ancient pollen clumps, suggesting flowers could have been part of a funeral rite.

To think about one of our closest human relatives out on the Eurasian steppe picking flowers that meant something to her, perhaps a specific memory that bound them to her father or merely possessed the aesthetic quality that she understood as honouring him, catches at the divine power of the primordial.

Nature is deeply implanted in mourning culture. The most common graveside offering is, of course, flowers. The laying of flowers goes back to the earliest humans and its specifics vary according to fashion, location and purpose. To me the cloying scent of lilies is guaranteed to bring on a migraine, but when bodies were prepared in the home this overpowering fragrance served an obvious purpose. Sweet-smelling herbs were also used in and on coffins to mask the smell of decomposition. Perfume and vibrancy have been traditionally provided by roses, lilies and amaranth around cypress, cedar and willow supports in Europe, delicate white chrysanthemums in Japan, and bright carnations and marigolds in the Americas.

Wreaths have an obvious symbolism of renewal and completion which many may find a comforting sight at a graveside. The ancient Greeks laid wreaths at the graves of early Christian virgin martyrs and in early modern England wreaths particularly commemorated the tragedy of death in maidenhood, especially wreaths of white flowers. For centuries, in Celtic and European communities wreaths were most often made from evergreen plants and shrubs, meaning appropriate tributes could be created during the winter months, the colour provided by seasonal berries, with the attendant symbolism of coniferous trees surviving through the harshest of winters heralding the triumph of the eternal soul beyond death.

Scotland has a strong tradition of melancholy folk songs wherein doomed love is both portended by and celebrated with plants and flowers. One ballad tells the fate of Barbara Allen, an uncultivated rose who spurned the advances of a besotted and (honestly, kind of drippy) young man. Only after he dies of unrequited love does Barbara realise her true feelings, and follows him to the grave with a broken heart.

> Barbara Allen was buried in the olde church yard,
> Sweet William buried beside her,
> Out of Sweet William's heart grew a red, red rose
> Out of Barbara Allen's, a briar.
>
> They grew and grew in the olde church yard
> Till they could grow no higher.
> At the end they formed a true lovers' knot,
> And the rose grew round the briar.

Sentimentalists could cry a river for Babs and Bill, a story that has everything for the perfectly piquant ideal of mourning. Out of rotting human transience, budding blossoming beauty. Out of steadfastness and heartsickness, the ultimate reward of the everafter.

It is the sort of sentimentalism that some grasp when forced to confront the reality of death, but there is also a grand tradition of the very opposite. Two Latin texts of the early fifteenth century known as the *Ars moriendi* ('The Art of Dying'), authored by an anonymous Dominican friar, depict death with unambiguous corporeality. The *Ars moriendi* was also propaganda; it warned against the deathbed temptations of despair, apostasy and avarice of one's material possessions, and by imploring renewed hope in God's forgiveness, was intended to console the dying. The inclusion of woodcut illustrations meant the message was widely disseminated to the literate and illiterate alike, and the tract had a transformative effect on the popular contemplation of death. By the end of the century these themes would coalesce in the *Danse Macabre*, a contemporary allegory that found widespread expression in art, drama and printed books. The *Danse*'s cavorting skeletons and defleshed corpses cackled at the viewer, for their inescapable message was the universality of death. King, monk, serf, child or beautiful maid, personified Death has no prejudice and leads them all Charlestoning towards a vacant grave.

There was something of these dark winter nights that led me just as willingly. It was there in the quickening of the blood, a stirring in the pondering of the fragility of life. I wonder if I would have been better adjusted if my grieving had manifested towards the former mode, that of floral tributes and sugary verse. On social media I followed pages dedicated to the vanitas picture: the still-life paintings that posed decomposing fruits next to sensuous blooms, delicate soap bubbles and ephemeral smoke mingling between depleting hourglasses and expiring candles, usually looked over by the eyeless gaze of a human skull, intended to remind people to shrink from earthly vanities and accept the certainty of death. So too did I understand the relics, the motives of collecting *memento mori*. I wanted something I could hold, a talisman of mourning that I could wave in people's faces. Increasingly I shared in that same morbid impulse that a couple of centuries past had kickstarted a whole industry.

As we touched on previously, the Black Death was a pandemic of such apocalyptic proportions that it demolished mourning customs the length and breadth of Europe. With the Enlightenment religious authority crumbled even further, situating what we might regard as 'modern' society for a highly commodified marketplace for mourning ephemera. One popular product was offered by the invention of the daguerreotype camera. Though cheaper than commissioning a painting, 'death photography' was still expensive; in many cases a person's only image was the cherished one captured after they had died. There is something about these photographs that never fails to startle me: because of long exposure times requiring extended stillness, in group portraits the dead subject is often the one sharpest in focus. Children are portrayed seemingly asleep with their dolls, or sometimes held up by their still-living siblings. If the eyelids could not be made to stay open occasionally eyes were painted on the film after being developed. It is uncanny and uncomfortable but I can understand it; in documenting the fleeting it offers something like control over a chaotic world of unforeseen tragedies and abbreviated life spans. For many, post-mortem portraiture offered the comfort of long term, a memory fixed forever.

Mourning periods can be rapid and restrained, or extended and extremely visible. The Japanese Buddhist Obon festival memorialises the dead on the first anniversary, then often the 3rd, 5th, 7th and 13th years, and on a further handful of anniversaries sometimes up to the 50th year. In contrast the Navajo time for mourning is four days, during which displays of emotion are discouraged, and afterwards the deceased is not spoken about again. This is not a lack of feeling but to ensure the spirit is not waylaid on its journey into the afterlife.

Others make remembrance a permanent alteration. In Fiji prior to the twentieth century the scars of mourning were permanent. In James Frazer's *The Belief in Immortality and the Worship of the Dead* (1913) the anthropologist records the customs of ritual circumcision and fingers being cut off in remembrance. Frazer notes one case 'after the death of a king of Fiji [in which] sixty fingers were amputated and being each inserted in a slit reed were stuck along the eaves of the king's house.' In a lecture on the topic he recalls some elderly members of the community had only a thumb remaining.

If these mourning rituals are the public gesture of deprivation or having had something taken, the excess of something can be equally weighty with meaning. Shy congregations just needed a little push. From ancient Greece right up until the beginning of the nineteenth century, to encourage everyone to let loose, professional mourners would be hired to howl and wail and perhaps claw at their faces and clothing for dramatic effect. Ritual crying traditions are not something that ever made it to Victorian England, however. The Victorians preferred the services of a funeral mute, hired to stand at the church door with a sad and pathetic expression. Hopefully the mute's dignified silence would rub off, as 1880s etiquette manual *Cassell's Household Guide* warns of the terrible alternative:

> It sometimes happens among the poorer classes that the female relatives attend the funeral; but this custom is by no means to be recommended, since in these cases it but too frequently happens that, being unable to restrain their emotions, they interrupt and destroy the solemnity of the ceremony with their sobs.

We can laugh at these etiquette books with their obsession with minutiae, excluding emotional women and detailing exactly the appropriate width of a black border on one's death stationery, but at least they gave some due respect to the understanding that the process of mourning might take a very long time. The privatisation of mourning has meant that while we are no longer comfortable with a space for plaintive community crying or even just wearing a certain colour for a certain period, somehow being two bottles of wine into scouring up and down every Cleethorpes street on Google Maps at 4am for a glimpse of Dad on his bike is fine, as long as it's out of sight.

On one of those explorations I discovered the front door of my parents' house had no door knocker, meaning the Google van had driven past on the one day in 2018 when Dad had taken it off to replace it with an antique Lincoln Imp one I'd bought him for Christmas that year. It was like a porthole into a dead timeline; he had probably just stepped in to get a Phillips-head screwdriver, so very close to being present, that I all but lost my sanity. It was the strangest memorial; captured without his or my consent yet the closest to my own personalised *memento mori* as I could imagine.

While grief may be observed in other species the instinct to solidify this emotion for long lasting contemplation and commemoration is very much human.

Memorials come in many guises and usually centre around three concerns. Honour, naturally, and on a proportionate scale. Specificity is also important – think of those anonymous piles of skulls in Europe's ossuaries and how the identity of their owners is lost to time. Lastly is the importance of location. Some of humanity's greatest injustices have been the removal of people from their homeland, severing their link to the burial grounds of their ancestors. The prospect of dying away from home can be a profound psychic burden; the exploited migrant Chinese labourers who were worked to death building the United States transcontinental railroad were terrified for their mortal souls, as burial in China is required for a spirit to ascend. One of the most depraved evils of American and European colonialism was the stealing of indigenous people for their human zoos, the remains eventually ending up as museum exhibits. None of this can be excused by cultural ignorance. British imperialists, for example, knew exactly the value of being buried on home turf, setting up hundreds of cemeteries across the empire under the Imperial War Graves Commission, to ensure that any Englishman who died while fighting abroad may spend eternity under a manicured English garden lawn.

Memorials can be on as gargantuan a scale as the Taj Mahal or as portable as the Korean custom of turning the ashes of loved ones into shiny blue-green beads. A scaled-up version of ash jewellery is the Neptune Memorial Reef. Remains are mixed with cement and used to build the columns and sculptures of this underwater mausoleum and man-made sunken city, off the coast of Key Biscayne, Florida. Family and friends can visit via glass-bottom boat or scuba tank.

When designing a memorial there is a tendency to confer angel status on the dead and present the loss as indelibly solemn. Which is why I love the Merry Cemetery in Săpânţa on Romania's Ukrainian border, which cheerfully memorialises its tenants in all their blood-and-guts materiality. Often literally: many of the 800 hand-painted and brightly coloured headstones depict the cause of death, such as that of one man who was run over by a truck. But that's not to say the memorials are tasteless – far from it. In their specificity they are highly intimate; no one-size platitudes, no hack 'rest in peace'. For over 40 years Stan Ioan Pătraş was commissioned by the people of the town to paint their loved ones doing what they loved in life, often with darkly funny limericks in local dialect. One reads: 'Ioan Toaderu loved horses. One more thing he loved very much. To sit at a table in a bar. Next to someone else's wife.' And why shouldn't a memorial provoke laughter? There is something revolutionary about having the unadorned truth of a life depicted on a death marker, to enshrine for posterity the humour that made a person human. Pătraş now rests alongside his works under a self-designed headstone, carried out by his apprentice.

The Merry Cemetery strikes me as far more meaningful than

the grand public cemeteries left over from the Victorians with their regimented grave art; a broken column for a life cut short, clasped hands for hope of being reunified with a spouse in heaven, a book to represent a scholar or perhaps a person who had lived a long and complete life. But there is one aspect of overblown Victorian mourning culture that I find surprisingly affecting.

At Marples Café on the seafront with Auntie Sarah, Mum and I had been talking about Victorian hair jewellery, the popular fashion of having the hair of your loved one intricately woven into a brooch, locket or set of earrings. It was a bit morbid, wasn't it? Without a word Auntie Sarah reached into her purse and handed me a small envelope. Inside was a perfect curled lock of my Grandma's hair. She had carried it with her every day since her mam's death.

And it shut me up. All that remained of Dad was his ashes in a cardboard tube that we had put at the back of his wardrobe while we thought about what to do with them. To me the ashes were abstract; they didn't seem to be 'him'. But here was a piece of Marie, a bit I remembered too, half golden half silver, and it was like a magic token. My dormant memories of her suddenly ignited.

I realised that the most successful monument is just a switch. The second death is the more final one; the death that happens when you are forgotten by the living. Whatever it may be that delays this is the only true memorial, whether it is losing a finger, visiting a grave 40 feet down with the help of an oxygen tank or sitting alone and holding your dead dad's pair of glasses as I am now, memorial is as personal and specific as the relationship you had and continue to have with your dead. There was no hurry to decide what to do with Dad's ashes. For now, I was his memorial.

If the Victorians were the punctilious and etiquette-obsessed captives to convention we imagine them to be, I have an unusual soft spot for them. They understood what performance can do. A circumscribed behavioural language around bereavement doesn't solely function as a tribute to the dead; it also acts as guardrails for the turbulence of the still-living. It lets everyone know what's what. A specific hat worn for a pre-arranged period of time tells others how they might expect the wearer to behave. Chances are he's probably going to be a bit of a drag. It follows that, after slipping it on, he too will adopt the same behaviour patterns for everyone's ease and convenience according to a collective social contract. Which is quite the feat for a hat.

To labour the metaphor: in the first six months I tried on every hat I could find about the place: the crisis manager, the busy organiser, the duteous daughter, the irreverent deflector, the estate settler, the intoxicant dispenser, the greased-for-efficiency emotional reconciliation machine. I truly believed I was doing well. But as any espionage agent knows, the best disguise is the one that doesn't announce itself in its hurry for credibility. I could never quite get the beret at a flattering angle, or else it pinched my ears or made my head look bulbous, as if I was attempting to conceal a tangle of spiralling thoughts and undigested pain, which was of course manifestly the case to anyone but me. I'd forgotten how to dress myself. My personhood was *en déshabillé*. I was an oversized shirt fastened up wrong, and there's you approaching with the incandescent spotlight of your neighbourly concern and I'm hopping from foot to foot and struggling with the buttons, frantic and scandalised that you should see any part of me exposed.

The months that I moved back in with Mum were characterised by the rumbling trepidation that I would run into someone, anyone, and so I decided that I should prepare what to say. It became a fixation, a scene of dialogue to pick up and idly script and re-script. For some reason the person I'd imagine running into took the composite form of my old primary school teachers or the parents of kids in my class, with whom Dad would have interacted at the school gates and on the birthday-party circuit. 'Responsible adults' I now see. If on the street I passed the actual kids themselves, now adults, I could just blank them, who cares, but not the mums. For what only now presents as extremely simplistic Freudian reasons, I needed to appear together for these hypothetical parent figures. I needed to be prepared for the performance. A collision could happen anytime and anywhere – say, the big Asda in Top Town:

> Responsible Adult: And how's your mum and dad?
>
> Me: Mum is well, thank you. [*Pause*] But I'm afraid that Dad is no longer with us.
>
> RA: Oh no, I'm so sorry to hear that.
>
> Me: Thank you. He'd had episodes of psychosis brought on by major depressive disorder for the past ten years, and wasn't of his right mind when he decided to take his life.
>
> RA: I had no idea. That's awful ...
>
> Me: I'm sorry to have to tell you this here [*gestures at cat litter*], but there is really no casual way to bring it up.
>
> RA: I'm just so sorry for your whole family. Please give my love to your mum when you see her. Rod was such a kind man, I remember him coming over to

```
   help Simon re-lay the roof tiling after
   that big storm we'd had ...
Me: That sounds like Dad, yes. Always
   helping people out.
```

Replaying this celluloid reel I see myself as remarkable in my fortitude, Ingrid Bergman as Joan of Arc. My skin glowing, my expression poised. My character-actor big Asda mum co-star taken aback by my grace and magnanimity.

'She is coping so well,' she'd later say to 'Simon', an invented confection of exemplar suburban fatherhood if complete roofing imbecile, 'it was like she was comforting me, not the other way round.'

In the end it happened only once, when I ran into the mother of a boy I shared years of swimming lessons with, and it went like this:

```
RA: And how's your mum and dad?
Me: Yes, good, yes, well, thanks, yes.
   I'll tell them I ran into you. Bye!
```

In traditional Jewish *minhagim* (customs), recorded in thirteenth-century German sources, a death in the home would be indicated by the pouring out of water. Jugs of *mayim she'uvim* (drawn water) were emptied on the threshold in part because its proximity to death meant the water was now considered undrinkable, but also to cover the sound should anybody inside utter the news and Satan overhear it. Crucially, however, it let anyone passing know that a death had occurred inside. As does the black ribbon hung from the front door in Honduras and El Salvador, asking visitors to tread quietly and not to ring the doorbell. In cities like Oakland, California, the tragedy of loss is made unmistakable and highly personal with the friends of the deceased commissioning hand-airbrushed 'RIP shirts' and wearing them for many months. Popular in areas particularly high in youth homicides, the T-shirts serve not just as a memorial but as a way to protest urban violence. I can't help but think these community-wide broadcasts are a lot kinder on the bereaved, sparing the grieving from having to voice their loss over and over again.

In many ways the unending list of strangers I had to tell about Dad as I unpicked his finances and direct debits was an easier task, not because announcing his death became any less painful but because I was saying it as the new person I had become, the only version now in existence. Friends were harder. They'd known me before. Anyone in the club will know this: in grief you will lose two to three otherwise healthy friendships.

Of course, my closest friends I called immediately and without thought; like reaching for an umbrella when the sky opens. But by your early thirties you tend to have collected a number of auxiliary friendships, from old jobs and friends-of-friends, who function mostly as nice but context-specific enhancements to your life. And like my physical grief reaction, extremes of agitated animation and bedbound paralysis, the task of informing people in my life of my new circumstances fell into the categories of all or nothing. I either rang you wailing or forgot you ever existed. Online forums often discuss losing friendships as one of the most alienating and upsetting side-effects of loss, an acute wounding akin to secondary grief. Rarely do people confess to how willing they might have been to let this happen.

I became hardened to solitude. I was still on furlough and had no reason to speak to anyone except Michael for weeks at a time. That suited me. I burrowed deep. No one could understand me and I delighted in it. Then on one of those merciless nights where it gets dark at 4pm I read an article that added an interesting perspective.

After working with the wives of servicemen missing in action during the Vietnam conflict at the Center for Prisoner of War Studies in San Diego in the 1970s, family therapist Dr Pauline Boss developed the concept of 'ambiguous loss'. Boss was interested in the experience of people whose loss was indefinite in some way. This may be literal: a wife longing for her husband's body un-recovered from war or a mother yearning for an abducted child. The loss can also be psychological, where the body is present but the person is perceived as psychologically 'absent' or having undergone a significant change in identity. For example, a loved one joining (or leaving) a religious cult, being the survivor of trauma such as a natural disaster or terrorist attack, or falling to drug dependency or other forms of addiction. But couldn't a life-altering bereavement also have this effect? The realisation was that in this scenario it wasn't me who was experiencing the ambiguous loss but all those who knew the me of before.

For particularly the first six months my inclination to hide came above all else. I wasn't a very nice person. If I could be bothered to reply when kind people messaged to ask how I was, it would be calculated in a way to disinvite conversation. I certainly wasn't about to ask others how they were, for while I resisted the unforgivable megalomania of believing mine was the worst possible incarnation of 2020 (no one had a good one except maybe Jeff Bezos and nasal swab fetishists), I certainly cared very little to be reminded of it. It was specifically the small things that turned me into a hissing goblin. I couldn't understand why someone was telling me about their boyfriend's rotator cuff injury or complaining about the surge pricing on their Cornwall holiday cottage, or how to make my face sit while they did.

Then from time to time there was this horrible impulse to provoke. To one poor friend I sent a screengrab from the horse-riding segment in *The Day Today*, one horse being named Massive Bereavement. Pleased with myself, sending up a familiar flag, the show we used to watch together at uni, deadpan and self-lacerating to get a rise. Reading back messages to another, I am by turns obstructionist, contrarian, melodramatic, and often pointedly rude. I don't know why I couldn't just say, 'I'm so sad all the time, and the endlessness of it frightens me so much.'

I set everyone the most impossible of tasks. To intuit my state of mind when that facility wasn't even available to me. There is a seductiveness to 'No one understands me.'

Two things can be true at once. In grief you can feel that the skin has been flayed off your body, your raw innards exposed to the grating wind. At the same time you can feel invincible, validated. *The very worst thing has happened to me, as I long suspected it would, and you all thought I was mad and paranoid! See, I was right all along!* Some years back I had lost a long-term friendship after a trifling disagreement that was, as it so often is, about something else entirely. I hadn't been able to reconcile this friend never asking after my Dad for fear, they said, of upsetting me and raking up settled soil. Now I felt grimly vindicated.

In Melbourne Richelle received either silence or free-associative WhatsApps from me at all hours. The time difference meant phone calls had to be pre-arranged, yet typing out a cogent message was often beyond me. I realise now she must have been sick with worry when I didn't respond for several weeks, but she never held it against me. Once I went silent for days and then dispatched an incoherent message to her about seeing my dad's toothbrush next to mine and becoming ashen with indecision on whether or not I should put it in the bin. In what would have been the middle of the night in Melbourne she replied:

> Do you remember when I left London and gave you
> my old raincoat, and in the pockets you found all my

disgusting used tissues? My mum laughed so much
when I told her because it reminded her of how after
Nana passed away we found tissues in all her jacket
pockets. It was equally gross and upsetting at the time,
but years later it is something Mum still smiles about.
That's a lot of emotions over a lot of years about dirty
tissues. It is not mad or abnormal for you to cram
a whole bunch of emotions into anything you feel like.

She didn't even try to address my dilemma, for of course it
was nothing to do with toothbrushes, and everything to do
with the invisible ties we have with other people. Dirty tissues
and a lot of years.

When you are tempted by the masochism of not being
understood, remember that if you are lucky enough to have
good friends they will want to understand you, and that is
more than halfway. Combat the impulse to isolate entirely.
There is succour in the act of letting people in.

But do meet them halfway. Just because you have suffered
a life-altering bereavement it does not mean that life has
stopped for anyone else. Other people will have successes and
failures, rough days and high points, lives that continue, and
you cannot just dismiss all this as beneath your threshold for
attention. There is a modern aphorism that says, 'It's okay not
to be okay,' but it's not okay to be a bad friend.

At the same time, if you have a friend who has lost a parent, sending two texts expressing regret and saying, 'Please let
me know if there's anything I can do, I'm always here,' and
then dropping communication for a year: absolutely fuck
that. A grieving person is living in a plane in which time has
concertinaed beyond recognition; they do not have the surfeit
of resources to come up with something for you to 'do' so that
you feel better about the situation. Community mourning
concepts addressed this, giving everyone defined roles and the

reassuring cloak of the ceremonial. Make it your business to find a role. It's easy, they are all the same, and they all have one purpose. To tend.

Scorched earth requires many hands to turn.

Widow's weeds and winter hags

In the perpetual fighting between the Oak King and the Holly King each can display his strength and has his turn to win out; neither of their respective masculinities is ever in question, for every year needs its light and dark, its waxes and wanes, its summer and its winter. Change the archetype to female, however, and you get Marzanna the Death Crone.

Marzanna the Death Crone represents winter or death across Slavic mythologies and, though she may have had some ancient associations of rebirth to counterbalance the death stuff, at some point in the Middle Ages any such philosophical tussling fell by the wayside: in these incarnations she is incontestably evil. During the festival of Maslenitsa straw effigies of Marzanna are imbued with the negative qualities of winter – cold, isolation, scarcity, darkness, illness, death – and carried through the town, set alight, then symbolically drowned in a river or pond for good measure. This performance of sympathetic magic, observed more light-heartedly today by Czech and Polish people, helped to banish the Crone and all that she represents to her lonely grave for another year.

Crones, hags, beldams, harridans; older women unsupervised by a man, or daring to outlive one, have historically been an uncomfortable fit to societies the world over. But first let's look at her patroness, the aspirant model and, as it turns out, quite unattainable ideal of feminine dedication and forbearance: the grieving widow.

The grieving widow is the pinnacle of feminine dignity; St

Bridget is Sweden's best-loved patron saint and later mystic, a woman who after losing her husband devoted herself to prayer and charity in commitment to him. In the West, doting widows are totemic and come in any colour so long as it's black; a tradition starting in Europe in the Middle Ages and reaching stratospheric heights of popularity by the nineteenth century. It is easy to conjure up a cloaked and veiled figure in 'widow's weeds', idealised but morose and strangely forbidding; just the silhouette of Queen Victoria in mourning is immediately recognisable.

That the monarch's remaining public life was spent in visible grief bestowed a certain solemnity and uncomplaining perseverance that some would argue still haunts the rafters of the English national self-image, yet at the same time it had the effect of suppressing all other personal identifiers she might have otherwise had. Here is a woman clad in black and experiencing heartbreak in the universal human way, and simultaneously her flattened aspect gives nothing, she is royalty in the remote and self-preserving manner required of the institution's survival.

Its effect on her subjects was not merely to inspire the uptake of visible mourning on an individual basis but supercharged mourning as a class signifier. Not everyone could afford a special outfit just for mourning, and the widow's dress inevitably became a visible status symbol. Its etiquette was highly prescribed; for the first year a widow wore heavy dull black crepe and a full veil whenever she left the house (which incidentally could only be for reasons of necessity, never 'frivolity'), while for the second year she might include a bit of black silk or, for a treat, even some jewellery that wasn't comprised totally of hair. The final six months were a heady carnival when to the black she might add a little grey accent, maybe even a ribbon of mauve or lavender.

White is the colour of mourning in many places, red or indigo in others. In Thailand, while general mourners wear black, purple robes are specifically reserved for the widow to define her sorrow as distinct on a spiritual level. White plaster mourning caps called *kopis* designate a widow in some indigenous Australian cultures, while in the Oro province of Papua New Guinea widows are garlanded with hundreds of distinctive grey beads, made from seeds of the *Coix lacryma-jobi* shrub or 'Job's tears'. After a period of total seclusion, a widow's slow recovery from her loss and restoration to life is symbolised by removing the considerable weight of these strings of beads. Just like the black gloves, capes and bodicing of the Victorians, devotional shedding and metamorphosis through transitional clothing seems to be an important part of a bereaved woman's re-inclusion into the community.

Ritual crying, as we looked at earlier, has a specific social function when applied to widows. A man whose death on the battlefield was truly tragic might have his bride fill a bottle, or lachrymatory, with tears, until his body was safely repatriated. Filling a whole jar with tears strikes me as bleakly impressive, but then historically widows have had a lot to cry about. Look closely among old gravestones and you might still find a deceased woman's name alongside the word 'relict', an archaic term for widow. It means 'remnant'. When her husband's death precedes hers, a wife is surplus, kitchen crumbs, a carpet measured wrong and left in the basket at the entrance of the discount store. Our modern sensibilities might be affronted by this but it was very much true; a widow knocking about the place was deeply inconvenient. So imperative was it that a deceased man's money stay within his family that many cultures had and have a tradition of levirate marriage, that is a widow married off to the brother or other male bloodline relative.

Or they could simply be shunned, disinherited and left to live in poverty and social abnegation. The solution? One was a historical practice in some Hindu communities, first recorded by Cicero and others from 300 BC, known as *sati*. A widow sacrificed herself by climbing atop her deceased husband's funeral pyre and going out with him. We can be charitable here by saying sometimes *sati* may have been voluntary. Ralph Fitch, a merchant traveller in the Mughal Empire, recorded the 'choice' laid out before one adolescent wife in 1591: 'When the husband died his wife is burnt with him, if she be alive, if she will not, her head is shaven, and then is never any account made of her ever after.'

Perhaps all this was why filling in the forms for Mum's 'widow's pension' made me disassociate a little. It was a dizzying anachronism. Like I was placing an order for an iron lung or applying for a hunting permit ahead of woolly mammoth season. It was strange to think of her like that, defined by the absence of something, as if the fact of Dad's absence wasn't obvious enough.

The fact is the vast majority of history's women needed a man to survive, and so as we might expect many folk tales focused on widows as money-grabbing and not to be trusted. Folklorists use the Aarne–Thompson–Uther Index to categorise folk stories, and category 1350 is the theme 'man feigns death to test his wife'. Tales of this type, and of type 1352 – 'widow mutilates her husband's corpse to save a new lover' – are plentiful, sometimes bawdy, but always the message is the same. A married man should never rest on his laurels; even marriage cannot always course-correct a woman's conniving nature.

Hang on though, we nearly forgot that other dimension of female economic precarity: titillation.

Romantics the world over have tried to capture in poetry and paint the elegiac beauty of a woman sobbing. Almost without exception these are young widows, ostensibly depicted in contemplation of the sublime tragedy of having lost so young, yet incidentally – the artist brings his paintbrush thoughtfully to the side of his mouth and leans in breathily – wouldn't you say she is also just a *little bit sexy*? Complying with a school's dress code, pursuing spiritual clarity by joining a religious order, undergoing years of education and training before enduring gruelling shift patterns and chronic low pay all to tread the halls of a hospital ward: there isn't a type of woman about which men have not immediately excavated for erotic potential. But the merry widow is nonpareil.

Folklore stories about just how up for it widows are abound. The story of 'Wooden Johannes' is one example from Germany, collected by Hans Wilhelm Kirchhof. A woman goes to bed every night with a lifesize puppet carved to look like her dear departed husband, until one evening, due to a farcical mix-up, a real man ends up in her bed instead, while the old widow pretends not to notice. The next morning the woman, cold after a strangely vivid dream and far more nocturnal exertion than is usual, wakes to find there is no firewood in the house. Except ... well, her late husband wouldn't want her going cold, would he? Wooden Johannes, we hardly knew ye.

As night follows day, expressions of female sexuality must be punished. Widows collected into harems for the use of the nobility was a practice recorded in ancient Egypt. Other parts of the world, including areas of East Africa, have seen the heinous ritual practice of 'cleansing' a widow with sexual intercourse by a man hired for the purpose. Still more superstitions are used as a pretence to humiliate, all underscored by widows' disgrace under the male gaze; shaving of her head, being forced to sleep on the ground and remaining unseen by men at all times.

But widows can be much more than oversexed money-hungry tramps. They can be akin to witches, and their presence can prompt not pity but suspicion. Dhumavati, the widow goddess of the Tantra, rides a chariot of black crows dishing out poverty and misfortune, but is also a figure of wisdom and ungovernable femininity. In the case of Marzanna her appearance inspires dread as it foreshadows misfortune, brings terrifying sleep paralysis and even, in a barely concealed euphemism, interferes with *other women's spinning*. Via these traditions women are told that their husbands are not safe around widows. Marzanna too is associated with the Roma myth of the 'enchanted huntsman' in which a man's soul is entrapped within the demon widow's magic mirror for the whole of winter. In the regions of Eastern Europe, where she is known as Mara or Mora, she stalks the frigid night to drink the blood of men or suffocate them in tendrils of her long white hair. She is the hag-featured 'mare' of the word 'nightmare'.

A pretty impressive reputation. To me at least.

'What do you think of the word "crone", Mum?'

'Well, it's not my favourite.'

'But it has positive associations too. "Croning" is the great rite of gaining wisdom, freedom and power ...'

'Yes, but it makes me sound old.'

Whatever I've been through, the physical effects that left me debilitated and barely able to work, the psychic alienation, the friendships I'm losing, the marriage I'm straining, the near-total disarray of my understanding of what happens when you die – the very worst of it has been watching my mum suffer. I worried so much about her, staying up late reading about 'broken heart syndrome', blazing through Wikipedia page links like Benson & Hedges. Every time I hugged her she felt slimmer in my arms and I thought about ways I might slip knobs of butter into her tea or red meat into her soup. It played on my mind that I had written down her new bank details and passwords so she'd have them handy, and how it would make light work for any conman from an Ealing comedy who might somehow get in.

'A few days ago I fell down the stairs!' she told me on the phone as if she'd misplaced her glasses on her head or dropped porridge on the cat and, comprehending for the first time that she was alone, I had one of those worrying fits that are only quelled by going very still and very quiet and then vomiting.

I was shoring up my remaining parental holdings. Wasn't this the same as treating her as a remnant?

This at least was a notion that Mum didn't see as entirely negative. After all, Mum and Dad had been married just shy of 35 years. An enormous part of an identity is stitched into a marriage of that length. I had lost one of my people and an important tentpole in my self-perception, but on top of that she had also lost her witness. A whole lifetime's bank of memories had suddenly become unverifiable.

'Remnant' could be taken in the sense that the person 'left behind' is a keeper of stories. A testifier. In English tradition the 35th wedding anniversary is known as the coral anniversary. Corals are organic structures made up of thousands of tiny components that over a long time become rooted by a firm skeleton that they create together. A mysterious symbiotic living memorial.

Once again I was coming to understand that when it comes down to it I will see my parents foremost as people who only exist or existed in relation to me.

I knew I wasn't able to understand it totally but I was sorry. So, so sorry this had happened to her. Because some of it really did feel like my fault.

In the days after Dad died a miscommunication between the coroner's office and the police revealed details of an injury, aside from the overwhelming number of factors pointing to it, possibly indicating a cause other than suicide. I relayed the news to my mother and watched her anguished face realign itself as hope went up like a flare. Maybe he had been the victim of an attack, or maybe it was an accident. We'd have to tell everyone, wouldn't we, set the record straight.

When the post-mortem clarified the situation I sat her down again and watched the same face as my words wrenched that hope away. After we'd finished crying I texted Richelle: 'It was like the last two weeks hadn't happened. Back to day one. Actually might have been the worst thing I've ever had to do.' I felt like I'd widowed her all over again.

To counter my distress I've plundered folk beliefs in search of a greater understanding beyond the four walls of my own head. But when it comes to widowhood here's one stock figure that, at least in our part of the world, has shrugged off many of these antiquated and often misogynistic associations. I am grateful for anything that lifts her burden, and that she might define widowhood in her own way.

That's not to say they are all bad. One exception is found in Chilote mythology of the archipelago off southern Chile, whose inhabitants *love* widows. Widows and their cats are important tools in hunting the mysterious *carbunclo*, a strange little rodent-like creature with a mirrored head that spits out gold and jewels to whoever finds him.

In the New Year, when lockdown adoptions had made the house pet a scarce commodity, Lewis and I took on the fanatical mission of finding Mum a cat. Finally, success: Henry was Mum's tiny ginger urchin who immediately became totally and pitifully obsessed with her. Us first round of children were no longer the yowling priority and whenever she plonked him onto my lap so she could go have a bath he passed the torment by crying and mooning dramatically at the door.

'I'll have to go,' she said, as we were discussing the content of the debut book of her first-born child, 'Henry keeps head-butting the phone out of my hand because I'm not giving him my full attention.'

'Maybe he has a good tip on some treasures,' I said, but she had already hung up.

Dad was supposed to retire today, 8 February 2021, his 65th birthday. After a life of toil he was supposed to be cashing in his dividend on the social contract he'd signed aged 14. He was supposed to be greeting what we call the autumn years, years to reap and rest. He wasn't supposed to go straight to winter.

February marks *Imbolc* in the Celtic calendar. It is thought that *Imbolc* was an existing festival associated with the goddess Brigid that later became Christianised in Ireland as the feast day of Saint Brigid of Kildare. Pagan Brigid brings poetry, protection, healing, solace; throughout rural parts of the country small four-armed Brigid crosses made from rushes are still hung in the doorway of the home. *Imbolc* is the first stirrings of spring, the lightening of evenings, the resumption of milking ewes, the blooming of the blackthorn promising the crop of sloes to savour later in the year, the first glimpse of snowdrops defying the frost. Softening. Unbinding. Yielding. Hope.

The clove of seasons. Cloven so wide a man could fall between.

I have Dad's last diary in my hands. The rest of the year's shift patterns are recorded in his studious script: always in yelling capitals, a lifetime's habit. Evidence of another, a pen nib pressed in so hard that the paper distorts, reminds me of the word I associate most with him. Deliberate. But here in my hands is the open provocation to that association. This calendrical countdown on the remaining days of work he had left to complete, double figures slipping to the single. Obligations that he didn't attend written by a hand that no longer exists.

OVERTIME 3 til 10?
SPECSAVERS – book
STAFF TRAINING
CHRISTMAS
HOLLIE BIRTHDAY (33)

Marks made when one finger was still clinging to the brink of the chasm walls.

In the back of this pocket diary is a mostly blank notes section that contains what look to me to be mystic runes but are probably circuit board diagrams, alongside notes that suggest plans to rewire the kitchen. An ouroboros of a biro low on ink. A phone number. I ring it; it rings out. I am a chicken scratching in the mealy dirt. How am I supposed to *perceive* anything, Dad, with these pickings? Isn't it incumbent on you, my ancestor – for I realise with a start that that is what my dead dad now is – to scatter little cuneiform tokens of meaning throughout my temporal landscape, for me to grandiosely seize and nimbly decode for everyone's satisfaction after you have gone? You, boy, quick, assemble the men, for I have cracked it: significance!

I am about to put it down when the back page flips open, and up in the corner are the words: 'WILLIE NELSON – ALWAYS ON MY MIND'.

I spend the entire day listening to this song. Brigid surprised London with an unexpected blizzard and so, on Dad's 65th birthday, I trudge around Kentish Town with my pink and bundled-up head laden with searing words of torment and apology. The song is really quite beautiful. I come at it from different interpretive angles, contemplate Nelson's gentle rasping rumination next to the Elvis Presley version (dreary), the Pet Shop Boys' (transcendent) and the industrial paint-tin-down-the-stairs pyro-clangthesising of German fancy dress troupe Rammstein, all to see if comparison might shake something loose.

Maybe I didn't love you, quite as often as I could have. For a meditation on the ending of a great love due to distance, changing feelings or just not saying it often enough, I'm struck by the lack of self-pity or protestation. Nelson's voice is made tender by his age, the regret in it absorbingly restrained.

Why this song? Did it remind you of someone or something? Did its message speak to you in some abstract way? Was it a favourite of your father's? Your mam's? It was released the week of your 26th birthday – was that a memorable one? Was that your happiest age? Before I existed? Was it the last song you ever listened to? Were you asking me to play it at your funeral?

You are always on my mind. Especially today. But mostly I just watched the sky split open and obscure the world in white nothing and wondered: *Where can you possibly be?*

It was the start of the anger. No, fury. Combustible like a front row of Wooden Johanneses at a Rammstein concert. I felt the anger wick the skin and render the fat, begin to char the bones of me. Roiling fury. That I didn't understand him at all, couldn't ever understand, because he'd left the conversation while I was still talking, the cycle incomplete, and looking back through ancestral rituals and folk tales that attempt to parse the black beyond was all well and good but it could only ever give me the sweeping universal, not the excruciatingly specific information that I craved. Nor could the slippers in the hall, the scribbles in a diary, the note the police haven't yet returned. The stupid plodding song of a dumb stupid DUMB old hippie? Touchpaper. I had no way of ever knowing what it meant.

The snow fell in sheets. I assumed snow falling after spring-heralding *Imbolc* was an inauspicious sign. Like, for instance, an immolation of bitter anger after months of, if not progress, fairly placid introspective collapse. Surely it throws the cycle out of kilter.

But it seems the ancients accounted for setbacks.

Imbolc is the time that the Cailleach, the weather-controlling hag and storm queen across Gaelic tradition, gathers up her firewood for the rest of the season. In some stories she is able to transform into a giant loathsome bird with a long wizened beak to do so. To ensure she has enough time to feather her nest, capricious Cailleach may decide to make winter last a great deal longer. If this is her plan she makes *Imbolc* bright and sunny so as to collect plenty of wood for her fire.

Therefore, if *Imbolc* is a day of miserable weather it would come as a relief. It meant the Cailleach was fast asleep. It meant that winter was almost over.

TREE OF GHOSTS

21°34'27.8"N 158°16'46.0"W
Hawai'i

IT WAS NEVER EXPLAINED TO me why I didn't have a mother. From the consoling faces of the women in the village I suppose I was meant to have come upon the reason myself. I knew that I was considered a *poor thing* and that if I didn't speak much and looked down at the ground it could occasion a fresh pomelo or a macadamia bun thrust into my hand from time to time. I had the notion that if I laughed too hard or looked too happy it would dishonour me, my family, somehow. But that wasn't all of it; as I grew in understanding I began to consider whether those sweet gifts were in fact votives. That the warm glances might be the shopfront for whispers around the village, whispers that the wrong one had been lost. That I hadn't been worth the trade.

My elementary school was the preference of the military families, being the closest to the ocean on the leeward side of the island. Nestled between O'ahu's two volcanic ridges, it was protected from the coastal winds in the fragrant basin of the pineapple plantations. My shyness had recently dimmed, making uncertain and exhilarating room for a new and hot temper. A clumsy corridor knock became a scuffle, became a barrette snatched from the glossy horsetail of blond hair that held it, became one of the American girls – for we didn't quite think of ourselves then as also American – tossing an incendiary '... jealous because she has no one to do her ugly hair! She doesn't even have a mom! Because she *killed* her!'

Not information altogether new to me, but to know suddenly that it was known, and just not the private reality I had come by degrees to acknowledge, caused the ground under my feet to become strange, misaligned.

At home, my face buried in my grandmother's lap, I demanded the full truth. Why hadn't she told me that me being born was the reason my mother was gone? I wailed, softening nicely into the indignance and its power. I clutched the only photograph I had of her for theatrical effect, a small woman with dark eyes and an orange dress sitting by a pool of water I didn't recognise. 'Because that isn't what happened,' Grandmother said. 'And she isn't gone at all.'

The next morning we set out for Ka'ena Point. Beyond the limits of our village we passed close to Kūkaniloko, the royal birthing stones considered the *piko* and centre point of the island, and home of many spirits of royalty who still watch over it.

'*Piko*,' said Grandmother, gesturing at her stomach. 'Belly-button.'

A blast of heat as we rounded the coast and the sea came into sight. Goddess Pele's preferred climate of intense sun, ferocious winds and salt spray had held off the tourists and their hotels on this side of the island so far. The only sign of other people was a couple of painted canoes baking on the volcanic shore, the fishermen themselves somewhere out of the high sun.

Seabirds skittered back and forth between the water and the cliff face of the Wai'anae Mountains. Beneath them Pacific storms had churned the skeletons of a thousand different reef dwellers into the fine dust that made up the dunes. Compact little shoreline shrubs with delicate flowers gave a patina of pastel to this otherwise bone-white shore. 'Ilima papa with its sunshiny yellow for lei-making, and for funerals.

And on the high bluff of the westernmost tip, one twisted candlenut tree, a bony finger pointing at the sea. It was here the spirits of the dead came to depart: *Leina a Ka'uhane*.

'The leaping place of ghosts.'

When we die there are three paths. The ghost is always wandering, Grandmother explained, smoothing the trunk of the strange tree with her hand. Given a chance they exit the body from the inner angle of the eye, the *lua-uhane*, and go wherever they please, even into the dreams of those who know them. If they can't get back, or if the person failed to honour his ancestors in life, these restless spirits can become *lapu*.

I knew about *lapu*, all the island kids did. The bamboo forest in the valley on the windward side and the screams of the banshee you could hear if you stayed after dark. The *huaka'i po*, night marchers, a procession of ancient warriors that could turn a person to stone on sight unless they were to lie face-down on the ground until they passed by. The green woman of Wahiawā Botanical Garden, whose own children had wandered off and were never found, and who took any child she came across there to replace them. O'ahu has always been full of ghosts.

'But your mother, she wasn't restless. It was just her time. She came right here to this tree, climbed the branches on the dry side, because that is the side that takes *'uhane* towards the beyond place.' This second path was a place of light.

A raft of white wings like two banana palms sailed over our heads.

I looked up through the spare branches to the sky. I knew about the third path. Every family has them, *'aumākua*, the ancestor spirits. They could be a shark or an owl or a mountain, and as long as the family continued to honour them the *'aumākua* would protect their home.

'She didn't die because she gave birth to you, girl. Her body was very tired and so her *'uhane* came here. We tried but it couldn't be coaxed back. Her spirit didn't want to walk on the ground, it wanted to watch you from the air.'

'She's in the air? She can fly?'

She smiled and looked past my shoulder. I followed her gaze to the rocks set back from the shore. There was movement in its crevices.

Not yet fledglings, the albatross chicks were still grey blurs. Blindly they turned their beaks to the sky with the sound of the colossal wings of the returning parent. The mother *mōlī*, black smudges round her dark eyes, her body cut like white marble. Almost her entire life was spent in the sky over the sea, just to feed her children.

In the small altar that Grandmother kept at home for our family's *'aumākua*, there was a small carving of a bird at the front, its eyes painted with the same dark diamonds.

Later, a lot later, for I was lucky enough to have a lot of time with her *kino* on earth, Grandmother lay motionless on her bed while I watched the *kahuna* work. She believed only this man could bring her back to her body, catching the reluctant spirit in an empty gourd and pushing it back in through the biggest toe, working to press the spirit further up the limbs, up to the heart. To tempt it to remain her body was wrapped in fragrant plants. Chants came next, a purifying bath. The hospital resuscitation had ended quietly too. That night she was in my dream smiling and drinking a cup of rum and so I woke up knowing it hadn't worked.

We did it how she wanted. The final piece of barkcloth is usually the honour of the son or daughter; I draped it around her shoulders and tied it in the middle. She was taken to the furthest cave so that her bones would be undisturbed and she would never become a wandering ghost. At the feast I watched the dancers tell a story of life and loss through the movements of their hips, the lightness in their arms and beckoning fingers.

That day I came here and touched the tree of the dry side and imagined her touching the other, soft and green, from the other world. Smiling and smiling.

'Travelled westward.' We still call it that. Do you know why? The path of the spirit always leads westward, so as to return to the land of the ancestors.

And one day, a long, long time from now, I will travel westward too. Or maybe it will come to be that I am a bird, or an octopus, or this rock we are sitting on. You can throw a lei of yellow 'ilima into the ocean that day too, if you like. Your grandmother and my grandmother and I, we will all watch. And you will know we are here.

SPRING

A FTER THE SNOWFALL IN LATE February, March came on like a tropical rash. By the end of the month an unseasonable warm spell had spread across the UK, reaching even to the temperamental east coast. Whether this impeccable synchrony with the vernal equinox, Ostara's festival of renewal and light, was experienced unconsciously, it was nevertheless clear in the national mood. People in England were once again free to mix with friends and family outdoors under the 'rule of six'. I returned to Cleethorpes like a homing pigeon.

Day-trippers to the Lincolnshire coast from the Yorkshire towns on the TransPennine line are known locally as 'comferts', being that they 'come f't'day'. Which is what my Uncle Jim called me, laughing, when I saw the fine weather outside and announced I was going to spend the day at the beach. Maybe in my years living away I'd forgotten the answer, but I couldn't at that moment figure out why it was that none of us ever thought to use the beach. Sunbathing and sandcastles were for the kiddies and the comferts. How absurd that the sand 800 metres from my mum and dad's front door was as clean and fine as any I had paid hundreds of pounds to sit on closer the equator. Granted the difference was usually the temperature, but that didn't hold quite true today.

I bought three cans of pink gin and a packet of Haribo Strawbs and set out my pitch on the quieter end, past the Ferris wheel and towards the sea wall. *Chemtrails over the Country*

Club had just dropped and, headphones in, I picked up where I'd left off with *The Body Keeps the Score*, amused that if I had written this scene these character extrapolations would read as too on the nose. Never mind; the point was I didn't have to think about anyone else for several hours. It felt like the first good deliberate solitude, not the cowering one I had adopted over the last six months. Full lungs of bounteous bright air, the feathery slip of the wind warm on uncovered arms, and my little boat bobbing along on a gentle blood-alcohol current, mild and analgesic.

Heat shimmer distorted the outline of what was looking more and more like a person. The shape levitated between where my toes were buried in the cool sand and the cluster of wind turbines grandstanding far out on the Humber bank, a fly on the lens of an otherwise faultless blue sky. I've never stopped finding it surprising just how far the estuary recedes, the expanse of sudden space strewn with the slimy piles of seaweed the tide forgot to take with it. Or how far you could walk out, if you weren't put off by the black Humber sludge. Further even than the red and yellow warning buoys anchored to the riverbed, making the now-unmistakable fact of a man beyond them appear comic in miniature.

The man was wearing Dad's coat. A mid-thigh-length hooded navy anorak with a red inner. Hair, as far as I could see, cut close and speckled black and grey. Carrying something in a plastic bag. I watched as he walked idly up one end of the sandbank, sometimes ending the length in a series of purposeful circles, before abruptly stopping and turning round to walk up the other. Steady and unhurried. The river was drawn back like bared teeth but it was on the turn, and the flood tide would come on quick. I was disconcerted, then desperate. Why wasn't he coming back in?

There is an old English coastal superstition that says no

person can die unless the tide is drawing out; if a sick man lives through one ebb tide, he will linger on until the next.

But surely that only applied if he wasn't directly in its path.

With a synchrony that felt planetary, as if I'd stood on the pier and blown on a conch to summon him, my friend Sean chose that moment to check in. My phone buzzed in my lap. A picture of his gleaming six-month-old, thick-eyelashed and perfect, and a 'How you holding up, mate?' I called him immediately, sobbing.

In the gravitational way of small towns Sean and I had collided with one another many times over the years. An orbital schoolmate and later colleague of Dad's who finally came to endure in true and mutual fondness even after I left home. He bought me my first ever Jack-and-Coke, not very long before I was permitted my last ever go on his drum kit. A former lifeguard, RNLI volunteer and eventual paramedic, if your life has been saved in North East Lincs in the past 15 years there's a good chance Sean had something to do with it. He has this placid optimism underscored by an earnest deference in matters of life and death that puts me in mind of a mascot bear of a national park, a beloved but respected authority in a brimmed hat telling visitors to 'Have fun out there!' but to 'Always remember to respect nature!'

'There's a man really far out, Sean. I've been watching him for ages. He's just walking aimlessly up and down but he's getting further out ... It looks like he's walking out to sea.' Frantic now and breathless, propped up on my beach towel surrounded by empty tinnies, Strawbs scattered to the four winds.

'Do I tell someone? He's going to get cut off. And not to sound crazy but, I mean, he looks exactly like Dad, I'm not kidding.'

Invariably Sean was there for me exactly when I needed

him. Those first miserable nights at the very beginning of 2011 when things changed forever, Sean was there for all of it.

Christmas 2010 had been an especially difficult one. Of course, I hadn't realised it was the 40th anniversary of my grandfather's death at sea. I came home to a dad I didn't recognise. Not the expected directionless anger and tense withdrawal but an unfamiliar and intense sorrow. I went to him, sat on the bed as he wept. About everything and nothing; that his father hadn't got to see him play football, about the nice time we'd had at Butlins when I was 11. I was mystified, for I was 21 and my head was unformed dough. I didn't know what a nervous breakdown looked like. I didn't know if I was supposed to do anything. *What* to do.

At New Year I returned to York, where Michael and I had just moved into our first flat, still dumbfounded. About a week later and *ah* : the call in the middle of the night, the chaotic stuffing of a suitcase, the first bloodshot train back to Cleethorpes. A sequence that I didn't know then would book-end the decade.

Those early days of 2011 had done something inexorable to his mind and, with near-total insomnia since Christmas, Dad had taken to long night-time walks. Only this time he hadn't come back.

I arrived home to much activity. Now I can recall it all only in a series of trancelike flashes. The house uncharacteristically full of people. Uncle Jim pacing the streets all night with a torch. Police dogs in the attic. Mum panicking when she couldn't find Dad's passport. Someone ringing Humberside Airport and the ferry port in Hull with a description. One of Dad's co-workers offering to drive out to the Humber Bridge. Why would ... ? Oh. Trying to peel off the contact lenses dried fast to my eyeballs. 'Reason to believe he might have travelled to Iceland.' Finding an enormous brass crucifix in the bottom of a sock drawer and letting out a spasm of laughter. The tidelines of drying sweat under my unwashed hoodie. Notes next to each of the landline phones warning of people listening in, or of covert cameras trained on the house: hints that the reality I'd assumed he and I shared wasn't a given. Stepping out into the pitch-black garden to cry and hearing the Coastguard helicopter overhead. Taking a white pill given to me by a woman I'd never seen before in my life who was drinking tea from my favourite mug.

To no one in particular I said I thought he'd probably walked into the sea. And then he walked in the door with a policeman.

Afterwards. After: the marks had been noticed. After: transporting him, improbably pliant and in good spirits, sitting up front in the riot van – the only vehicle available – laughing and chatting about football with the police officer, while the only space for Michael and me was in the back, where we were untethered and rolling around in a metal box that smelled of piss, Michael trying to stop my head hitting any sharp corners as I tried to quell my hysteria to inaudibility, convinced I was brushing insanity. After: blustering into an acute crisis inpatient facility staffed with kind eyes and lanyards and turning him over on his first psychiatric hold, wondering how I (a child!) could have a deciding role in this, and shouldn't I ask an adult, and actually where even are we actually and why am I being handed his belt? Afterwards. Afterwards Sean scooped up what was left of me and took me home.

On the way we stopped at the grubby pub where it turned out Dad had been hiding between wandering up and down the coast each night. He had rented a room for seven nights in total; thankfully he had been picked up near the docks by the police before the reservation was up. I had my first sense then of being on the clock. We had been just a few days from tragedy. Later the intervals would shorten.

Michael went into the pub to retrieve Dad's belongings

and Sean and I sat in the car. It was the first time in several days that the ride had stopped and I had space for thought. None of them were good. I started to cry.

'He'll be okay, Hollie.'

Sean had been present at so many brushes with death, so often he had been part of the life-raft for the desperate and afraid. A lot of the time Sean's were the only reassurances I could tolerate.

The surge tide encloses the sandbanks of the Humber at frightening speeds. A change in the wind blowing paddle-boarders into a shipping route. Patches of quicksand in which struggling only serves to trap a person tighter. Every few weeks the RNLI has to go out for a dog-walker or a group of kids cut off from the shore.

But listen, the man on the sandbank was okay, Sean was telling me. He may look to be in his own world but he knew exactly when to turn back to beat the tide. He walked out most days, members of the public were always reporting him and the lifeboat station knew all about him. They always kept an eye out anyway, don't worry.

Nevertheless, Sean stayed on the phone with me while I watched the man casually retreat as the waves rolled in.

For not the first time I apologised. My floodgates, historically compromised, were nowadays easily breached.

'Don't apologise,' he said. 'Hallmark of being in the club, isn't it?'

When we were in secondary school Sean had lost his mum to cancer. Only right then did I comprehend the parallel between his formative bereavement and my dad's loss at the same age.

'I don't want to say I'm glad you are in it, because it's just shit, isn't it, but if I have to be in the club at least I already know someone,' I sniffed, laughing slightly with the post-cortisol comedown.

That first time Dad went missing Sean got off a 12-hour shift driving an ambulance and got straight into his car and continued looking for him. Ten years later he received the news of Dad's death as he was in neonatal intensive care, red-eyed and awake for the entirety of the two days since his beautiful little boy's troubled entry into the world. It seemed to me I was always meeting my old friend here, in this space of life and death. Between the clove of worlds.

The breeze had turned to a chill but after I hung up I sat on the beach a while more. I was surprised that I had never put it together. How similar they were. To channel grief at almost the exact age into saving the lives of others. Would it be too poetic to venture a factor in this shared impulse to be topographical? It after all had manifested in the same way; they both rescued from the sea.

Why did the man walk out to greet the oncoming tide every day? Courting the peril that everyone who grows up here knows could be one muddy misstep away. Maybe in the pull and wane of the tide he found he could better appreciate the inevitability, the unseen whirr of the cycle, that speaks to something ancient and, in our time, all but abandoned.

Tidal waters and restless sleep

As with any shoreline, Cleethorpes beach has a shifting, chimeric quality. Once the means of survival for the tiny fishing community settled there from the earliest of the Norse raids, over the passing centuries it saw growth mainly through cottage industry, with little family-owned stalls selling cockles and oysters lining the length of the seafront. Then with the coming of the railways and the Victorian invention of 'leisure' Cleethorpes almost overnight became a health resort and fashionable sea-bathing haven. I wonder what the old cockle fishermen would have thought of the fine ladies taking in these so-called medicinal waters. They would likely be wary. For as far back as records go the waters off Cleethorpes have hidden a surfeit of mysteries.

There seems to be something amiss off the Humber estuary. Over the years the sea has spat out various troubling ephemera onto the coasts of north Lincolnshire; in 1870 a ghost ship absent of its crew; in 1901 a headless body; some 20 years later a cargo of thousands of onions washed ashore like an invasion of sea urchins; and in 1953 a greengrocer named J.R. Pye, declared dead on the sand, a verdict he contested in person the following morning at Louth Town Hall.

One of my earliest memories is the sight of ten thousand beached starfish as far as I could see, so abiding perhaps because of the unforgettable smell of them crisping in the sun. At particularly low tides tree stumps from a Neolithic drowned forest can be seen protruding from the mudflats. The uncanniness extends to the sky above the brackish water: ufologists cite the many corroborating reports of a large spherical object visible for more than an hour over Cleethorpes promenade in 1956, and picked up by radar at RAF Manby, as verifiable proof in their cause. Some blame the 1970 disappearance of an American fighter-jet pilot, who reportedly saw orb-like objects hovering over the estuary before his equipment malfunction, on something akin to a 'Humber triangle'. Unexploded Second World War mortars and mines turn up with some regularity and, in 2020, a complete Bristol Type 156 Beaufighter rose up from the riverbed, cockpit mysteriously empty but its ordnance still live. Human feet have washed up more than once; one still contained within a size-9 Reebok. On the more plausible end of the spectrum, beached minke and even sperm whales are sadly not uncommon but in their impossible scale, no less striking.

Much of this flotsam has a reasonable explanation. But it

doesn't change the ingress of the inscrutable symbology of the sea washing up in my subconscious. Its dangers and peculiarities have been rising up in my dreams for as long as I can remember. In the wake of Dad, I dreamt of the sea every night. Many of these dreams unfolded along the same lines.

A wall of water 200 feet high surging towards Cleethorpes promenade. Floodwaters with unyielding efficiency laden with strange debris. People scrabbling for higher ground as Dock Tower threatens to become the only marker of the sunken town. And in every version Lewis, perennially six, has let go of my hand and is nowhere to be seen. He is a mirage in a raincoat and wellies, glimpsed among the chaos of the splashing crowd but always just out of reach. Or I yank him out of the vacuum of a whirlpool only to have our boat begin to capsize; underneath a dark shape circles. It's always Lewis being snatched away by the tide, taken off by a wave or swept into a storm drain, and I am always unable to do anything but watch a pair of little pink hands pinwheeling in the froth.

Tides have fascinated humans of every age, observing and recording their movements in order to explain them. To the priest and the poet the tides may variously evoke antediluvian judgement, mortal helplessness and despair in the face of God's inscrutable wrath. But they are also cleansing; floodwaters rise to wash away the impious and unrepentant. The tide is destructive yet regenerative.

Though I grew up seeing the coast get smaller and larger twice daily, I have only recently discovered that different places have different numbers of tides, anywhere from one to four. This is due to a complex dance involving the push and pull of both the moon and the sun, a question of vibrations and reflections bouncing off continental shelves and folding the tide over and back in on itself, accelerating and decelerating with a temperament of its own. It follows then that water is the symbol of the subconscious mind, its ebbs and flows, allusive and fluid and ever-changing. In literature it has equally denoted wildness and internal tumult or birth and rebirth, in religion the reckoning as well as the baptismal. For the sailor the tide table is a map and a gospel, and its correct interpretation dictates whether a navigator and his crew might live or die.

As a barrier between the land and the sea, residing not quite in either, the coast summons comparisons to other inscrutable realms: that between sleep and wakefulness, life and death. Many figures of folk tradition tread this damp sand. Selkies, the seal-people of Celtic–Norse waters, cast off their seal skins to walk the shore in human form. And a bewitching form at that; it is said that no man can resist the soulful brown eyes and sweet song of the seal maiden. Tales of romantic encounters with selkies are knitted into the lore of communities in Orkney and Shetland. Though such unions were not always happy; a selkie can be taken as a wife simply by hiding her seal skin to ensure she is unable to return to her home. On blustering Orcadian nights the selkies trapped on land will sing their heart-rending homesickness.

The Blue Men of Minch, a pack of marauding Hebridean faeries with skin personifying the sea (perhaps originating from the Picts who stained their bodies blue with woad), prowl harbours for incoming boats to capsize for sport. Entire communities are cursed for overfishing and abusing the generosity of the sea. The lost city of Ys, formerly the jewel in the Brittany coastline, was swallowed up by the ocean, due to one princess's failure to respect the might of the Iroise Sea by opening the levee in order to steal her lover into the fort. Indeed, the outline of the Humber region is always in flux, with some sunken towns losing their battle as recently as last century.

For those not put off by its volatility or by the mysteries it conceals, living by the sea can come with its perks. I didn't have to go back far into the Heenan family tree to find one of us on the grift. Michael Heenan, my great-great-grandfather, was a fisherman out of the Humber port. Haddock wasn't the only thing he transported: in 1899 he appeared in court on a charge of smuggling more than 50lb of tobacco. Smugglers flourished the length of the North Sea coast, a criminal enterprise but understandable given the hard lives and lack of opportunities of the people there.

Estuary waters are bountiful in other ways. Along with its contraband the churn of the tidal water makes Cleethorpes beach a particularly good spot for finding hag stones. Smooth pebbles with a naturally bored hole through the middle, hag stones are protective amulets against witches, and are tokens to bring fortune, cure ailments and quell storms. To ensure a ship returns safely, a hag stone was tied to a ship's mast or nailed to its hull, or kept on the bedpost of a bed to which a man away at sea wished to return.

The second time Dad became ill was 2013. I had come home again, stomach full of viper-toothed dread. We monitored him very closely while we decided if he needed to be committed. In the meantime, Michael and I decided it was best to keep him distracted so we took him to the Smugglers, a pub facing the slip road down to the beach, for scampi and chips. Dad was quiet in a way that worried me more than the talk of being bugged and spied on, and he spoke only to say that he had found a shell on the beach on one of his all-night walks. It seemed important to him that I have it. It may not be a hag stone but I have rubbed it so much, holding it as I do now, in a circle so that the middle now threatens to be pushed through. Maybe I didn't do it enough. The storm in him didn't quell.

So much of my life has been spent in proximity to the beach looking into the horizon it's no wonder my sleeping self so often returns me there.

On board the *Titanic*, water has breached the hull and it becomes apparent that the only hope of saving everyone on board is to solve a series of intricate puzzles. Before me blocks and levers are painted with unrecognisable runes that I keep fumbling. The other hand worries at the spinning helm, and – oh, of course – little Lewis has blundered open the cabin door and is immediately thrust back as the icy water slams his flimsy weight against the rivets of the steel hull. I look down at the puzzle pieces in my hands and see that they have turned into a knotted ball of eels.

'You've scaled up,' David observed when I recounted my latest dream. 'Now you're the captain. A captain that literally drops the ball.'

'Of eels …' I mimed, defensively.

'Out of your depth.'

Right.

'*Going down with the ship …*'

Yes, okay. So my unconscious is not the unfathomable complexity I had assumed it to be. I was apparently flattering myself. The *Titanic*? The *Titanic* is big. The *Titanic* is the twentieth century's most colossal symbol of hubris and inevitability. *Titanic* was also the highest-grossing film when I was ten. I was a tad embarrassed about the basicness of my metaphor factory.

What I was interested in most was the omission. If I was having such vivid dreams hinging on failed vigilance on a titanic scale, why did they not contain the subject to which they so obviously pertained? I was also having a repeating dream of a gorilla lurching around the house, unpredictable and ferocious, but when it was quiet we sort of learnt to live with it in a state of casual tension. This was a barely concealed stand-in, but it was the fact of the stand-in that made me feel guilt and embarrassment. I could only let Dad into my conscious mind through the shroud of analogy. It seemed so cowardly.

Another: I am splattered with gore, supporting John F. Kennedy as we make good our escape from Dealey Plaza. A hand to his head, he asks if it's bad. I dab at a trickle of blood on his cheek and ignore the back of his head flapping open. He is clearly getting woozy so I tell him to recite presidents starting with George Washington. He does well, reeling them off in a Boston drawl. Vehicles speed past and he mistakes it for a motorcade. But no, the procession comprises ambulances and police cars. Later I find fragments of skull in my pockets, my shoelaces, my hair.

'Picking up the pieces,' pronounced David.

Joan Didion talks about life unfolding in the wake of her husband's death with 'the nonsequential inexorability of a dream'. The sinking of the *Titanic*, the assassination of JFK, the unstoppable surge of a tsunami; pull any image out of the flipbook deck and find it dripping in iconic horror. Because, of course: my loss was commensurate on this historic scale and my subconscious kept returning to them to change the course of their inevitable unfolding.

In the last few months Mum, Lewis and I had all experienced striking sleep disturbances that went beyond the usual nightmares. Mum recalled lying in bed unable to move while being abruptly pulled upwards by a pair of disembodied arms and hearing the words: 'I've been waiting for you.' It was a glimpse into something Lewis had long suffered with: sleep paralysis. I was shocked to learn it had happened to him a few times a week; eyes open but hopelessly immobilised. Some experience it as an 'old hag' who sits on the sleeper's chest with a terrific pressure. For my part, on top of the vivid dreams of tsunamis, I was experiencing regular hypnopompic hallucinations – that is, the type that occur in the transitional state between sleep and waking. Drenched in sweat I lie awake next to fully fleshed figures that aren't there, and often water lapping all around the bed as if I am on a raft. Unable to move my head I turn my gaze to the pillow next to me, to see a pallid bluish-grey baby lying on the pillow inches from my face, staring emptily at the stars.

The breadth of folklore around the 'hag' experienced during what we now term sleep paralysis is testament to the universality of this terrifying experience. In Kashmir the sensation is caused when a *pasikdhar*, an invisible house goblin, attacks in the night if it is unhappy with its accommodation. To break the spell of the Latvian *lietuvēns*, sufferers are told to move the toe on their left foot, a practice you'll find recommended by the sleep paralysis Reddit board today. Though a seemingly universal phenomenon, curiously some cultures suffer more than others. A recent survey of a group of refugees from Laos reported a hugely disproportionate amount of old hag sleep paralysis, as being displaced means their ancestors' spirits aren't there to protect them.

So we know that there is a link between sleep disturbance and unrestful ancestors, or at least our perception of them. In *Making an Exit*, a superb study of how different cultures connect with their dead, Sarah Murray meets a Vietnamese teacher named Nyuyen Thi Thuan who experienced debilitating migraines and vivid dreams about her deceased father, recently buried. In these dreams she would see him clutching at his head and trying desperately to tell her something, though she could not understand him. In Vietnam it is common to exhume a body sometime after burial in order to wash and arrange the bones for final rest. When her father's body was exhumed, Thuan saw that a tree root had grown though her father's skull. The bones were collected and reburied and Thuan's headaches and distressing dreams disappeared immediately.

The dreaming mind is something over which we have no control, which is why beliefs that some people can receive divine messages or predict the future persist. The dream experience may have given rise to the notion of the human soul, and fired the imaginations of early people in understanding the bodily realm and the 'something else' as distinct universes. Proof, no less, of a spiritual dominion. The Hawaiian term *Moe'uhane* means 'soul sleep', where long-dead ancestors could be met in dreams and pass on specific information.

We would never find out the time of Dad's death. Later the inquest would narrow it down to a window of between 4am and 6am, but I know what it is. It's 5.25am. I know that because that's what time I woke up every day for months, still tasting the sea.

Ghosts, visitations and the spirit medium

I knew it was only a matter of time before I had a dream about Dad. I thought that when it happened it would destroy any fragile serenity I had managed to contrive. It didn't. Something entirely unexpected happened instead.

In the dream, a group of people were gathering around a hectic table set for a meal. A great heraldic crest hung on the wall behind. Dream logic meant I was aware that some of these people were living and some were dead; a few of the older ladies I didn't recognise but I knew to be relatives from many generations back. Everyone was animated, pouring tea for one another and happily passing plates around. I spotted Dad straight away and took a vacant seat next to him.

''Ello, Hollie!' he said, in a timbre familiar only to me, but so very achingly familiar. He was grinning. Tanned; I felt he must have been gardening. I asked after Grandma.

'Yes, she's alright. Couldn't make it today – her and me dad are actually getting remarried later!'

'Wait – what? You can do that here?'

'Yeah, you can do whatever you want!'

I passed a bowl of something warm and buttery down the table and we settled into blessedly mundane conversation. I admitted I had been a bit stressed with the seemingly unending job of settling the estate and how much easier it would be if I could have just asked him whenever I had got stuck. Later it would be these details that would feel the most meaningful to me, because rather than any grand declarations or metaphysical insights it was far more plausible that we would discuss the admin.

'Did you find the stuff about the mortgage protection insurance?' he asked, disassembling a sandwich and inserting Colman's mustard inside.

'Yeah, don't worry, it doesn't impact the inheritance tax threshold. Actually, Dad, while I have you – it'd be really helpful if you could remember the date you paid the mortgage off? There's so many bits of paper, I can't find it anywhere.'

'Hmm, 2005, I think, but I'll get back to you on that.'

At that point Nanna, Mum's mother who died quite suddenly during Dad's first period of illness in 2011, leant over. Cheeks popping in colour, eyes sparkling, voice conspiratorial.

'I had this friend who found a life insurance policy she knew nothing about after her husband ... you know. Sixteen million pounds, I think it was.'

'What? *Sixteen million pounds*, are you sure about that, Nanna?'

'That's what she said, love.'

Dad's eyes went wide. 'Worth checking that, Ju—Hollie, sorry.'

'Dad we're not getting sixteen million pounds, you weren't a fucking racehorse.'

He laughed hard at that. 'Alright, alright.'

Tea was over and everyone was getting up. This was the only chance but it took everything within me to ask. He was putting his jacket on but I couldn't let him go without knowing.

'Dad – is it cold?'

'No.'

'Is it dark?'

'No. Well, sometimes but that's fine, it's not scary.'

'Are you alright there?'

I don't know what he replied as I was already awake and crying.

The dream was extremely vivid; I can picture it as well as yesterday's memories. But that isn't what made it different. I don't expect you to come with me on this. I'm not sure I know quite what happened next, or that anything did.

I'd given up on sleep after that and sat up in bed listening to a podcast through headphones, trying to calm down and block out the night's intruding images. I began to feel the sensation of someone blowing air into my face. It would stop for a few seconds, the length of an inhale, and then happen again. It felt distinctly directioned, so that after a while the right side of my forehead was perceptibly colder than the left. How it would feel if a person standing at the foot of the bed was unable to speak but needed to get my attention. So fleeting and small-scale an experience that I doubted my own veracity at the same time as knowing the fact of it was as solid as stone.

Anomalous experiences in the wake of a bereavement have been the subject of several studies. In his 1971 landmark paper 'Hallucinations of Widowhood' Dr W.D. Rees reported that of the 293 widows and widowers he interviewed across Wales in 1971, nearly 50 per cent claimed to have 'felt the presence' of a dead spouse or close relative. More recently, researchers at the University of Gothenburg found that over 80 per cent of elderly people experience hallucinations associated with their dead partner in the four weeks following their death, as if their full comprehension of the fact was at a time lag. In both groups up to one-fifth reported they had witnessed a physical manifestation, whether or not they used the term 'ghost'.

What fascinates me is how differently this cross-cultural experience is interpreted by the beholder. In a Japanese study that revealed up to 90 per cent of recent widows had 'sensed' their deceased, few if any expressed fear or worried what this phenomenon might say about their grip on their sanity. It simply didn't occur to them; in Japan ghosts are understood to be all around. Contrast this with what Sigmund Freud, arguably the predominant influence on modern Western ideas about the interior being, has to say on sightings of the dead. In the essay 'Mourning and Melancholia', he determines such encounters should be deemed pathological, 'a clinging to the object through the medium of a hallucinatory wishful psychosis'.

First-person accounts often compare bereavement to losing a limb. People reach for this analogy as the only fitting approximation of the pain and profundity of their loss. Our brains hold an internal map of the body but following amputation this map isn't immediately updated to reflect the body's new reality. Consequently, amputee patients with phantom limb syndrome continue to experience bodily sensations, anything from an itch to actual pain, located where the absent limb used to be. Because this is obviously disorientating, sufferers may avoid as much sensory information as they can to protect themselves from contradictory information; if they don't look at their missing arm it can continue to exist in their mind as complete.

To me this could not be more relatable. To save myself confronting the reality that Dad was gone I avoided certain topics of conversation, even within my own head. I sent Michael into the shed to retrieve the lawnmower when the grass was getting long rather than cross that threshold of Dad's former domain, cobwebbed as it was with his absence.

So then it is true to say the human brain and the culture in which it operates can literally summon and animate our ghosts. Whether we suppress or embrace the sensing of presence is almost out of our hands, a series of delicately weighted apothecary scales between internal regulation and perception of social norms. Ghosts do not require you to believe in them. As such, anomalous experiences, whether embraced as the foundation of a community's understanding of its place in the universe or dismissed as fanciful 'ghost stories', tell us a great deal about our own feelings on death and what comes after.

Apparition, phantom, poltergeist, spectre, wraith; the restless dead are woven into the folk cycle of almost every culture. To some beholding a spirit is a shocking aberration, like a sudden nosebleed, the terrible comprehension of chaos oozing through the divide. In medieval Europe the ghost signalled only torment or temptation. To others, however, their appearance provides comforting proof of an afterlife. One endearing belief in many Muslim families is that the smile of a baby or the look of serenity that often falls over the face of the dying is due to their being on the precipice and sighting spirits beyond it.

A favourite trope from Shakespeare to Dickens is the ghost that points the spindly finger in accusation and condemnation. Ashliman finds many of this folk tale, type 4025, most often where infanticidal mothers are haunted by the ghost of a murdered child. In Iceland phantom children point out who left them to die of exposure on the glacier, driving the woman to madness or suicide. Or the spirit might take possession of a weakened moral character (or what we today might call mental illness) such as the *dybbuk* of Kabbalah Jewish mythology. Becoming possessed by the *bhoot*, a white-clad spectre identifiable by its backwards-facing feet, is a great fear across the

Indian subcontinent. They are said to seek out milk in which to bathe, and consuming *bhoot*-contaminated milk is a surefire route to requiring the services of an exorcist.

Still more ghost types are spite-filled beings envious of the living who must be placated in offerings and dutiful funeral rites. Other ghosts give it out. Fans of the gothic haunted house may be disappointed by the lack of jump-scares in one of the earliest, the tale 'Ali the Cairene and the Haunted House in Baghdad' from *The Book of the Thousand and One Nights*. On a visit to Baghdad a trader named Ali, destitute at spending all his inheritance on getting drunk with his friends, enquires about a particular house and is told that it is haunted by the supernatural spirits called *jinn*. Anyone who stays the night there dies before morning, their corpse dragged out by ropes as the local people are too scared to enter. Using his wits Ali spends the night and is rewarded for his courage; the *jinn* welcome him and give him a large amount of gold. This is the opposite of a cautionary tale of many ghost stories: mournful souls lingering in purgatorial doom who offer an example to live out the remainder of one's life in such a way as to escape the same fate.

I gorged on these traditions, finding something humbling in the sheer breadth and variety of something I basically took wholesale from horror films as stock characters. In the absence of any idea of what happens when we die, I understood that if the universe was truly infinite any, and all, of these stories must be true somewhere.

According to many traditions the human spirit is eternal, but the particular interpretation of the many groups who make up the nations of Indigenous Australia strikes me as particularly beautiful. When a soul leaves a body it becomes part of the elements of nature called the everywhen, or the Dreaming. The Dreaming is a poetic realm resistant to proper translation, the interconnectedness of nature and ancestral spirits beyond space or time. Some communities will cease to use the person's name once they have settled in the Dreaming, very much leaving behind the body.

The Egyptian Book of the Dead, in contrast, shows the spirits of the dead relaxing in contemporary fashions, just sitting back and having a nice embodied time of it. Ghosts likewise had a physical reality in the afterlife of ancient Sumer and Assyria, and families would be expected to make regular offerings so as to better their living conditions. If they didn't, illnesses could be sent from the ghost in retaliation. The Latin *spiritus* for 'breath' or 'vital essence' indicates a more ephemeral haunting, and indeed figurative ghosts only really happen in Middle English records from the fourteenth century onwards. However, there were also stories of decidedly bodily ghosts, pale and mournful but solid. A spate of Victorian reports had the ghost needing to be wrestled to the ground until a priest could come and take a confession.

Many traditions formed with the intention of keeping ghosts away. Weeping too ardently, failing to open a window after a death or speaking ill of the dead are all ways of asking for a haunting. It could also be quite literal, though; bodies have been found in Sweden and Denmark up to the nineteenth century with their hands and feet bound together in order to stop them rising from their graves. If the visitation was inevitable sometimes it was better to just get it over with. Like *Samhain*, in which the souls of the dead were unleashed to revisit their former homes for one night, the Chinese observation of *Zhongyuan* ('The Festival of the Hungry Ghost') is a special night during which restless ancestors seek hospitality and amusement before being persuaded back down to the lower realm. A feast is given in their honour with the caveat firmly stated that they must then exit until the same time next year.

Despite their diversity these traditions attest that all humans carry ghosts around in their living bodies, the fingerprint impressions of those who have influenced and touched us. In all cultures and times there is something here that won't go away, some irresolution trying to be expressed, the continual return of the repressed.

For phenomena considered rare and out of the ordinary, it's striking how often people volunteer their own experiences when the subject is brought up. Auntie Sarah, for example, after I handed back her loop of Grandma Marie's hair over tea, launched into a story that riveted me. As a pre-teen, she said, she used to knock about with a group of older girls, looking to stave off the after-school boredom by whatever means necessary. One day the group were discussing something covertly, excluding Sarah on the basis that she was too young to understand and 'would only bugger about'. Sarah swore she wouldn't, but when they shared their plan, that after school they were to get the bus to Cleethorpes to visit a spiritualist medium who was appearing at the church hall that evening, Sarah tagged along 'with the express intention of buggering about'. It was too perfect; the medium was a rickety old dear in witches' rags and the congregation were rapt in ridiculous reverence to her.

Sarah sat smirking and swinging her legs as the 'witch woman' walked theatrically about the crowd. Until she stopped dead in the aisle next to Sarah's chair.

After a pause the old woman reeled off a series of statements as coolly and factually as if she had been reading a weather report. This child's dad was dead. It had happened in water. The nearest land was Iceland. She even spoke the name of the ship, though as Sarah didn't know this detail at the time the name *Northern Queen* meant nothing to her. What did mean something, producing a hot, tingling recognition, was the gesture the woman was repeating. She pulled at the neck-line of her dress, describing it as tight and uncomfortable. When he died John had been wearing a thick wool jumper, chosen, naturally, for being his warmest. Before he had returned to sea Marie had repaired the neck, making it ever so slightly too tight. He had been bothered a little by it and was forever pulling at its neck.

Sarah had been late back and girded herself for a telling-off. Instead, after confessing to her mam all about the witch woman, Marie asked to go with her next time. The mediums alternated, and this woman was on every other week. When they went back two weeks later the medium wasn't there. During that week she had died.

The gasp I gave at that almost too dramatic detail was all the prompting I needed to try out the spiritualist churches of London. Inside a series of similarly neat but dated tabernacle-like buildings on residential streets I joined the congregation to witness 'demonstrations' of clairvoyance. I approached each one with not just an open mind but almost a willing gul-libility. I wanted to be impressed, I was a cold-reader's perfect mark.

Now imagine how triumphant it would be here to relate my own uncannily accurate readings. How a detail plucked from beyond that only I could have known had changed my life. But regrettably, time and again, I found nothing to con-vince me that contact with the spirit world was possible.

Many of my encounters were mystifying but not in the narratively satisfying way I had hoped. In a north London ser-vice that began bizarrely with Kylie Minogue's 'Spinning Around' and was attended by a labradoodle hoping to be healed of arthritis, the medium wished to pass on a message to a person in the room 'who was Jewish', which the audience, with hostages' willingness, eventually agreed was for a woman whose house, as far as she could remember, might have once been owned by a Hasidic family. A clairvoyant in Notting Hill cancelled my private reading due to 'unforeseen circumstances' and I texted this with delight to everyone I knew. Another in Stockwell told me deliberately to stick to 'yes' or 'no' responses, so as to properly demonstrate his abilities as a conduit. Unfortunately, so little of the reading had any recognition to me that I began handing over information simply because I was bored and wanted something to show for my tenner.

To each I came with specific questions to allow Dad to prove it was really him: what film was Mum watching when she went into labour with me? Which Beatle did Lewis play in his Year 5 talent show? That one was a gift; a one-in-four shot. Wrong every time. The sense of feeling around in the dark, though reasonably entertaining, was frustrating, but it served to convince me that no one I met in the spiritualist movement had been out to con me.

Until one demonstration. A medium focused in on a young couple in the room, and said there was a toddler with a rainbow lollipop standing next to them. The little girl, the medium said, wanted to thank them for making her short life 'so sweet'. The woman, barely in her twenties, silently wept as her partner laid his arm across her hunched shoulders. I felt suddenly disgusted with myself and the performers on the church's small stage, grief vampires all, and myself a deplorable voyeur in a private sorrow.

There have been conmen extorting the grieving for centuries, but there are many other explanations at the sceptic's disposal. External stimuli, from spiking electromagnetic fields to infrasound so subtle the human ear doesn't register it as audible, could explain the sensing of a ghostly presence. Humidity changes can expand wood, air pressure fluctuations can slam doors. Internal mechanisms that are only just becoming understood can throw systems haywire and produce all sorts of hallucinatory and auditory effects. The same mapping misalignment that is thought to cause phantom limb syndrome has been demonstrated to go further, to 'map' the presence of an entire body which the brain can only logically place outside of our own, resulting in the uncanny sense of someone nearby and watching us.

Hallucinations, furthermore, are far more commonplace than most people think; up to 10 per cent of the population have experienced a hallucination in their lives, unrelated to any substance or onset of mental illness. Visual distortions can be produced by carbon monoxide poisoning and are a little-known side effect in pharmaceuticals as common as aspirin. Meanwhile, it is well documented that the human mind is a bundle of prejudice: false memories, grief hallucinations and confirmation bias can easily explain these experiences. Asking us to disregard the terrible creatures produced in hypnopompic and hypnagogic states is to ask us to disregard what we can see with our own eyes.

And that's before we add in psychological stressors. Grief, yes, but also common, everyday fear of our own mortality. The paradox of why we are drawn to stories of hauntings is that they are simultaneously frightening, exhilarating and a strange comfort. An encounter can tip into existentialist anxiety but also equally into the comprehension that there is a grey area between life and death, the ultimate balm. It may be because I was seeking them out but it felt to me that reports of ghosts rose considerably during the pandemic. Perhaps we were all inside more and so could hear the noises that might ordinarily be missed, or perhaps a parade of ghosts materialised by the séance-pull of collective worry. This may explain the documented resurgences in the spiritualist movement after anxiety flashpoints or times of political uncertainty, such as the aftermath of the Second World War and the months following the 9/11 terrorist attacks.

Pareidolia is the tendency to find meaning in meaningless things, something many of us will have encountered by finding 'faces' in anything from architecture to a yoghurt lid. Most of the time there's so much going on that the brain chooses what to give our attention to and must fill in the rest. Low light heightens this effect, as does insufficient sensory information or when the body is fatigued or under stress. This is why no one ever seems to see a ghost in daylight in a new-build or at a football match; your brain is much more likely to misfire when you are alone, scared, or in the dark. The instinct to 'trust our senses' is so strong that we tend immediately to jump to the conclusion that what we have seen must be a ghost. It's easier to believe than that your brain is lying to you.

We are complicit in the manifestation of ghosts. When one person is gone the between-world of habitual life remains, for a while, intact, even with the full comprehension and acceptance of death. Spaces and objects continue to implicate them. The 'we' things: a sofa once shared, an old film often watched, a side of a bed unoccupied. The first photo I took after hearing Dad's body had been found was of his empty chair in the living room. Such things imply the possibility of a presence, they have potential. And this potential is diffuse and unrelated to time, not simply a matter of presence or absence. These ghosts are magically untethered, and as valid and as real as we need them to be. Reality is no match for love.

Since Freud's pathological reading of 'wishful psychosis' the West has to some extent now caught up, with the continuing bonds theory posited by grief experts Phyllis Silverman, Dennis Klass, and Steven Nickman in 1996. This theory holds that when someone dies our relationship with them doesn't. There is no culmination to grief that concludes with severing ties in the present. Perceiving their presence, whether we use the word 'ghost' or not, can be more constructively considered as messages from our own psyche.

My dream of Dad over dinner was scripted perfectly. Of course it was. I conjured it using data from 32 years of character study. In every way that matters the episode was 'real' in that it was a perfect facsimile of him, a post-mortem memory. A new chapter in our continuing bond.

At the reception of her wedding to Dad, Mum turned round and momentarily saw her long-dead grandmother a little way off, sitting at a table and smiling. Auntie Sarah and my cousin Gemma both swear to catching the scent of Tweed, Grandma Marie's signature perfume, in the living room of the house they inherited from her, many years and many renovations after her death. My friend Carly recently stayed with her family in a rented cottage the night before her grandma's funeral, and at 11pm all of them could smell the toast and jam that her grandma would habitually make before bed. I don't care to know the explanation for any of these. In their intimacy they feel authentic in a way that paying a bloke in a back room in Stockwell to make cryptic pronouncements never could.

My visitation breaks the first rule I've always had of ghosts: that any encounter which takes place in a bed, sleep being that great deceiver, can immediately be discarded. The room could have had a quirk of airflow that didn't require a window to be open. My overwrought nerve endings could have been misfiring, the weeks of pounding stress leaving my internal facets fried. It was St Mark's Eve, the night second only to All Hallows' Eve in proximity to the dead, in which superstition told the dead could speak the names of those who would join them, and I had been reading ghost stories.

Still, I eventually did find the bit of paper confirming the final mortgage payment. The mortgage was paid off in 2005.

Natural healing and the storyteller's medicine

Aside from the handful of countries that do not follow the Gregorian calendar, wherever you go in the world April seems to be the month of cheery and convivial festivals.

In England the cuckoo is the bringer of spring; towns such as Marsden in West Yorkshire still hold an annual April Cuckoo Fair in which a giant effigy of the bird leads a town procession in celebration of warming days. Japanese Buddhists celebrate Buddha's mid-April birthday in a haze of pastel blooms called *Hanamatsuri*, or the Flower Festival. Even in the medieval idealisation of rural toils, a trope known as the 'Labours of the Months', April was a light one, limited to the planting and enjoying of flowers. April is the traditional New Year in many South and Southeast Asian cultures, based on the sun's entry into the constellation Aries, and is marked by water festivals in Myanmar, Laos and Thailand, with hose-pipes wielded by neighbours in good-natured public water fights. West Bengal, Bangladesh and parts of Assam designate April for sacred bathing and house-cleaning, and spring-time cleaning is an important preparation for the Jewish Pesach, or Passover. Walpurgis Night, meanwhile, has many variations throughout Central and Northern Europe but often involves lighting a bonfire to drive out any lingering winter spirits overstaying their welcome. Glasses of mead are also raised to the magnificence of the cherry tree in blossom. The April-time Roman festival of Floralia was all about games, pleasure-seeking and spectacle; historian Suetonius recorded the festivities in 68 AD which featured a tightrope-walking elephant. Even better, Floralia was distinctly a festival of the plebeians (commoners), meaning no stuffy overlords to harsh the vibe.

Because my thoughts are so distorted by the 2020s-fication of persisting in a bodily form known as 'self-care', when I read about these traditions I imagined how each would be boiled down into pleasingly formatted Instagram posts. Reductionist digestions of ancient and nuanced modes of human existence outlined in a coral sans-serif on lavender. Demon-casting, mead-downing, water-frolicking – any one of them could have their essence distilled into the favoured homilies of the moment: slow down, embrace light, cleanse your space, invite freshness, *seize your joy*, the last slide revealing it to be an advert for subscription heartburn gummies specially developed for INTJ fire signs with 35 per cent off your first box, use offer code 'refluxqueen'.

Whether it was my astral connection to seasonal rhythms or my algorithmic marketing fingerprint something was seriously out of whack, because I was feeling nothing of the optimism and renewal that either promised. Comprehend a cherry blossom? Win a selection of gut re-magnetising #plant-mylks, simply follow our brand partner and like this post? I'm sorry but that tightrope is barely off the ground, and would it kill the elephant to smile?

Half a year into The Grieving and my routine when Michael was on late shifts had become to drink by myself and think about nothing but myself. About how much smaller my world had got, or how I would never get off SSRIs. I would dwell on the thought that even if I lived for a very long time and received everything I could ever want I would perhaps one day be 85 per cent happy, but never fully, not after this. Talking this over with David once a week made me feel that my insights on my misery were profound, important. I'd save them up specially, turn over the delivery in my mind. But when I lingered for just a minute between brilliant observations I knew I felt something else too. Indulged.

At what point does talking become rumination? Ruminants are animals that regurgitate and chew over old material.

I am not suggesting that talking therapy is not a vital resource that should be widely and cheaply available, but there has been a recent trend towards therapy as a panacea to all possible types of malaise. Though I am speaking only of my own case it still feels a contentious opinion that my almost-constant desire to stay in bed is not a symptom that I am overdue a self-nurturing 'bed day' but a tendency towards paralysis that needs to be resisted if I am ever to build any resilience and rejoin the world. Restating my sadness, anger and disorientation didn't make these emotions less true, so why was I still talking about them? Yet I persevered with therapy largely because 'going to therapy' is the metropolitan dictum held above all else.

And then my workplace, via which I had been entitled to a number of free sessions, failed, as I had hoped, to support a continuation and I, an unmanifested punctured tyre of a girl-boss, realised I could not afford David.

Right, fine. *Embrace change.*

Grief after all is not a pathology but a commonplace human experience, and not a new one. For 'therapy' my ancestors (Celtic peoples on Dad's side and the Danes on my mother's) would have had only what could be gathered from their natural landscape and the passed-down wisdom with which to mobilise it. Uncharitably we often suppose that civilisations that existed before the modern era were too busy surviving to bother with introspection, but this is too simplistic and too cynical. Hardship cannot have been the only concern when we have jewellery, toys, decorative arts, songs and oral poetry that show that people have always externalised those meanings most important to them. Couldn't this be considered in the sphere of therapeutics? Most Celtic art is non-figurative; could its characteristic triskelion and interlocking spirals have been favoured as a reminder of the constant turning year, the macrocosm, the human tendency to endure?

'Coping' may be a modern invention, developed alongside the rise of individualism encouraged by a capital-centred labour model, but prior to this different virtues existed: stoicism, forbearance, faith. Somewhere in the last half century we forgot that verbalising pain is not the only option.

So, I decided, I would shut up and try the alternatives.

I started with my black bile. The centuries-dominant 'four humours' theory suggested an imbalance in my melancholia that needed purging, with the gold-standard treatment being blood-letting. This was a problem, considering the general shift towards medicine that actually works, but I did manage to find someone claiming to be practised in the ancient art of 'leechcraft' operating out of a boat in Mile End. On checking the website the business had unfortunately become one of the casualties of the pandemic. No word on what happened to the leeches that could not be furloughed and had to be 'let go,' which is also the reason I won't be approaching that other very 2020s self-care prescription – wild swimming – downstream in Limehouse Basin any time soon.

An unsatisfying start, and it had given me a new image that needed exorcising, so I booked into a transcendental meditation centre near Highbury Fields to clear my head. I squatted on a pouffe while a lady with a calming voice invited me and the other assembled students to relax. I only became aware I had fallen asleep when I woke up surrounded by other silent students, unsure if the big dose of cog-loosening CBD oil I had taken beforehand had resulted in the sleep-talking it often does in me, and I was too embarrassed to return.

Luckily my next commission was with the acupuncturist's table, where sleep was encouraged. Acupuncture is said to activate key meridians along the body. After sending me to blissful sleep with needles stuck in my back, legs and scalp, the practitioner in the Traditional Chinese Medicine method offered me tea and, having accepted my card payment of £45, told me that in fact 'laughter was the best medicine' to all of my coalesced ailments. She recommended *You've Been Framed*, nightly. While I could swallow the bitter herbal loose-leaf I'm afraid I failed in this half of the prescription.

Lured by my keyword googling like moths to a Himalayan salt lamp, adverts for botanical doctors and naturopaths in my area began fighting for attention, suggesting I try wheatgrass enemas and drinking my own urine. *I may be a metropolitan white woman looking to be exploited by the very treatments I am happy to appropriate, but I'm not a chump!* I thought as I clicked on a website offering ozone therapy, in which the toxic gas used for disinfecting hospitals of superbugs is injected intravenously.

Perhaps something a little less invasive. Sounds couldn't cause any harm, surely? The gong bath, or sound healing, is a fairly new therapy, but the use of sound and vibration for meditation and ceremonial purposes has a long history. There is science to support the gong bath as a healing modality, being that music has been shown to activate the body's rest-enabling parasympathetic nervous system and has a demonstrated connection to emotion. The chance that I might tap into arrested emotion while lying on the floor of a small church off Shaftesbury Avenue was made more likely by the ritualistic tone set from the beginning. It should have been strange to make a bed and lie down next to strangers, our bodies radiating headwards from the three instrumentalists and their strange apparatus in the centre of the room, but the flickering candlelight and burning clary sage made everyone behave with a quiet reverence. I nested into my blankets and put a mask over my eyes.

What happened next was one of the most extraordinary combinations of sensations I've ever experienced. That the symphonic waves came from all directions seemed impossible.

I resisted the urge to peek as a string of bells seemed to snake around my feet. This combined with bodily sensations that prickled and thrummed, and were not always entirely pleasant, made me feel enveloped as if in the belly of some large thing. Only some of the instruments I could place: the strangely human warble of the Tibetan singing bowls, layered like a choir, and the unmistakable ululation of throat singing, a mode of folk song traditional to the Mongolian and the Tuvan people of southern Siberia. And, of course, the imposing vibrato of the largest of the gongs blooming and retracting like rolling thunder. The earliest Chinese tam-tams were used to signal workers in from the fields up to five miles away. Being just metres from where the soft but powerful mallet rained down it felt as though the dull pulse was coming from within my own rib cage.

A stream of alien noises by turns thrilling, ecstatic, soothing and menacing but never failing to hold my attention. I found by concentrating on my eyelids I could make explosions of colour ignite with each chime or drone. Eventually they organised themselves into the lurid pink-and-brown 1970s pattern I recognised as the square of old carpet that Dad would haul out the shed on sunny days to form the foundation of a Wendy house or another building project. When it was over I opened my eyes to find that somehow I had ended up in the foetal position. Next to me I saw that my neighbour had been crying.

This beautiful stillness lasted a long while, but it made me want to move my body. Whenever I am on a yoga kick I love the way my spine feels tall and my joints limber, but the Sanskrit meaning of the ancient Vedic discipline is a spiritual and meditative practice of 'yoke' or control, whose bodily contortions are not something to strive for above all else but all in the ultimate cause of stilling the mind. This is the bit I've always been bad at. Attending online 'grief yoga' was perhaps the closest I have come to understanding the *ujjayi pranayama* or 'ocean breathing' technique, and I grasped a few moments during which focusing on my breath really did empty my head of thoughts. And then I was instructed to close my eyes and pretend to be a sea sponge, which prompted a stream of thoughts, mostly questions. *Does a sea sponge have eyes? What do I do with my arms?* Muting the rest of the session to google sponge facts I read that if you whizz up a living sponge in a blender, in time it will reconstruct itself. Fair play to my teacher, I did zero yoga beyond learning to breathe, but circuitously I did learn a solid analogy for grieving. You'll have to excuse me, I'm a sponge in a blender.

Maybe that was it, I just needed the warm woollen cardigan of a good metaphor. Grief culture is full of metaphors. There's one about a box with a bouncing ball and a 'pain button' inside; as the ball shrinks it smashes into the button less often, but it's no less painful when it does. It's a tidy image. Others less so. Grief is a rowboat, is a new pair of glasses, is a half-torn kite, is a chest of broken ribs; tears are the language and grief is the book. The internet is extraordinarily insistent that grief be considered like glitter. I'm not sure why. You'll find some in the shower and it'll make you think, *Huh, where did that come from?* I suppose that rings true but I'm not entirely sure what to do with it. Another widely shared post said that grief is like 'a draughty house', but I was crying at the time and misread it as 'haughty horse' and spent too long, brow knitted, pondering what that could possibly mean.

See? You can have grief be anything, which is why I found this aspect of grief culture so annoying. Take a wisdom pellet, the dose same for all, and ascend the next rung of understanding.

Intellectualising suffering worked for the Stoics, the third-century Hellenistic philosophers who maintained that through fortitude and self-control a person could achieve equanimity whatever life's highs and lows. This is akin to the aphorism 'This too shall pass', originating from a fable told by the Sufi poets of medieval Persia, in which a sultan demands his wisest advisor conjure words that are always appropriate, no matter if the moment be happy or sad.

If feeling better was all in the mind maybe it would be best achieved by total removal of somatic sensors. With that in mind I turned to floatation therapy.

Within a private chamber I enter a tank filled with water and Epsom salts designed for complete sensory deprivation. Inside this alien pod is the first time I experience true pitch black; moving a hand in front of my eyes has no effect. The soundproofing is so total that very soon I can hear my own heartbeat. And the water is kept to exact body temperature, giving the sensation of genuinely floating in three-dimensional space. I emerge from the liquid dark as relaxed as from an expert massage, but I can't say I came to any profound revelations or ever really turned off my whirring monologue. Maybe it takes practice. And being enabled only by access to a technologically advanced egg that retails for around £30,000 I realised I might have swung past my aim to restore a closeness to nature by some way.

All these interventions that skirted around the natural in some way or another and I'd missed the obvious one: literally going to stand in it. Last time I'd done that I'd had a panic attack so total I didn't leave the house for three weeks afterwards. So I was apprehensive. I thought I would try again but with guardrails, by joining a 'forest bathing' group on Hampstead Heath.

Forest bathing is the Western approximation of *shinrinyoku*, the Japanese practice that melds mindful meditation and nature. As it draws on the Shinto religion and its tradition of animism – that non-sentient things possess an essential spirit, particularly true of trees – forest bathing makes an elemental sense to the Japanese in opposition to, for example, Michael, who on hearing why I was going up the Heath warned that 'those ponds are filled with Weil's disease, you know'.

No, there isn't actually any bathing in forest bathing. Rather a gentle walk with a small group of others wanting to connect in some way. I hadn't noticed before now but being made to focus on the ground I saw that crocuses had sprung up everywhere, firmly announcing the season. Our session was facilitated by the calming presence of a forest guide named Estelle who crafted meditative exercises for us with the intention of slowing down, engaging all the senses and connecting with the frequency of the natural world. One was simply to find a spot on my own by the lake for 15 minutes and look at how the water changed. I was struck by just how much was constantly in motion; the reflected sky was like silver foil until its gentle undulating rhythm was interrupted by an improbably glamorous mandarin duck softly landing.

Told to wander off and bring back something that caught my attention, I happened upon a bright blue pebble the size and shape of a wren's egg, a jewel half submerged in the sandy soil. It made me think of Easter, naturally, which made me think of the wheel turning the warming days. I told this to my group as we ended the session in a circle while Estelle served us all burdock tea, pouring the first cup into the roots of the giant ash tree between us. She was in a light jacket while I was in my impractical winter coat. I confessed I had been so disconnected from nature that rather than go outside to figure out what coat to wear that morning I'd looked at a weather app.

'You need all five senses engaged to notice those changes in season,' she said, tactfully.

Proponents of forest bathing champion the proven health benefits of phytoncides, the chemicals leached in the forest's aroma, which may provoke an anti-inflammatory response and have a mediating effect on cortisol levels. But for me forest bathing won where mindfulness didn't, simply because it gave my frantic mind stuff to look at and listen to. In meditation you are told to return to your breath, which just reminds me I can always, and eventually will, stop breathing. Forests, oceans, soil and sky however will outlive me, and I find a logical comfort in that.

I hopped down from the Heath more relaxed than I had been in months. Last time, in Sydenham Hill, I'd been a wreck. Why had this experience been so different?

In the explosion of the wellness industry in recent years there are two things that have been embraced above all else: 'natural' and 'ancient'. You might see *shinrin-yoku* described as the 'ancient Japanese art of forest bathing', but it isn't: it was coined by the head of the Japanese Ministry of Agriculture, Forestry and Fisheries in 1982 to restore flailing visitor numbers to the country's national parks. But it works.

It works because when we interact with therapeutics, part of the application is the story we tell ourselves about it. Perhaps more than anything else, when we use nature for healing we tell ourselves that story. 'The appeal to natural goodness is among the most influential arguments in the history of human thought,' writes Alan Levinovitz in *Natural: The Seductive Myth of Nature's Goodness* (2020), going on to argue that such is the status of this belief that 'natural' can be considered a religious term. Given the churn of self-help books in recent years it is clear that nature's evangelism continues to draw converts.

Nature feels orderly so we perceive wisdom in its transitions and endurance. But nature is ambivalent to people. Could it be said that this ambivalence to human suffering makes it akin to a god? Take the preponderance across world cultures of the 'enchanted wood' trope. Forests represent real or imagined danger (we talk of being 'out of the woods') and have prompted cautionary tales, such as 'Red Riding Hood' and 'The Babes in the Wood'. They are magic, according to anyone who figuratively or literally might 'knock on wood' for good luck. 'The woods have ears', just like a god, and like a god they are capable of offering transformation, sanctuary, adventure or danger. They have the ability to transport from normal human experience, but their ambivalence towards us makes us desperate to understand this backdrop to our world. Norse myth and legend had the gloomy black woods of Myrkviðr, the Romans the semi-mythical Hercynian mega-forest that reportedly stretched from northern France to the Carpathian Mountains and housed unicorns, and in Arthurian cycles the verdant Brocéliande is a majestic forest populated by fairies and shapeshifters.

Nature is humankind's most enduring fable. Embracing nature was central to the Romantic movement that swept across Europe partly in response to the rationalism of the Enlightenment. Levinovitz points to the power of metaphors that figure nature as indispensable for our understanding of reality, and such metaphors are threaded through the fabric of a culture, a theory formalised by what later became known as cognitive linguistics. Nature is not a static object but a story itself.

It strikes me that our use of nature in this way is supremely solipsistic and rooted in privilege. Only those protected from nature's ravages can possibly romanticise and idealise it. It may even be considered offensively myopic; if nature's powerful healing properties were true rural workers the world over would be buzzing off all the dopamine and never suffer depression. Taking the cure of nature also centres humans as entitled to it as rightfully ours. And so we are in the interesting position of being the antagonist in the story of ecological collapse; we see nature as our cure when we are also its poisoner. Holding these two positions is an instinctive denial of death: just as we block out our own mortality, so too we pretend our compulsive consumption is not hastening the premature end of our species' presence on the planet.

I think the reason I felt hobbled in Sydenham Hill and fulsome on the Heath was the permission to rewrite my story of myself experiencing nature. I had told myself the shallow story that I needed 'to get back to nature' with the expectation of immediate relief, but Estelle had taught me to meet the forest with no preconceived notions and feel what was there to feel. The Heath would have been the same that day whether or not I was there. That is a peace-giving thought. Against my instinct, borrowed from the grief world, to 'prove' all I needed was old cures and wisdom, maybe nature's indifference was what I needed to learn. No amount of wild swimming, being stuck with pins or drinking piss was going to cure me. I needed to detach from the idea that there was some succinct lesson to come from my grief. For now, it just is.

Storytelling is a universal restorer. When Cicero lost his beloved daughter Tullia from complications following childbirth the Roman statesman and orator was plunged into deep depression from which his only consolation was in the 'healing arts' of reading and writing, his now-lost *Consolatio*. Stories are used to permit and contextualise grief, as in this Brothers Grimm retelling of a folk story that had existed in Germany since at least the thirteenth century:

> There once was a mother of a seven-year-old boy, the perfect son in every way.
>
> One day tragedy struck and the little boy died. The woman wept night and day and could not be comforted.
>
> Not long after the burial the spirit of the boy returned to his home and began to play as if still alive. But these visits did not stop the woman's tears, and when the mother cried, the boy cried as well. When morning came he would disappear.

On one of these nights the boy appeared with the white shirt in which he had been laid into his coffin, and with a burial wreath on his head. He knelt at his mother's feet and begged, 'Oh Mother, please stop crying! My shirt is wet and heavy with your tears. The weight keeps me from going to heaven.' Startled, the woman stopped crying.

The next night the child came one more time, smiling widely. 'See, my shirt is almost dry, and I now will be able to rest in my grave.'

The mother, having grieved for her loss, was now ready to live on without any more tears, knowing her son rested peacefully in the afterlife.

This poignant tale tells of a loss utterly without explanation yet nevertheless characterises death as a divine release from the tethers of the world. It has a strong social and cultural function: the mother has the story of her loss reframed and in doing so informs the reader that it is okay to move on. Stories themselves become a type of folk medicine.

It probably speaks for the popularity of groups such as Survivors of Bereavement by Suicide (SOBS) and others, which I avoided for so long out of fear and a vague sort of embarrassment. When I finally went along I found a simple truth: that people need to tell stories about their dead, and that is at least as therapeutic as any medication, structured therapy programme or nature-based intervention, whether prescribed or not. The UK bereavement charity Cruse supplies storytellers in hospitals; aside from the ritual of sharing and retelling, listening to another's voice is grounding and connecting, particularly when we are feeling weak and vulnerable. When I was a kid I used to make my mum read the same stories to me over and over, and as I got older I would self-comfort with books in the same way. At the heart of grief and consolation is a paradox: despite it being a universally experienced phenomenon we all consider our grief unique. To voice the personal and have it reflected in the collective canon fulfils both these paradoxical needs.

Stories even change the human brain. Trauma and pain are experienced in the sensory part of the brain but when we digest the how and why of our experiences, i.e. through our own internal 'storytelling', these stimuli become ordered and narrativised, prompting them to move to the permanent storage area of the brain to become fully incorporated into memory. That we tell ourselves stories in order to live is not just a Joan Didion quote for tote bags. Sufferers of Cotard's syndrome, or 'walking corpse syndrome', believe that they are dead because the feelings capacity, located in the amygdala, has been suppressed in some way and all that is left is pure thought. Human consciousness is essentially a narrative with feelings attached; remove this and the 'story' of the self-unspools. Some Cotard's patients have died by starvation, believing that since they are already dead they do not have to eat.

Does it matter in whose head the story is stored in order for it to be 'alive'? Story is an outward act of memorial, as shown in this folk story from West Africa:

A great warrior did not return from the hunt. His family gave him up for dead, all except his youngest child who each day would ask, 'Where is my father? Where is my father?'

The child's older brothers, who were magicians, finally went forth to find him. They came upon his broken spear and a pile of bones. The first son assembled the bones into a skeleton; the second son put flesh upon the bones; the third son breathed life into the flesh.

The warrior arose and walked into the village where there was great celebration. He said, 'I will give a fine gift to the one who has brought me back to life.'

Each one of his sons cried out, 'Give it to me, for I have done the most.'

'I will give the gift to my youngest child,' said the warrior. 'For it is this child who saved my life. A man is never truly dead until he is forgotten!'

I wrote. The Dead Dad Diary became less about me and more an exercise in recording every story I could think of. I brought full colour back to memories grown sepia by time. I recorded everything told to me about Dad that I wasn't there to see. As a kid, sacking off church to collect brambles round the back of the British Legion to sell door-to-door. Dad and his siblings' childhood violence; the time he shot his sister Sarah in the side with an arrow so she bit him back, rough justice settled with them both trying to hide the substantial bloodstains to avoid getting a good hiding. Taking Mum to York on their honeymoon. A work do at which he got too drunk to notice he was in Cleethorpes's worst nightclub and, in an image unfathomable to me, was observed punching the air to Born Slippy in jeans and loafers.

It helped also to imagine stories at a remove from mine. I wrote daydreams, little fables: about a daughter burying her father upright in a tree to honour his beliefs, another explaining what comes after death to her own daughter on a Hawaiian beach and invoking the interconnectedness of the natural world. I staged them in places where humans are not the overseer or controller but where nature exists in tandem, in places far away but graspable in their emotional familiarity. It meant I could tell the story to myself that my suffering wasn't singular, that people have been losing their people since people were around and those people had carried on. Later I read *The Mess Inside: Narrative, Emotion, and the Mind* in which Peter Goldie, a philosopher of emotion, observes that in grieving we examine the past in a special way, coming to apprehend the change in reality by degrees like accepting a missing limb, while at the same time storifying our memory. He draws a parallel between grieving and use of free indirect style in literature, a mode of writing that combines internal and external perspectives. In my little notebook this is exactly what I was doing.

This too shall pass. It is the notion that everything elapses and that the present moment is all you ever have. Stories have the power to transcend this; they are a type of magic able to reanimate even our most long-rested dead.

Here be dragons

On 1 November 1937 John Heenan, aged 12, swam 440 yards in 14 minutes and 23 seconds. A praiseworthy score, according to the Grimsby and District Schools' Sports Association, but not quite a record. A few years earlier in 1932 his big brother Walter had beaten his time by five seconds.

With just the two of them, John and Walter are unusual in a family line that favoured the Quiverfull approach to procreation. Both sons were born to a trawler engineer gainfully employed during Grimsby's boom years, a time when the town was suffused with optimism as it realised its destiny in becoming the biggest and busiest fishing port in the world. Only a few years apart in age, both athletic, keen swimmers, it's hard to imagine the two not growing up close. When on shore leave from the Royal Naval Patrol Service perhaps Walter snuck his younger brother an underage pint in the Corporation Arms, or in another of the pubs in the shadow of Dock Tower where the port's seamen and dockworkers rushed to spend their wages.

'Churchill's pirates' they were called, the men of the trawlers requisitioned for convoy duty and anti-submarine and minesweeping operations off the British coast during both world wars. Many of the crew were ex-fisherman and the boats themselves adapted trawls, whalers and drifters, giving the RNPS a reputation of the somewhat ramshackle. Nevertheless, the work being hard and dangerous, these men were universally considered courageous. And not without reason. By the end of the Second World War the RNPS fleet out of Grimsby had lost more vessels than any other branch of the Royal Navy.

One of them, the 507-ton trawler HMS *Stella Capella*, was torpedoed by German submarine U-701 on 11 March 1942 off the coast of Iceland. In just two and half minutes she sank to the seabed, taking 23-year-old engineman Walter Heenan and another 32 of Churchill's pirates with her.

There is scant material on John and Walter, precious few photographs, but somehow those two school swimming certificates survived. Dad kept them in a folder at the back of his wardrobe and the first time I knew of them was when we were cleaning it out in the spring following his death. Two brothers, champion swimmers, lost their lives in the same biting waters that refused to give up either body almost 30 years apart. 'No grave but the sea' is the naval phrase.

That the sea is full of the dead is a dread that lurks in every sailor. Trying to sleep amid the creaking and groaning of a pitching ship provides fertile ingredients for thoughts of death.

In Japan the waters contain the *funayūrei*, indiscriminately vengeful spirits of dead mariners, that during storms will fill boats of the still-living with ladlefuls of water until they sink. To protect themselves sailors would have a bucket without a bottom on board to hand out to any spectral entities they encountered. Though legends of the *funayūrei* emerge before Japan's Edo period at the beginning of the seventeenth century, the myth of the murderous drowning victim has refused to lie. After the sinking of the passenger ferry the *Tōya Maru* between the islands of Hokkaidō and Honshū during a typhoon in 1954, a disaster that killed more people than the *Titanic*, strange gouges were discovered on the vessel's propeller. These were attributed to fingernails, fuelling the belief that the *funayūrei* had pulled the ship down into the abyss. More recently, after the devastation of the 120-foot-high tsunami that smashed against the north-eastern coast of Japan in 2011, a whole region drowned by floodwaters is now said to be haunted. Sightings of some of the 18,000 victims were seen across Ishinomaki in the weeks after the catastrophe, including dripping-wet figures appearing at doors, confused why their former homes no longer existed, and more than one instance of a taxi driver inadvertently picking up a customer before having them disappear, leaving behind only a puddle.

Terra incognita, the early cartographers called it, those lands uncharted by human exploration during the Age of Discovery. But the bodies of water in between have always remained a mystery. The unfathomable deep has weighed heavy and given rise to all sorts of imaginative speculations. Impossible colossi of teeth and scale sending men out of their minds and their bodies into the briny beyond; ships tossed in the tempest swell, a paroxysm of an angered God, and swallowed in a single gulp; drowned cities of purloined treasures and magnificent underwater kingdoms populated by seductive hybrid beauties covetous of mortal souls. If the surges and recessions of coastal waters signal inevitability and God's judgement, the open ocean is a vast wilderness in which anything in the human imagination, or beyond it, could feasibly dwell.

Hafgufa, for instance, is a monster of such vastness that when it is stationary around its home between Iceland and Greenland it can be mistaken for an island. The Norse *Jörmungandr*, meanwhile, is so big it encircles Earth and grasps its own tail, which when released will precipitate Ragnarök, the end times. Shapeshifters are common to much of water lore, whether the Chinese Dragon Kings that could leave their underwater palaces and transform into human figures, or the water horses that emerge from the spume of the waves and go by many names: kelpies, *bäckahästen, nøkken*. They could be the alluring sirens of antiquity and mermaid-like *jengu* of Cameroon, or hideous sea hags with supernumerary appendages and mercurial tempers. Or they could be much smaller in scale, though no less vexatious. A *kappa* ('river child') is an amphibious *yōkai* or mononoke demon found in traditional Japanese folklore. *Kappa* behaviour varies in charm; they can be mischievous pranksters or malevolent avengers. For every tale of them looking up women's kimonos there's another of them drowning a child or eating human flesh. Even today, signs warning about *kappa* appear by bodies of water in some Japanese towns and villages.

A letter sent from John to Marie while on the way to fish the White Sea off north-west Russia in September 1970 reports that the *Northern Queen* had had a mechanical breakdown and was sitting immobile in the bay of Honningsvåg, the northernmost city in Norway. An engineer had been sent for but, nonetheless, 'It looks like being a long trip,' John wrote, 'I would say 6 or 7 weeks.' You can picture a sailor presented with the same landscape day after day letting their imagination run away from them. Certainly, it made John ruminate about home, writing: 'I never knew how I missed the kids until I came back to sea.' He was stuck for those weeks over the very waters that, 1,000 fathoms deep, lived the most famous of the *monstrum marinum*, the kraken. Many men have succumbed to 'calenture', a madness that strikes a man while staring too long into the horizon and, convincing himself he sees land, jumps straight down to Davy Jones. Estranged from the familial and at the end of the world, a man's thoughts can turn to great questions that the endless sea seems naturally to provoke.

The oceans represent a psychological opposite world to ours, a notion which explains the tendency for the notoriously superstitious sailor never to invoke what on land would be considered good fortune. On board, the word 'rabbit' was never spoken, for it foretold disaster at sea, despite carrying a 'lucky rabbit's foot' when on land being commonplace. Seagulls, storm petrels and gannets all had superstitious power as they were believed to carry the souls of dead mariners and could bring on bad weather if not properly respected. Other superstitions commonly held are about the colour of the sky, never launching a voyage on a Friday or allowing a woman to set foot on deck, and the talismanic power of tattoos to protect from the treacheries of nature and enable a sailor to always find his way home. The sailor floats between two worlds, his wisdom-based practicality that helps him navigate and survive is held in balance with a respect for augury, magic and monsters unknown.

I always had a sense of the potency of water and the sea in Dad's imagination. On one of his birthdays I deviated from the customary gift list of liquorice allsorts and bought him a small wooden nautical calendar I saw by chance in a second-hand shop. By twisting the polished brass dial the calendar is correct for 50 years. I remember intuiting it as risky, that this object engraved with reef knots and anchors might provoke something of which I only vaguely knew the parameters, but I think I was trying to communicate that I was cognizant, that his preoccupation hadn't escaped my notice. He looked at it for a long time, passing its weight from hand to hand and then thanked me, and I assumed it would disappear like the other confusing tat I'd chanced he might like. But no, it lived on his bedside table for the next 15 years.

There was another way in which he gave away his fixation. It was something that bound us and eventually something I came to resent.

As a kid I loved to swim. I don't remember ever learning how; I must have learnt to be comfortable in the water very young. I can only think that was because Dad took me swimming from when I was tiny. Junior swimming lessons were a lark; me and Dad against the other kids and their parents, in games that revolved around blowing bubbles, collecting floating puzzle pieces and pretending to be snapping crocodiles. I was strong, quick and unafraid of heights, diving from the top board. Most of all I liked to float on my belly and surveil the pool through my goggles, pretending to be a manatee.

As I got older things became more formalised. Fun swims became lessons. A Victorian tiled swimming bath, its changing rooms horrifically open-plan. Lessons were around swimming lengths in races against much bigger children. Repeating form, length after length until my lungs burned. I still remember standing on the side and waiting for my race, shivering, skin barnacled with goosebumps. The playful thing I loved became competitive, the swimming teacher brusque and unpleasant.

I began to dread those two hours of swimming after school on a Wednesday. Each week I would develop a stomach ache that would churn all day. Once the pain stopped me eating breakfast or lunch and later that day I fainted; I was delighted as there was no mention of having to go swimming after that. Unfortunately, I couldn't seem to replicate it. As the school years wound on Wednesday anxiety became all-consuming, a black hole that vacuumed the entire week. Still, I wasn't allowed to stop. I was too small to be anything special but they needed girls under 12 for county competitions. I demurred.

Competing would mean training and more lessons and that horrified me. Dad wasn't happy.

'I can swim! Really well! Why do I have to keep going to lessons?!' I would cry, make a scene.

'You'll go because I've paid for you to go.' He would yell, slam things.

The lessons cost £2 a week, the same as my pocket money. I offered to offset it and he told me off for being smart. I wasn't trying to be, I was just miserable. It became a weekly war.

One Wednesday Dad was distracted talking to another parent as the whistle blew and I saw my chance: I sailed over the water in a perfect long dive, front-crawled the full length in surely my personal best time, hoiked myself out of the water and ran to the changing rooms, into my trainers, jeans and T-shirt at an Olympian clip and ran out the school and half the way home. There he screamed and screamed at me but I'd decided finally I wasn't going back.

Now I know all those horrid swimming lessons were shoring up a superstitious belief that family members could be snatched away and drowned at sea. Given my dreams it is now clear I inherited the same fears. Us kids learning to swim was a preoccupation for him because it was rewriting history. His losses were like a submarine on the ocean floor, silent and imperceptible to radar, until it sent its depth charges on anniversaries or furtive walks around the docks at night. Perhaps it's also why that first time I immediately concluded he'd walked into the sea. I settled on the expression 'lost my dad to suicide' ultimately because I think of him something close to lost at sea. It has the same scale, the same impossible magnitude. Hamlet, contemplating self-destruction in his 'To be, or not to be' soliloquy contemplates taking 'arms against a sea of troubles'. The sea of course is not an external factor but Hamlet's own mind, an adversary that exerts as much pressure as an ocean.

Dad worked for the council in a leisure centre for many years, and in that time prevented the deaths of numerous people who had got out of their depth, often the young and the vulnerable. Sean told me how Dad had got his nickname at work – 'Super Rod' – by clocking a toddler dipping below the surface and struggling to breathe and, rather than take an extra 0.5 seconds to alight the tower, diving from its very top.

A lifelong blood donor, one of the saddest and longest-lingering regrets was knowing how his manner of death prevented donation of his organs. There was something sacrificial in his sense of giving, beyond gallantry. A bodily compulsion to help.

It's what I think about when I recall what I've come to regard as the illuminated manuscript of his bravery. I say recall like I was there, but I wasn't. Like all legends it has been passed around and perhaps the edges are worn, but it is now so known to me I can summon it like a memory.

Up past the sand dunes of Cleethorpes, past the marshes and the marina at Humberston with its white boats, is an untouched little stretch of coast called the Fitties. A man has been taking a bike ride when he sees the white piths of splashes he has become honed to recognise. The current is unpredictable here on the turn of the coast, not like the protected shore along the promenade, and can be deceptively strong just under the surface. Flashes of colour, a blur of a small hand. A weak spot in the continuum where life and death is wafer thin, the present and future at a hinge.

I realise in my mind I've turned it into a *Tintin* comic; Dad is standing on the dunes with a '!' over his head. A mother in a newsprint polka-dot dress turning slowly, her smile dropping, the next panel has her rising from the sand, blanched in horror. The actual rescue is momentary, the mother utterly absorbed in her daughter, the little girl sputtering and then wailing in incomprehension with the same lungs that moments earlier came close to being deluged.

On a night that felt like biblical floodwaters had come, judging by the great blobs of raindrops being flung at my window, I decided I would find this little girl. She would be a shibboleth, the comprehension of the continuation of her life enabling me to better understand the ending of Dad's.

I asked anyone who had been told this story for details that I was too young or uninterested at the time to recall. Unfortunately there were precious few, only that she was pre-school age and the year might have been 1996. I took to Facebook, even attempted an appeal in the local paper, spending obsessive hours in search of her. Despondence set in when this scouring, admittedly an exercise in distraction, came to nothing. It had already slipped through my fingers, and with horror I saw I had failed to have this story chronicled. It had been less than a year and this piece of lore was already dead.

When I was the same age as this child whose identity I would never know, I was Dad's study aid. He would have to do regular first aid and water rescue tests and would practise on me, having me drill him with questions and putting me in the recovery position on the living room carpet. I felt special and close to him, trusted with something important. But then I got to a certain age and didn't want to help anymore. I wanted to watch *Malcolm in the Middle* and play Snake on my new phone, and so that little ritual of ours died. When he performed those life-saving skills next time it was with far higher stakes on a little girl who wasn't bored and aloof but terrified and grateful.

A man protects Britain's shoreline during war and pays with his life; a man goes to sea to provide for his family; a man returns a drowning girl to a grateful mother. Folklore does not need the details that I, biographer, become fixated upon.

They just need to be retold and shaped by the retelling, rounded like a stone in water.

The Chilote, the indigenous islanders of southern Chile, those whose folklore I found to be almost unique in its positive portrayal of widowhood, had another comfort to offer me. Being a collection of islands Chiloé Province has its own distinctive mythology divergent from the mainland and is particularly preoccupied with the sea. One of the most well known is that of the *Caleuche*, a ghost ship. Phantom ships manned by skeleton crews, damned to an eternity at sea, such as the legend of *The Flying Dutchman*, inspire terror, but the *Caleuche* is more complex, its name translating as 'the ship of transformed people'.

All is calm, the moon a placid face over the yawning dark, when the sounds start to swell as if from the water itself. Music, lights, laughter: a party. And as an all-white ship appears, almost glowing in the reflected light, it's clear a lively time is happening on board. Then once again it fades out, celestial and intangible.

The crew are said to be victims of drowning, revived into a strange kingdom free from the ravages of pain or old age. Some say they can transform into dolphins or shapeshift on land. Onlookers should hold their breath if they spot the ship. Failure to do so means they may be left without the power of speech or minus their sanity. However, the crew are honourable; seafarers never cease to be of service, and a hereafter of duty is the only one that makes sense for them. They man the *Caleuche* throughout the night, appearing and disappearing on the bays and lagoons between islands, rescuing victims of shipwrecks or, where they cannot, recovering the dead and granting them eternal sanctuary and the camaraderie of sailors. The Chilote can rest knowing their ancestors guard them from the mercurial seas while comforted that their dead loved ones continue in the afterlife forever spent in parties and celebrations.

The Chilote tradition taps into that opposite power of massive forces, the ones that speak of the rains coming and drowning out all but the worthy, or the fountain of youth bringing immortality, the regenerative and healing. Among these positive readings they landed on a story by which to recontextualise their grief.

I still don't dream of Dad much, and my visit to the tea party was the only one in which he spoke to me. I continue to dream of great waves and violent storms almost nightly. But one dream of the sea felt a little different. The waters were still and the night was settled in fog, and as I sat on the shore there was the noise of happy activity on the wind. Some way off a vision of silver sails, lit from within with candlelight. Only one figure was out on the deck. He was walking back and forth, like the man I had watched on the beach. I looked down and I was holding a nautical calendar, it was stuck on 2020, and I looked back and squinted: it was dark but I could see the figure standing still on the deck just watching. A small group came out, maybe two brothers, placed their arms around the man's shoulders, and led him back to the party.

'It's amazing we're here at all,' said Lewis, squelching a trainer out from the mud.

I'd been telling my younger brother about my research, all the prematurely dead people in our family. About Emma killed by the last childbirth of many; the too-young men claimed by the sea; the first wife of a great-uncle who suffered terribly and, dismissed by doctors, may have taken matters into her own hands. More widely diasporic Heenans: one apparently the victim of Australia's first serial killer.

Thin wisps of clouds trailed across a blue sky and the air tasted of copper and sea-grit. Not far from the Greenwich Meridian line the promenade gives way to an expanse of marshland that curls round like a great beckoning finger, enclosing an altogether different beach. This is Humberston Fitties, 'fitties' being an old Lincolnshire word meaning 'salt-marsh'. The sands here are buffeted by dunes springing with cattails and spiky grasses that as kids we ran around and hid among. That it is regularly cut off by the tide gives it both a tranquillity and a certain wildness.

Lewis and I were ignoring what the universe was taking great pains to tell us: the map from the coastguard that I had printed off, showing the recommended route; the lady in the coffee shop confirming the shortcut was not a shortcut at all; a mud-splattered man walking his disappointed dog back from attempting it; single flip-flops abandoned to the sludge, as potent a warning as the actual signs proclaiming the multiple hazards outright. And yet presented with a natural path through the marsh we found ourselves blithely taking it. As I say, a family with weak survival instincts.

We were trying to find something I had read about during lockdown and had never known existed. Spotting its cumbersome shape rise out of the dunes beyond the saltmarsh and looking so very in reach we took off over it, lulled by the deceptively flat terrain. The May sun was rising and the distant sounds of people making full use of the Bank Holiday wavered on the glittering wind. Beltane, the fire time.

Oily black mud slopped over our shoes but the progress was quick, until we met a problem. Something we hadn't seen from the path were the large fissures in the bogland, and the one we had arrived at looked deep, steeped with water a cloudy greenish-grey. The sides were collapsing inwards.

'We should turn back and go round the proper way. This is so dumb – we are going to regret this,' I said.

'What! No, that'll take ages. We'll be fine!'

As we both mentally measured the run-up we'd each need, I was once again surprised at my brother's height. Lewis being an adult was a point of amnesia to me and I was often caught out by it. I could easily conjure the time he got Fuzzy Felt stuck up his nose and the vivid memory of Dad holding him by the ankles as Mum dusted pepper up his nostrils to make him sneeze it out. Or dressed as the red Power Ranger for his eighth birthday. How he was always collecting rocks and sticks, and how he would do the tricky levels on *Crash Bandicoot 3* for me. Sometimes I felt a bit dizzy when I remembered he was now a man with a beard and an accountant.

It was only in the first few days of his new fatherless reality that Lewis turned 30. Turning 30 feels to me as much a milestone as turning 21 did a generation ago. Poor Lewis, no one was in the mood to do anything. His birthday and its insistence that life carried on was not one we were yet ready to face.

It seemed like another echo. I'd been collecting them. I couldn't help it. Dates, patterns, parallels, chimes from beyond, time bent in on itself. Useless data that in its aggregate felt like it should add up to something.

I swilled the numbers around in my head: 2020, Lewis turning 30, it had been 50 years since John had been lost at sea, lost in the same sea as his brother 30 years prior. Dad had been 64, his mother had been 64, 64 was twice my current age. Numerological synchronicities, echoes pulsing like sonar or like rings in a tree trunk.

'It's just *weird* though, don't you think?'

'Yeah, I guess.' He was playing with a film camera, waiting for a seagull to become artfully angled in the sky.

'Like, I bet if I sat down and compiled all the death dates of the family – I dunno, maybe there'd be all these ... patterns.'

He lowered the camera and gave me a dubious look. We had arrived at another creek. A flip-flop was stuck perpendicularly like a grave marker. This one looked like an even bigger jump and there were finger marks in the clay. Like the pony that had got stuck a few days before, I imagined having to be winched out by a small team and making the evening paper.

'If I fall down there I'm not confident you could pull me out.'

'Nah, I reckon I could, you are quite small.'

Before I lost the nerve I took the biggest stride I could manage and cleared it, though an uncertain landing splashed a thick brown soup up my leggings.

I had a bolt of déjà vu to the time when Lewis had become stuck in the wet sand and Dad had had to sacrifice his wellies to free him. Now here he was more than capable of doing the lifting. A quick calculation: no, Dad would have been about 36 then. Finding patterns was as much about discarding the data that didn't fit.

It has a name, this tendency to perceive meaningful connections between unrelated details and random events. Apophenia. Some might put it in the same wheelhouse as recognising faces in shadows as the ghosts of our dead, an uncannily accurate reading by a psychic medium or the interpretation of certain dreams as meaningful.

2020. I should have expected it. Why hadn't I? Dad always had a head for dates. He knew how old his dead relatives would have been at any given time, like he had an internal hourglass he upended on anniversaries. It is wrong to say he 'chose' anything about his death, because his choices were distorted by illness, but I couldn't escape the idea that I should have been on high alert that whole year. Ten years since his first attempt, this time 50 years since his own dad, dates piling on top of dates. The term *Apophänie* was coined by the German psychiatrist Klaus Conrad in his 1958 publication on the beginning stages of schizophrenia. Could it be that a habit that starts out as comforting, keeping and reciting a list of numbers like a spell, eventually feeds a delusion? Here I was grasping at dates and festival markers, just like him, trying to find meaningful connections in the murk on as unstable a footing as the one we were walking.

Lewis on the other hand seemed completely uninterested and was barely listening to my babble. We had reached the sand, which was soft and bone-dry. Two Second World War forts stood out in the mouth of the river Humber and the horizon was clear enough to see the lighthouse at Spurn Point.

There's a photo taken here that I love, of Dad no older than two, all fat cherubic arms and dungarees, plonked between his parents on the sand. Marie is keeping a watchful eye while John is peering over horn-rimmed glasses and very intently digging a massive hole. In a picture of 1950s recreation he has rolled up the arms of his starched white shirt but has not even loosened his tie. You could swap out the figures. Dad looks so much like Lewis did as a tiny boy. I got the head for dates and signs but from this angle, May Day sun shining bright above, Lewis is beginning to look more and more like him. Especially the eyes.

I wondered what else was contained in that masculine inheritance beyond genetics.

It is an area that has been given credence lately, in the rise of a new field of biology called epigenetics. Specifically, proponents believe, traumatic experiences in a parent can be passed on as biological 'scars' to the children, via tiny chemical tags that alter how a gene is read without altering the genome itself. It is a revolutionary claim, counter to the understanding that DNA is the only mode of biological inheritance and has launched the idea that trauma can reverberate down the family line. Evidence cited include studies of mortality levels in children of prisoners of war, cortisol levels in descendants of survivors of the Holocaust and the much-cited case study around the Dutch famine of 1944–5 which claimed that a link between hardship and malnutrition could be traced even through to grandchildren. Crucially, as the epigenetic effect is hypothesised as a modification on the Y chromosome, the expression occurs in males only. More recently the field has been re-examined with evidence to the contrary coming to the fore, claims the evidence is circumstantial, and that the mechanisms implied by studies into this burgeoning science are simply not plausible.

Regardless of the debate, the idea that we carry the signature of our ancestors' pain as their living memorial has a strong emotional magnetism. But echoes of trauma needn't be physiological to exist. It could be said that stories are the ultimate epigenetic transmission. That troubled me.

How Lewis was doing was an ambient dread that I had carried for the last eight months. In the pages of the Dead Dad Diary there is a lot of fretting about Lewis. Those early days he had sat with me and listened as I cried, in frustration at the funeral delays, in the disorientation of the viewing, in drudgery and despair. But for the most part he didn't talk to me about how he was feeling, nor had he since. I had back-channelled for status updates from his patient and unwavering girlfriend, Isabella, but Dad's own grief response had been to bury it deep and the thought pattern of generational trauma and the possibility of it being passed on to my brother was, when I wasn't having dreams about him drowning, keeping me up at night.

My own instinct was to write it all down, which I had come to believe was an exercise in switching the mess of information into a narrative, to tell the story back to myself. But actually I think I am writing this book *for* Lewis, the only other person who knows what it's like to have lost this particular father. The only other candidate for a life's witness is a sibling and by committing these events to print I am verifying them with him. Doing so is perhaps an attempt to demonstrate to him that some cycles are not inevitable.

I never asked him but I wonder if Dad dreamt of the same floods and typhoons and having to rescue Lewis as I did. He went to every one of Lewis's football matches, took him to pick out his first guitar, went to his gigs when he was older and rang me all the time to ask if he was alright. I know that I baffled Dad right from the beginning: a firstborn's mantle. Lewis though was sweet and kind, a perfect little boy and a mild-mannered man, far more patient than me when it came to sorting out our parents' Wi-Fi problems. Better than me with Dad in general, for they could sit placidly together, Lewis tinkering with a musical instrument, Dad reading the paper.

Lewis was 18 when Dad first became unwell and I made the unilateral decision to keep the more lurid details from him while I took care of everything. I now wonder whether that was a kindness, or if perhaps it took away something of his confrontation with it all. The instinct is to shield him from pain, in the same way I'm always shielding him from floodwaters in my dreams. If I hadn't always insisted on intervening he would have floated on his own.

I remember planning the funeral and feeling exasperated, and not a little ashamed, that I didn't know which song by the Supremes Dad would most have wanted played. I went up to bed angry that he'd left me this task on top of everything else and then listened in the dark while Lewis, down the hall, went through every song in their back catalogue to find the one with the right sentiment. I see now that I underestimated him in so many ways. There was an ocean of difference between the last three generations of men in my family. My need to verbalise everything was just that: my need. Even after all those alternative therapies I had fallen for the fallacy that healing was counselling or nothing. But this year Lewis had begun to find it in his own meandering way, by making music and creating things.

Our pilgrimage had been satisfyingly hard, which is probably half the point of pilgrimages, but we had reached it, our destination out on the sand. It has several names, though the Buck Beck Beach Bench is the most pleasing one to say. The Pirate Bench is more descriptive, looking as it does like a disassembled galleon rising out the sand with its centre mast spearing the air, a tangle of netting in its wake.

This unofficial landmark reportedly began when a dog-walker built a small makeshift bench as a rest stop. Soon others began adding to it. The bench, though it can hardly be called one anymore, became a sort of half-open hut in which you can shelter from the wind and look out at the whispering waves. A tattered Union Jack torn in the salt wind stands at the highest point as windchimes and dangling shells tinkle in the breeze. Pinned to the walls are photos and messages from Melbourne, Tokyo, South Africa, among crosses, tyres, lobster pots, ropes, a life preserver and other maritime detritus.

In time the bench metamorphosed into not just somewhere to rest but a community art project and, eventually, a collaborative memorial. It started with dogs who had accompanied their owners here; there are many dog tags and collars hanging from the planks overhead. Though it has been around for years this word-of-mouth landmark only became popular during the first lockdown, when people used their allotted exercise time to visit this strange monument and leave something behind. Perhaps they were also brought there by the feeling of unmooredness that struck us all during that time, or the grief that struck some of us.

In its life it has been washed away by storms and tidal surges and rebuilt several times. Its renewal is indefatigable, each time unseen hands collect debris not claimed by the waves and reattach it all. The bench becomes bigger and more eclectic. The way the late-afternoon orange light hit it now was like it was on fire, lit from within.

May Day is the opposite point on the wheel to its autumn counterweight, *Samhain*. It is a high point, the beginning of summer and a fire festival to celebrate life in its fullness. Rituals centre around fertility and growth; the fires, smoke and ashes of the *Lá Bealtaine* or Beltane bonfire are protective of livestock, crops and the family. The world is once again young and green. But it is also a doorway, another proximal window into the next world. The Welsh *Calan Mai* holds this special time to be *Ysbrydnos* or 'spirit night' of ghostly activity. I lit a candle at the monument but we didn't need a fire to feel the closeness to the dead; there were messages all around.

'RIP DAD, SAIL SOMEWHERE NEW' read one of them, carved on a piece of driftwood. 'GRANDAD' said another. 'BILL – 25 YEARS GONE BUT NEVER FORGOTTEN' looked to be a piece of fence-post. A wooden heart with a poem about sitting in a garden without the one they wish to be sitting with. One giant antler, purportedly in memory of Neil. A plank carved with the word 'ZIHUATANEJO'. I had no signal but in the pub later I would find out this Mexican town is a sanctuary dedicated to the goddess Cihuatéotl. The Olmec, the first major civilisation in Mexico, considered her the mother of the Earth and goddess of the valiant dead; mothers who died in childbirth and warriors who died on the battlefield.

Synchronously, I had brought a marigold from the garden with me, the flower of the Mexican Day of the Dead. I placed it on an upturned plant pot next to a shell I'd brought from home. All of us had developed a habit of picking them up on beach walks and so a little collection had always lived in a basket in the garden. I had no way of knowing but perhaps this perfect white whelk was one from when we were kids on a bright Bank Holiday like today, found while Dad buried Lewis in a big hole in the sand. In time it would be washed back into the sea.

We didn't talk much, but standing side-by-side we read every single message. When I turned round Lewis was taking a photo of something I'd missed, or maybe overlooked because of all the contributions here this one was the saddest. A pair of children's shoes.

Along with my offerings I had brought a skull-and-crossbones flag to add to the top, but I needed Lewis's help to place it. He took it out of my hand with the same exasperated noises that Dad made when I came to him with something broken, a sort of pantomime exhalation, a good-natured roll of the eyes. Like picking through 50 very similar Motown songs, Lewis was, like Dad, a person who preferred tasks, not words.

Conscious of the tide times I thought we should start heading back, though we would emphatically not be taking the 'shortcut' this time. As we took one last look at the bench and turned to head off up the shore we heard a dad pointing out the flag and telling his kid this strange pile of items was indeed a shipwrecked pirate ship. 'No way!' came the reply.

We both laughed. I saw I had my chance to say something.

'We could, if you wanted, come down here together, you, me and Mum, and build a sandcastle, adding some of Dad's ashes. I'd check the tide times, obviously, and we'd build it down by the shore. And just wait for it to come in.'

I was keen for him to know that it didn't have to be soon. The funeral had been a solar plexus thump; the scattering of ashes could be something else, happy even, and that would only be possible when it was possible.

'I thought we could bring a picnic even, have some drinks.' I was worried then that my idea would strike him as un-solemn. Getting drunk on the beach. Sticking Dad into a plastic bucket and tapping the top with a spade. *Shit.*

'Yes, I like that,' he said quietly, looking forward. 'It was his happiest time, I think. And it's a gentle way to do it. The tide just ... washing away.'

I think Lewis turning 30 in the miseries of the first few days upset me so much because Dad did not have a son in his thirties. So how could I be standing here now with a brother in his thirties? It was like we had become asynchronous. Lewis and I were on a different trajectory than the 2021 we would have had. How many more birthdays would he have without him? How many more turns of the wheel?

We look for patterns in numbers, dreams, half-glimpsed figures in shadows and experience a bolt of liquid terror when we see a person who resembles our dead out walking around in the world. Folklore fulfils this human need for the comfort of categorising and by naming our fears, conquering them. Strange things at sea need an explanation, when perhaps they have less to do with monsters and angered gods and more with bridging our divides and our peculiar brains comprehending their own mortality. I'm not as certain as I was that there's a beginning and an end, that death might better be described as becoming asynchronous from one another for a period. The more our ancestors are shored up, by remembering, chronicling and speaking their names, the more they are likely to withstand the frothing fingers and the insistent claws of the tide.

Summer is well and truly on the ingress and the saltmarsh is glowing bonfire-yellow. The wind is picking up sand into my side vision, but I can see there is a man walking quite far out. I don't turn to look, partly because I know he will turn back, but also because the concreteness of having someone next to me keeps my spiralling thoughts in check. Having a witness gives you that. Knowing that when the tide turns I am not alone.

BLEEDING TREE

52°01'31.6"N 4°47'42.5"W
Nevern, Wales

WHEN THE FIRST OF US put down roots the land here was already a manuscript of footsteps. Men spied the depression like a sparkling green gem from the lookout of the Preseli bluestone crags and picked their way down to the valley with conquering strides. It was not long before the men found reason to war between themselves and then different men came and they warred with them instead. Those came up the *afon* in their long boats and stood their timber fortress against a dorsal of slate. Later they rebuilt it from stone. It lasted a heartbeat, just a century, until it burnt to the ground.

Listen. The shuffle of the breeze whisks past the harp-shaped hills and softens over the pool in the river's bend. A ring of Pembrokeshire sessile oaks casts shadow over the water, sunless and bible-black, as dragonflies bother its surface. Goosanders blaze a quiet trail of light under the stilts of a motionless egret. On the woodland floor the twitching of beetles disturbs sorrel, wood anemone and blue violets, and sways the fronds of hay-scented ferns in tumbling rhythm.

A magician produced marvels here and so they built him a church. Now men sleep around me in soil beds where no flesh decks the bones, and stones that bear their name cling at angles to the undulating churchyard as if in dissent: death shall have no dominion.

My father stood in my place then, when there were wolves still in Wales, observing the comings and goings, the feasts and the famine. Sometimes fishermen of Merlin's pool – named for another magician – skipped the sabbath to fill baskets with juddering lamprey. They would be taken home to soak in their own blood for several days, then to become a banquet. Other times – times of want – people turned superstitious and returned to the heavy wooden doors with their boils and pustules speaking of last rites.

Listen. Those bluestones up in the hills are gongs. Struck with a mallet they ring out like church bells. Back when my father's father stood here the musical stones were pried from the earth and taken along the Golden Road. Heaved between the rocky tors, hauled through the lair of the terrible boar named Twrch Trwyth and wrenched past the lozenge of stones in the shape of an eye, a lantern song in the darkness, to make the circle in Salisbury.

Listen. For hundreds of years this church was on the pilgrims' trail and sometimes I can still hear the thump of their tread. In parables of sunlight they came in procession and stopped here, by the waymarker Pilgrim's Cross that is carved into the rockface, to kneel and pray and rest. Thousands of feet have warped the slate steps on the south side, on the way to ask St David to relieve the burden of their sins.

There are no pilgrims now but people still come by to see the famous Nevern yews. Usually they have heard of the one in particular that bleeds.

Listen. To the many stories there are about me. That the unguent blood that swells from within me falls to the ground in sympathy for Christ on the cross. That I bleed in sorrow for a local monk taken for a crime for which he was innocent, that the clay at my roots is made of hangman's lime. That I won't stop bleeding until a Welsh prince is installed once more at Nevern Castle. Or that a fairy queen named Viviane tricked the magician into giving up his secrets, and uttering the charm of sleep she entombed him in a yew to die, and I am that tree. That story would make me older than the church. Not quite.

Listen. *Hen wlad fy nhadau*. The land of my fathers. A force that comes up through the centre, a green fuse. Time passes. The green fuse gets lit again. We shall keep growing up from the centre, regenerating, dying, living, bleeding.

Look. The blood is life.

SUMMER

I've always loved looking at photographs of my parents from before I was born. The one of Mum in a white party dress sitting in Nanna's 1970s flock-wallpapered living room on her 18th birthday, reaching for a glass of Babycham just outside the frame, a timid study of adulthood. Early-eighties Mum and Dad sitting together on a pub banquette, her eyes glistening as he makes her laugh in some private joke, both oblivious to the relative catching a new couple's candid moment and creating a periscope for the kid they end up making.

Studying these pictures indulges an irresistible nihilist fantasy wherein I never existed. They speak of a world that is pure optimism. No one takes photos at a funeral; leaf through any family's album and it's all christenings and dripping ice-creams at the zoo, school summer fêtes and fizzy wine around a firepit for someone's 40th. Taken alone this intrinsically biased palette of cobalt high noons and fantastical pink dusks it is perfectly plausible that the two of them were constantly happy, with none of the earth tones of dreary responsibility and ordinary work drudgery that I knew accompanied my arrival to muddy the sublime composition.

My favourites of Dad are a series in which he is wielding a sledgehammer as he demolishes what was the old outdoor toilet and coal shed that came with every pre-war terrace. There is a gaping space where the kitchen window should be, as if the house is slack-jawed at the scene of destruction, gormless at the young conqueror with a builder's tan standing atop the rubble with a look of contented exertion and a head full of plans for the future.

We rediscovered these photos when we were selecting some to take along to the wake, and Lewis said that it was because of these images that he believed for many years that Dad had built our house himself. A sweet child logic but I think we both realised then he had touched upon a deeper truth. There was something about that house that was constituent to Dad and his sense of himself. He might as well have been part of the brickwork.

Home ownership occupies a very specific place in the British psyche that almost evades translation. It is difficult to unpick what is a sincere and understandable desire for security and the laying of roots from the non-consensual participation in the 1980s programme of the dismantling of the alternative. With it came the incubation of a culture of hostility towards those in receipt of state assistance and the lauding of asset speculation that changed forever the yardstick of success: 'An Englishman's home is his castle.' Although Dad opposed the regressive and divisive cruelties of Thatcherism, he wasn't inured to its ideals, and so buying a house, even a wreck, was a milestone and a triumph. It was somewhere to install the family he was about to make for himself.

But no sooner had he filled a skip with chunks of masonry and Victorian plumbing and closed up that shrieking maw of a kitchen window did the house begin whispering demands. The entire interior required damp-coursing and plastering. The old coal fire needed gutting and replacing with gas before winter. A tiny parlour had to be smashed through to make the kitchen a liveable size, the circuitry rewired from two bedsits to one family home. There was no bath. A modest income from television repair, supplemented with another from a betting shop, soon to be curtailed by pregnancy, didn't stretch far. Kids appeared and demanded bedrooms. Priorities slackened. Maintenance trumped improvement, homeliness came a distant third.

A decade or so passed. Things broke, through age or wretched children. The walls remained unpainted, carpets unlaid. Single-glazed windows rattled and draughts of unknown origin snatched doors violently shut. We were loved and nourished and looked after, but in that house I always felt an unsettlement and precarity to the way we lived. Mum made curtains and papered cracks with her art; in his room Lewis did the same with drawings and later prints of his photography. One summer I took a bedsheet and tie-dyed an enormous swirling vortex and was surprised when Dad let me hammer in hooks to cover an entire bedroom wall with it.

The house was always cold, but with the tectonic pace of Dad's consultation on any major home improvement, the progress towards central heating was a snail crawl that lasted until I was in secondary school. Many of his tirades I listened to from the top of the stairs involved the state of the house, with the running theme of our carelessness and ingratitude.

We should paint the kitchen yellow, I suggested once, after seeing it on a sitcom. 'Who's going to pay for that then?' Dad scoffed. The pressure of mounting 'jobs' weighed on him like landslip. Throughout my childhood I mistook it for embitterment but with hindsight he was more likely petrified that if he capitulated to any sort of luxury, or simply the notion of a job being 'done', that some burst pipe or rising damp would necessitate the floors being ripped up and an unforeseen cost that could sink us. Better then to make do with token furnishings in unadorned rooms and sit tight for developments.

And yet he poured enormous effort into the garden. At the gable end of a small ornamental wall he put in a little seat and carved into the stone the words 'HOLLIE'S STEP' where I would perch and watch him like a queenly gnome. The construction of a rockery was hard work but the pleasure he took from selecting hardy little shrubs to nestle in its recesses was uninhibited and genuine. Behind that he built a trellis for the climbing roses that after a few years covered the whole shed with sprays of pale pink. I would collect the fallen petals to make 'perfume', a soup of brown water whose recipe could include whatever else was on the ground of the small unspoilt Arcadia that I took for granted: purple aquilegia, apricot begonias, little clouds of sweet pea and fizzes of busy Lizzie. Dad helped me plant a sunflower and took over watering when I was too lazy, helping it grow into a 10-foot totem with a sinister eyeless head that turned with the sun. In one corner a hydrangea cutting from his mam's garden had turned into a monster and bees flitted between it and the lavender bush, the lot encircled by a gargantuan Virginia creeper the colour of hissing embers.

Every day of summer I would wake to the hum of the hose-pipe and the luscious smell of wet soil. But his real pride was the peonies. When they flowered in early summer he would let us all know and sometimes I would dutifully accept his invitation to go outside and smell them. I remember watching him doing the washing-up while staring out the window to the peonies struggling under their enormous weighted heads. When he finished, he went outside and stood there some more, just watching them, from time to time touching the dark glossy green leaves and buds like clenched fists. The overwhelming scent of a peony still damp from the shower of a watering can is transportive for me even now.

Many of my early memories are in the garden and the sun is always out. Dad saving me from a bee when it flew up my floral dress. Wincing as he removed a splinter from my foot with tweezers. Kicking a football between us in the alley. Cutting the corner of my lip on an ice pop and feeling the sugared sting. Magic FM and the caw of seagulls. Every surface lurid and thrumming with insects, sticky with Cherryade residue, smelling of barbecue smoke and citronella. Everything too loud, too vibrant, too full of life. The Māori have a maiden goddess named Hine-Raumati who in her youth and vitality is the personification of the summer. Other solar deities are often depicted with overspilling baskets of ripe fruit or golden maize. But these are the sounds and smells and sense memories that would be the tokens to summon my own particular summer god.

The garden in full summer swing had a natural rhythm, but the house looked over it like a cold tomb, groaning and demanding.

When Lewis and I left home our parents finally had some breathing space, which should have delivered more time and more resources. But the paralysis remained. Mum knew how heavily it weighed on him. This symbol of pride and dignity became a burden, and eventually something approaching a prison.

Following his breakdown in 2011, Dad's insomnia, led by intense depression and the first rumblings of disordered thinking, had him clawing at the doors. Mum had begun with hiding the kitchen knives, garden tools, anything that looked like a ligature, and eventually locked them both in at night and hid the keys for his own safety. She couldn't stay awake and watch him all night but she could do that. Understandably, he found this intolerable.

It is the first true summer's day and my skin is pinking. The wrapper from the Cornetto I am eating has blown into the rose bush and in retrieving it I have cut myself on a thorn. A bead of blood like a ladybird. A trail of ants is marching over HOLLIE'S STEP and I try to regard the house as if it's my first time seeing it.

It looks like any turn-of-the-century terrace. Off-white render on the outside the colour of a bleached skull. On top is a decommissioned chimney stack from which a seagull squawks. The walls that enclosed him, the world getting smaller and smaller, until the only space remaining was inside his own head. Unlike the ephemerality of the garden where I sit now, a house is solid and immovable, like circular problems that only reveal themselves in the dread and damp of winter.

Dad would have spent a lot of his retirement in this garden. I wonder if he liked gardening because of the dependable renewal. Maybe he needed to see life coming back again and again against the odds, after the frost.

I suck the blood and look up at the house in which I grew up, knowing one thing to be true. He ended his life just weeks before his retirement, because that would mean a death-in-service payout to his family. I look at the house, and its horrible power. Dad's death means I might now be able to buy one too.

His quietus make: On suffering and suicide

One summer's day my family witnessed a suicide attempt.

Mum and Dad were visiting London and we had done the tourist route: a morning stroll in Hyde Park followed by the Natural History Museum, past the pelicans at St James's Park to board the Thames Clipper at Westminster. The boat takes care of the rest in quick succession: the London Eye, Embankment, Tate Modern, Shakespeare's Globe. It was mine and Michael's first real showing-off of our new home and I wanted my parents to be impressed.

Though we were sitting on the top deck in full sun, we didn't see anything happen. Just a gasp, followed by a synchronised turning of heads. Dad stood up first and had moved to the railings before I had even lowered my camera. When someone is in moving water milliseconds can obscure even the most spirited thrashing.

I whipped my attention back to the front as loudspeakers declared an emergency. They grew louder as the Metropolitan Police Marine Unit boat, reacting in mere seconds, advanced towards us.

'Rod!' said Mum, who had clocked what Dad was gearing up to do. He was already slipping out of his trainers and testing the wooden railing for grip.

Then the rescue boat was upon us. Had it had taken a few moments more he would have gone in. I looked down at the churning green water and felt sick. Even the strongest swimmers are dragged down by its powerful current.

They had located her in lightspeed time and were working to fish her out. A young woman about my height and size, she should have vanished into the heave with little resistance. The winch on the boat was powerful, effortlessly lifting her and the two orange-clad rescuers either side. We locked eyes. The look on her face will be with me forever, as will the sense of having imposed myself on the most private of moments.

What happened next bewilders me to this day. A cheer went up across the top deck of our boat, another tourist boat opposite and even the spectators on London Bridge, on which seconds earlier the woman had herself stood. Not just a cheer but a hoot, impassioned clapping. The speed and capability of the coastguard had been astonishing to witness so close, of course. But Michael and I exchanged glances. Did they not see the bag tied around her slight waist and weighted with concrete? I thought about her just minutes earlier evaluating each piece, passing it between her hands.

Like everyone else, our day continued. Mum, Michael and I were dazed. None of us knew what to say, how to get the conversation light again. Dad, however, was exhilarated. Unfortunately, the pub in the shadow of the Tower of London that I had picked for lunch was called The Hung, Drawn and Quartered. Above the bar, like a dismal punchline, hung a noose.

'At some stage of evolution man must have discovered that he can kill not only animals and fellow-men but also himself. It can be assumed that life has never since been the same to him,' wrote the psychoanalyst Erwin Stengel in 1969. Stengel reasoned that the understanding that one can cause the end of one's own existence is a threshold of sophisticated thought that sets humans apart from other species. Evolutionary psychologist Nicholas Humphrey dates this discovery to no more than 100,000 years ago. Suicide is a relatively new behaviour. Though however maladaptive the act might be in an evolutionary sense, once sparked into being it could not be un-known.

It's an evolutionary touch point not just on a macro level but also the developmental. There will have been a time when you did not comprehend this extraordinary and terrible potential within yourself. The comprehension of death itself may only have been very recent to you, at least consciously. Within our cellular fabric, of course, we are constantly dying and replenishing.

Opting out is not conducive to a functioning community. So, like guardrails on the Golden Gate Bridge, we put up cultural barriers. These mores against suicide spread through folk knowledge and religious orthodoxy.

Some Mesopotamian and Egyptian civilisations thought demonic influences caused depression and sucked from the sufferer the will to live. Early Chinese medicine considered listlessness and incapacity to enjoy life to be the result of either moral turpitude or insufficiently honouring one's family in current or past lives. Suicidal feelings were partly the fault of the patient, his failures of self were an open door to bad influences.

In the Abrahamic religions to die by suicide is a sinful and selfish act. Those who rejected the almighty's gift of life were condemned. Culturally this was enforced by giving individuals who committed this so-called unnatural act an unnatural burial. Such people were often denied funeral rites and burial on consecrated ground. A combination of eternal damnation, public exile and reputational damage to the surviving family acted as a strong deterrent for anyone who might be considering the option.

To underscore this censure, or to prevent any unquiet spirits troubling the living, in Britain it was common to bury the suicide dead under piles of stones or with a stake driven through their heart. Up until the Burial of Suicide Act of 1823 it was a legal requirement to dispose of executed criminals and suicides at night and outside the parish limits at crossroads. This may have been born out of superstition, an attempt to confuse any ghost from finding his way back. However, another interesting theory aligns the practice with that of certain Teutonic groups who customarily used crossroads as the location for their sacrificial altars. Burial here then was an especially ignominious one, disassociating it from Christianity and linking it as much as possible with the heathen pagan.

Ghosts of the ostracised and desperate haunt the margins of death registers. One of the saddest stories I came across was that of Betty Corrigall. Betty lived on the island of Hoy in the Orkneys, Scotland, until her death in the late 1770s. At 27 she had become pregnant by a whaler who deserted her and fled back to sea. Unmarried and steeped in shame, Betty could see no way out but to end her life. Naturally the devout authorities of the island refused her and the unborn child a Christian burial and her resting place, unmarked, was the peat bog bordering the hamlet where Betty Corrigall was forgotten.

In 1933 labourers cutting the peat for fuel uncovered a

long box and, hoping for treasure, opened it. Inside was what looked like a sleeping young woman, long dark hair coiled round her slim shoulders, the skin tinged with the colour of the peat but otherwise perfectly preserved by the conditions of the ground. The callous elders had made sure Betty could not escape condemnation even in death: in her casket they had laid beside her the noose she had used.

Sadly, the people of Hoy were still unmoved and, after the police in Kirkwall had ruled out a crime had taken place, Betty was reinterred. But the 150-year-old sleeping beauty known as 'the Lady of Hoy' turned into legend, and during the Second World War English soldiers garrisoned there sought and found Betty once again. Morbid curiosity led more groups to dig her up and rebury her, and her corpse soon deteriorated. Finally the officer in charge put a stop to it and had her laid to rest under a concrete slab. There she remained. It wasn't until 1976 that an American minister heard the sad tale and organised a Christian service and a headstone. Betty Corrigall's story, tragic though it is, ends with some manner of redemptive arc.

Ten months on and it was only now with these accounts of historical record that I felt able to turn my mind to the act of suicide. The stories about death, bodily disposal, mourning and memorial I'd been finding were useful up to a point, but they stopped short of the true search I was on. I needed to understand what had led him to it.

It is a common misconception that suicide rates are highest in winter. Multiple studies have shown the peak actually falls in the summer months, but there has been no conclusive explanation, only hypotheses about compounded social disconnection made more stark during good weather. The dismal truth is that at every turn the *why* evades answers.

Crossroad burials indicate the social reasons around why someone might take his or her life: shame, community exclusion or an internal sense of religious shortcoming. There were plenty of deterrents heaped on top; like the *felo de se* tenet in English common law which said that the assets of anyone who died by suicide would be forfeited to the Crown, even if it turned the surviving family out on the streets. In France Louis XIV mandated that the body of someone known to have died by suicide be drawn face-down through the streets and then thrown into Paris's landfill.

This condemnation was not just coded in law but also in folklore. In nineteenth-century Slavic folklore a woman who turned to suicide after being jilted by a lover or becoming pregnant outside of marriage became a *rusałka*, a mournful entity who stalked Eurasian waterways entrapping people in her long coils of green hair. In parts of rural Spain there still exists the tradition of the *ánimas*, a procession of cloaked figures forming the *Santa Compaña* (the Holy Company) who have been roaming the night since the thirteenth-century introduction of the concept of Purgatory. The *ánimas* are trapped in this limbo state due to dying by suicide or other heretical reasons and may offer the passer-by a candle; if taken the unsuspecting living will see his flesh decay and fall from his bones and be forced to join the restless mass of the *ánimas* for eternity.

This thread of shame continues to run through cases today, playing a part in those social factors to which they are most often attributed: isolation and loneliness, bankruptcy and the perception of 'failures', substance abuse and, especially in the younger online generation, bullying. Alongside this is the concept of suicide contagion, with studies showing that reading about the topic, news reports that mention details such as method, or a celebrity dying by suicide, all contribute to an uptick in numbers. Around the world 1.4 per cent of all deaths are attributed to suicide annually, and up to 20 times that number for suicide attempts. It remains the greatest cause of violent death, between 800,000 to 1 million people a year, more than wars and homicide combined. These statistics shock me not just for their breath-taking number but for what they conceal. From the outside Dad had no 'reason' to kill himself. He was privileged in that he had a family that loved him and visited often. Sisters that he saw and spoke to all the time. Colleagues who thought the world of him. He was weeks away from retirement. The mortgage was paid off, kids settled and in gainful employment. He had none of the comorbidities that can accompany internal struggles – addiction, alcoholism, money problems, divorce – none.

That's why it takes the perspective of considerable intimacy to spot what is happening. And also why so many people 'miss the signs', as is wholly understandable, and blame themselves for it forever.

Émile Durkheim, the great scholar of suicide, determined four types of self-killing: the altruistic, egoistic, anomic and fatalistic. There are many cultural examples of altruistic suicide and martyrdom in which the act is codified as ennobling of the victim. Japan has a long association of suicide bound up with honour; the ritual disembowelment *seppuku* of the warrior samurai class as preferable over surrender, and the *kamikaze* pilots and *kaiten* human torpedoes used by the Imperial Japanese Army towards the end of the Second World War. Rarely documented but known across East Asia and the Himalayas are the *sokushinbutsu* mummies. As an act of asceticism a Buddhist monk would reject all food and water so as to bring about self-mummification. Suicidal acts of protest are also associated with Buddhism. The 1963 self-immolation of Thích Quảng Đức in Saigon was an act of dissent against religious persecution by the South Vietnamese. Rather than shameful, the monk's suicide, which made front pages around the world, has come to be regarded as an impassioned *cri de cœur* and an altruistic sacrifice for a collective cause.

Though I couldn't help being fascinated with these stories of self-sacrifice it was alongside an increasing discomfort. The implicit suggestion was that the opposite number, the 'egoistic' suicide, is a cowardly abjection, a solipsistic opting-out.

It was coming up on a year and I hadn't really stopped drinking. Perhaps one of the pros of grieving while on furlough, though it could equally be a con, was that I simply had nowhere to which I was required to turn up sober. A gratifying narrative arc would enjoy a lapse into blackout here, a rock bottom before a redemptive return, but I'm afraid I can't satisfy that. It was immoderate moderation. I drank a half to a full bottle of wine a day because I was bored. Then, one June day, as I walked past a supermarket display of pint glasses and golf caddy mugs, I realised why I had de-progressed. Father's Day.

Naturally the occasion called for a box rather than a bottle. When I got to the self-check-out in the Co-op I realised the 3-litre box of Shiraz had been barcoded as a single bottle, and a cheap bottle at that. I quickly picked up another, the limit to what I could carry, and after breathlessly reporting my findings back home, I immediately went back and cleared the shelf.

Dad would have been delighted by this. Nothing gave him a kick more than having needled out a discount. It had long irritated me, the way he listed the exact mark-down on everything, how he stocked the freezer with yellow-stickered goods. When I was younger I thought it gauche, because for a few years I was the type of pretentious shit who thought things gauche. But as an adult I just got incensed by the inefficiency of it all.

'Look at these cherry tomatoes – 19p!'

'Wow. Yeah.'

'They are really sweet! Have one!'

'I've just woken up, Dad.'

'I got extra so you can take them home in your suitcase.'

'We have cherry tomatoes in London, Dad.'

'But they're all going mushy and need using up today. Only 19p a punnet!'

For his 60th birthday I took him and Mum to the Hampton Court Flower Show but I genuinely think his becoming qualified for various OAP discounts was his favourite thing about turning 60. Papa's Fish & Chips on Cleethorpes pier now included a cup of tea and a free pudding. He had a bottomless enthusiasm for having got a good deal.

Since he'd been gone the yellow stickers had taken on a new significance. I had moved back to London but was back in Cleethorpes regularly, where I kept myself busy by cooking for Mum. Dad knew all the staff in the Co-op because he turned up at the same time every day when they were marking stuff down. He wasn't pushy but he knew when and where to be first in line and he'd developed a jovial 'me again!' rapport with everyone there.

Filling my Bag for Life with my sneaky haul, I wondered suddenly how long it had taken for his absence to have been noted. 'Haven't seen that yellow sticker man much lately, have you? I wonder where he is?'

Yellow stickers were how I knew he was alright. If the first thing he said to me off the train was that he'd got a catering-sized tub of peanut butter in, because you like that don't you, and for only 59p!, but you have to be quick because it goes off tomorrow, then I knew he was okay. When I sat at the kitchen table as he pottered about and I was unable to ask out loud how he had been doing, his yellow sticker reports stood in for more difficult conversational assessments. It was how I knew for the time being that he was invested in the world, because the cherry tomatoes were on the turn and needed eating.

Melancholia. For many centuries a patient presenting with a combination of mood disorder and one or another adverse physical sensations would have been termed 'melancholic'. In premodern medicine melancholia was a state in which 'black bile' was dangerously overrepresented, displacing the balance of the four humours. Hippocrates' diagnostic criteria was much like we might figure depression today: poor appetite, abulia (lack of willpower), insomnia, irritability, anhedonia (inability to feel pleasure), agitation and despondency. The four humours theory was of course incorrect, but that melancholia was no less serious an affliction for it being an illness of the mind was a progressive idea. The prescription was exercise, music, hydrotherapy and even an early form of behavioural therapy, wherein health-seeking actions were rewarded.

Of course, if the cure for melancholia really worked then suicide would have ceased long before the fall of Rome. The problem with despair is that it is a unique prison, a soul buffeted by 'the thousand natural shocks / That flesh is heir to', as Hamlet terms it in his famous monologue, a pondering around the nature of suicide. What man would bear 'the whips and scorns' of earthly existence, he reasons, 'When he himself might his quietus make / With a bare bodkin?' (i.e. a swift and decisive end with a dagger). What prevents this is not knowing what comes next, and this immobilisation, Hamlet believes, is the bedrock of human despair.

It is this atavistic understanding that captivates the human conscience in mythic stories of unendurable torment. Take, for instance, the myth of Sisyphus, sentenced by the gods to push a great boulder up a mountain every day only to have it roll back down at night. It is not the physical torture but the starting from scratch every day that outrages us: an analogy for the daily battle between remaining on the precipice of a known misery, or jumping into an unknown void.

The act of suicide as a reasonable and/or defensible response to suffering is one that has been debated by philosophers from a range of moral and theoretical positions, variously taking into account personal liberty, life's purpose (or existential absence thereof), the social contract, and the rejection of the divine gift of existence. Picking through them all I have even less of an idea of what I think than before. What made the most impact was stumbling across the reviews of *Final Exit: The Practicalities of Self-Deliverance and Assisted Suicide for the Dying* by Derek Humphry, founder of the assisted-dying pressure group the Hemlock Society. Humphrey's controversial 1991 book provided information to those seeking to end their own lives, from the position that since we are born without our permission, so life is ours to end. The one-star reviews are tough to read. Many of them are by grieving relatives, laying bare the unmistakable fact that suicide can never be described as an act taken in isolation.

Trying to square the illogical with logic sends me into challenging waters. Because any philosophical despair that Dad experienced wasn't the sum total of his suffering. His pain was not just of the spirit but of the body too. So I cannot avoid the conclusion that his act was not completely irrational.

Daily for years his sciatic nerve tortured him, twisting his back and upper legs with spasms of pain. He scoured every conceivable medical intervention and approached every specialist. Sometimes the pain had him laid up for days. He had done everything right, kept fit and active. He rode his bicycle everywhere, jogged, swam lengths before work every day. But day by day his mobility was diminishing.

On top of that were the side-effects of the medications.

Antidepressants are well known for weight gain, which he attributed to his increase in back pain. Antipsychotics, meanwhile, left him drowsy and listless. Once he described the experience to me as 'not living'.

Dad's mostly intact him-ness was what I found so hard, because it showed none of the unravelling I would have presumed would happen before a suicide. He had the presence of mind to look into pre-paid funerals. I found documents and articles on transference of finances to a spouse after death, with key bits highlighted. He arranged all his financial affairs in a labelled envelope for me. There was also a letter from his MP in reply to a letter he'd written about the assisted suicide debate (presumably in favour given the tone of the reply), dated March 2012. And on the night in question he disappeared with everything he needed and hid from capture and to ensure his privacy. As painful as it is to confront, it was very clear this wasn't an impulse that came out of the blue.

I couldn't confront his suicide without also confronting his knowledge that he would probably never be totally physically well again. Which opened up a periscope through which I didn't want to look. I might recognise the desire just to call it off. The anticipation of relief. The allure of sleep. When you spend a lot of time trying to access the psychology of the suicidal mind, it is unavoidable to recognise when rational thought goes into the so called-irrational act.

In the 2006 documentary *The Bridge* a film crew documented all the suicides off the Golden Gate Bridge for a whole year. I am still not sure what I think of the film and urge you to seek it out only with extreme caution. However, one scene struck me as totally unlike any other reporting I have encountered on suicide and suicide bereavement. A woman visits the bridge and looks over the side from which her sister had jumped, and calls it extraordinarily brave. It made the loss no less heartbreaking or the grief less acute, but the woman could appreciate that whatever internal mechanism by which her sister had been guided, the step itself was enormously weighty. A person in a burning building jumps not because death seems suddenly appealing or because the terror of jumping is any less intense, but because the fear of not doing it is worse.

In cases of despair, rather than of delusional or disordered thinking, the ending of one's life unavoidably requires a clarity of mind to deliver. It is a mind of invisible agony that has become unendurable. Durkheim wrote that it can be considered 'not an act of despair, but of abnegation': a renouncing of pain, a break from the prison. It was no less real a prison because nobody else could see the bars.

That the act of suicide can come from a complex combination of factors is usually considered an enlightened modern view. I came across one example, however, that shares this remarkably progressive stance, and it comes from the tenth century.

The *Kalevala*, a collection of epic poetry and ballads compiled from oral folklore, has been hugely influential on Finnish culture and national identity since its first publication in 1835. Runes 31 to 36 tell of the tragic life of a figure named Kullervo. Kullervo's misery predates even his own birth; while still in his mother's womb the entire tribe is slain by the rival Untamo clan. He survives, but into a life of slavery and grinding toil. Finally Kullervo finds happiness when he falls in love with a homeless beggar; her misfortune mirrors his and they feel bound by destiny. However, the object of his love turns out to be Kullervo's sister, whom he presumed had been murdered with the rest of his family. Confronted with her unknowing incest the young woman is consumed by shame and drowns herself. Kullervo finally explodes in anger for the injustices he has suffered by the cruelty of the Untamo tribe, and vows revenge. Using his latent magical powers he destroys the Untamo line. Afterwards a nymph tries to direct Kullervo to a sanctuary in the forest but instead, with great distress, he finds the place where his sister ended her life. Furious, he takes out his sword:

> Thereupon the youth, Kullervo,
> Wicked wizard of the Northland,
> Lifts the mighty sword of Ukko,
> Bids adieu to earth and heaven;
> Firmly thrusts the hilt in heather,
> To his heart he points the weapon,
> Throws his weight upon his broadsword,
> Pouring out his wicked life-blood.

It is a scene of passion but also one of triumph. In a life of trauma, persecution and isolation this final act can be said to be the only freely chosen one of Kullervo's short life.

Let me say it plainly for the avoidance of misinterpretation: in no way am I lionising suicide as a heroic act. There is certainly no shame in the near-universal contemplation of it, or indeed in its completion. But there is no space for glory either. Intervention is always possible, there is no lost cause.

That said, I can't pretend that these stories told by ordinary people, probably as a way to understand a suicide in the community, didn't give me a great deal of comfort. The tales that make up the *Kalevala* were in existence at least 1,000 years ago, crafted by an unknown number of unknown authors. The drive to make sense of seismic life events is something to which anyone navigating suicide loss can surely relate.

Narratologists believe storytelling began soon after our development of language, around 100,000 years ago. If we take evolutionary psychologist Nicholas Humphrey's theory that the human brain became sufficiently sophisticated to discover the concept of self-killing, it is likely folklore began at the same point in human development as our comprehension of suicide.

The *Kalevala* is taught to all Finnish schoolchildren and the characters and stories are deeply enmeshed in Finnish national identity and civic behaviour. The *Kalevala* and other sagas provide a map for progressive understanding of how mental illness and suicidal behaviours may be brought about by circumstance, at odds with the official condemnation of suicide as deviant. In Kullervo's tragic tale there is no moral weakness. He is an honourable man and true to himself and his family. It is the wickedness of a rich warmonger that conspires to make his life one of violence, injustice and strife and, eventually, to become intolerable. Ancient listeners to the story understood that a combination of interiority and social pressures lead a person through their life choices, that choice itself is an illusion. In Rune 36 Kullervo's suicide is very much considered in terms of his childhood trauma. It is heartbreaking to me that this understanding is a thousand years old.

But the model has its limits. As with any suicide the conditions were complex. Like Kullervo, Dad's was a loss involving many factors, some of which were experienced in his mind only. I still had questions to ask. What, for instance, does it mean to have your mind turn against you?

Midsummer madness

Midsummer, around 21 June every year, is a festival of the senses. It often falls on the astronomical beginning of summer known as the solstice or longest day. Debate remains over whether ancient peoples had fixed calendrical customs around it. In England recognisable midsummer celebrations may have only occurred after the Normans arrived. By the late fourteenth century these festivities had become increasingly rowdy and, in London, required watchmen to carry flaming torches to keep everyone in check. During this fire festival bonfires were lit as a protection from evil spirits as the sun turned to face its decline to the year's dark half.

Summer's peak then is also a precipice, and this paradox comes with a woozy disorientation. The year's longest day meant all the more time to give in to pleasure as summer's last hurrah. So say the fae-folk of Shakespeare's *A Midsummer Night's Dream*, whose mischief potions wreak havoc on the mental states of mortals just for their own entertainment. Modern paganism's transmutation of the festival, called Litha, very much leans into the mystique, sensuality and hedonism of the strangely elongated day. After all, the wheel only teeters in this position once a year before the warm evenings begin their demise; why not mark it with magic and masquerade, dancing and disinhibition, in soon-to-be skeletonised forests?

The summer solstice was also an event in which those given to eccentricity might tip further in its direction. Shakespeare's 'Midsummer madness' turns up again in *Twelfth Night*, in reference to Malvolio wearing outlandish clothing that everyone else takes as evidence of his insanity.

Madness has been characterised by senses in overdrive. Its representatives in folklore are creatures of intense feeling becoming too powerful and then deranged.

In the pantheon of ancient Greece insanity and unreason is personified by a group of spirits called the *Maniae*, the origin of the word 'mania', and with the goddess Lyssa, who embodies madness, frenzy and rabies; cleaving the minds of gods and men alike. While Vedic mythology has the *pishachas*, demons of glowing red eyes and a taste for flesh who haunted crematoria and graveyards. If you retreat without being eaten try not to look back – the *pishacha* will turn out the contents of a healthy mind onto the burial ground.

In some contexts the 'fool' was romanticised. During the Feast of Fools a peasant was appointed the Lord of Misrule, a sort of permitted lunatic given fleeting impunity to panto-mime ecclesiastical rituals and lampoon the clergy at court. A 'lunatic' was so called for having slept where the beams of the moon could hit his head, and the proximity between the lunar cycle and lunacy persisted well into the nineteenth century. Others in history have transcended the derogatory connotations of insanity to achieve a sort of divine madness, usually of religious ecstasy. In such examples the visible symptoms of mental illness are interpreted as evidence of a divine connection or abilities in prophecy, indicated for instance by the speaking of tongues. Then there is the unavoidable label of mad in the context of othering. This is the madness of 'primitive' peoples, used as pretext for imperialist subjugation for centuries.

Treatments for anything from light eccentrism to full-blown psychological disturbance have the world over encompassed expulsion, exorcism or imprisonment, as well as medical interventions such as herbal emetics or trepanation: the drilling of a hole into the living skull in order to let the 'bad spirit' escape. In Enlightenment Europe many towns had a 'fool's tower', like the Narrenturm in Vienna, and no facility casts a longer shadow than London's Bethlem asylum, better known as Bedlam. Forced sterilisation of the mentally unwell is a crime that haunts many regimes.

Madness is not static, but a push and pull between the sufferer and the society in which he exists. This is the foundation of Michel Foucault's *Madness and Civilization*, in which he argues that various cultural, intellectual and economic structures determine how madness is experienced and interpreted. Take the examples we looked at before concerning visions, 'ghosts' and other anomalous experiences. Depending on time and place such experience could mean you were bound for the asylum, or they could mean a healthy and comforting connection to your ancestors.

Following this thread I found a fascinating study. Researchers at Stanford found that individuals in the United States who presented with hearing voices, most often described such voices as stern and authoritarian. More often than not the sufferer found the voice frightening. A subject pool in Chennai, India, meanwhile were more likely to describe the voices they heard as benign. These voices could help them solve problems in the home and bring comfort during stressful life events. Some specified the voices were recognisable as members of their deceased family. Why the difference? The researchers offered an explanation: 'Europeans and Americans tend to see themselves as individuals motivated by a sense of self identity, whereas outside the West, people imagine the mind and self interwoven with others and defined through relationships.'

In the UK we'd like to imagine that things have changed since Bedlam. Most people recognise that words like 'crazy' or 'insane' are no longer appropriate. If asked, the majority of people would agree that sufferers of mental illness should be treated with compassion. But have we congratulated ourselves on becoming enlightened simply by getting the language right? Despite mental health awareness ballooning in the last decade it is much overlooked how different conditions are discussed in the public sphere. The fact is that while disorders of anxiety and panic, depression and, to some extent, obsessive compulsive disorder have benefitted hugely and rightly from increasing social understanding and accommodations, other more visible conditions are still considered unsightly and something to be feared. A person acting erratically in a public place makes people behave with revulsion whether or not this person is prone to violence.

Dad's major depressive disorder was at times so severe that it brought on episodes of transient psychosis. The symptoms he experienced could be frightening both to him and anyone nearby. He never posed a threat to anyone other than himself, but nor was it, despite the campaigns, 'just like breaking a leg'. Presenting at A&E would not have got him the treatment he needed, which would probably have required lifetime management of monitoring, therapeutics and medications. In our underfunded healthcare system it is not a case of simply 'asking for help'.

Each episode the onset of symptoms accelerated. The deep depression came first followed by a trickle of strange behaviour. I tried to keep abreast of clues: the word 'entrapment' or 'surveillance' written on the shopping list sent me on a rummage through his bedside table. Ironically I would attach meaning to things that were probably benign, our paranoia feeding one another like midsummer madness.

Mum was privy to his more baroque delusions. 'They are coming for me,' he'd explain when she asked why he was pacing about, 'I can hear them outside.' 'They', as is common in delusions of persecution, was the police. They were staking out the house from unmarked cars parked for too long, or people who he didn't recognise walking on our street and glancing at the house in a way that he considered to be menacing. A new security camera outside his work upset him greatly and once I deeply regretted explaining what the Google Maps car was doing driving around. The crux of his worries seemed to be either that he had committed a crime many years ago and had forgotten about it, or that the authorities needed a scapegoat for an unsolved crime and were fixing to gather his DNA in order to falsely charge him with it. After his first psychiatric hold, going back to the in-patient facility would only make his DNA easier to collect. He was sure he would go to prison for the rest of his life.

To live every waking and un-waking hour with that fear must be close to the limits of what any human mind can bear. Being caught in a trap by state oppression, exiled by public condemnation with no course of redress, banished to a tiny cage to be forgotten is agony on a primal level. One would do anything to escape it. I have wept so many times thinking about his isolation. It is difficult to think of him thinking we, his loved ones, did not believe the mortal danger he was convinced he was in.

There was also a huge amount of forgetfulness on his part. Whenever Mum or I reminded him of something unusual he'd said he would dismiss it. 'Oh no, I didn't say that.' But it wasn't just forgetfulness, it was deceit too. It is probably what family members of sufferers of altered realities find the most difficult. His capacity to conceal meant that I didn't trust him, and his comprehension of that meant a mutual suspicion that any family would find challenging. It was painful to think that his acuity and meticulousness in taking steps to conceal, qualities so aligned with my internal portrait of my clever and tenacious father, meant that this version was in some way still present. He knew enough to know that we found his thoughts illogical, and perhaps occasionally had the strength of mind to know himself they were. It might have been easier had he been fully taken over by some demonic force, as his condition might have been diagnosed a few centuries ago.

But we are not our thoughts. In between episodes Dad had significant periods of apparent placidity and motivation. Sometimes these periods were made possible by antipsychotics and antidepressants, but equally there were periods of wellness when he did not take regular medication. I now know of course that mental illness is a game by degrees; in the last ten years of his life he was never all well or all ill. The fire of trauma may die down but it never ceases to smoke at the edges, ready to take again with the right fuel.

There's no point pretending it was anything other than very hard on us all as a family. Surely, I thought, I could discover the right combination of words that would end the spell of conspiracy. On the phone to Mum I understood the limits to what she could do alone to bring him back to reality, at the same time as being frustrated by her lack of superhuman ability. To Lewis I downplayed many of Dad's symptoms, especially the ones that made me uncomfortable. I am guilty of lying by omission. But mostly I was immobile because I was scared of a man who looked like my dad – who'd cut the umbilicus and taught me to use a spoon and clapped at my graduation and held my wedding bouquet while I made final adjustments to my dress – periodically occupy the body of someone else.

In the *Vita Merlini*, the twelfth-century biography of Merlin by Geoffrey of Monmouth, Merlin reels after the bloody battle of Camlann, which ended with him ruling over South Wales. This is no glorification as in other Arthurian cycles, and what is particularly unusual is the description of the effect the war had on the hero. 'Winter will be hard but not as hard as living among the savagery of people, therefore let me be,' Merlin says, and, grief-stricken and traumatised by seeing his comrades slain, he retreats into the Caledonian Forest. Merlin was a prophetic sage but after his withdrawal into the woods he was considered swallowed up by madness.

Does Merlin's retreat into nature console his madness or burnish it? The folklore of many cultures has time and again chosen the forest, and specifically the tree, round which to base this exploration.

Generally speaking, when discussing suicide it is inadvisable to talk about method. Most charities for mental illness advise this, primarily because discussing methods may make the act itself appear more feasible and increase the chances of an attempt. Nevertheless my preoccupation throughout this year must be pretty clear by now. Aside from reading about the folklore around them I dreamt of trees constantly. Trees looming over me, trees rising out of the floodwaters. I was both drawn to woodland areas and anxious at the thought of being among them. Trees hang heavy with the weight of the saddest of ends. A ligature cast in desperation over a branch likely predates recorded history.

What is perhaps the oldest of all methods has a prominent place in ancient lore, part of the story of existence itself. The foundation of all that exists in Norse mythology is Yggdrasil, the world tree. An immense and sacred evergreen ash, Yggdrasil holds up the nine worlds that make up the ancient Norse conception of the cosmos. The gods dwell in the heavens at the top, connected by a rainbow bridge to the realm of humankind in the middle and, beneath the tree roots, the underworld, where a dragon named Níðhöggr sucks the blood of the dead. The name of the tree in Old Norse is commonly accepted as 'Odin's horse', or the hangman's horse, meaning gallows. In the poem *Hávamál* from the Poetic Edda, Odin is described as having 'hung on that windy tree nine long nights', a slow, painful suicide in order that he might learn the meaning of the runes. What's striking are the parallels between Merlin's 'threefold death' in the pursuit of occult knowledge and Odin's self-sacrifice. In both mythic traditions ritual death is finally brought about by hanging.

But in the Norse the most prominent aspect is the tree itself, Yggdrasil. Followers of the Odin cult hung *blót* (sacrifices), both human and animal, from trees in holy groves, not as punishment but as the most powerful form of offering. Those whose death was by hanging, whether accidental, self-inflicted or sacrificial, were consecrated to Odin. It was considered a noble death.

By the fourteenth century moral condemnation of suicide was the dominant European worldview and its imaginative vision of the afterlife is best represented by Dante Alighieri's

The Divine Comedy. In the *Inferno* Dante placed those who had died by suicide in the seventh circle of Hell. The Wood of Suicides is where they are transformed into gnarled trees ('deform'd / And matted thick: fruits there were none, but thorns / Instead, with venom fill'd') for committing the sin of murder of the self. In Canto XIII Dante travels through the accursed forest which is guarded by vicious harpies that feed on the leaves of the trees, ensuring eternal pain and torment to those entombed inside. This scene was portrayed by print-maker William Blake in *The Wood of the Self-Murderers: The Harpies and the Suicides.* Blake chooses a specific moment to illustrate: Dante's plucking of a branch and the plaintive cry of the imprisoned soul – 'Wherefore tear'st me thus? Is there no touch of mercy in thy breast?' – suggesting that his era's moral position on the act of suicide, five centuries later than Dante, may have shifted in sympathy.

Trees that bear strange fruit can have dangerous and magical applications. It was said that if a hanged man's blood, urine or fat deposits were spilled on the ground underneath there would grow a mandrake, a human-shaped root that would scream and thus had to be harvested carefully so as to make use of its black-magic properties. The left hand of a hanged man could be turned into a 'Hand of Glory', coveted by burglars who believed the token would allow them to pick any lock. It had to be harvested fresh, shrouded, pickled and dried in the sun. Pieces of an executed man were also believed to treat a whole range of ailments and sufferers attended pub-lic executions, slipping the hangman a coin for access to the corpse. Even the gallows itself had curative properties. A piece of gallows wood could be worn around the neck to defend against ague (fever), while inserting splinters into the mouth was said to cure toothache.

The gallows are first and foremost associated with crime and punishment. In this way the gallows may be understood as a caricature of the life-giving tree. For centuries the end of the road in the English judicial code was the 'Tyburn Tree', London's infamous scaffold from which the condemned were taken to be executed in public. Research has suggested that countries that continue to or have in living memory used hanging as a method of capital punishment tend to have a low rate of hanging suicides. This may be because such suicides came to be culturally regarded as shameful.

A notable exception is the Aokigahara 'suicide forest' in Japan, a country that executes around 15 people a year by this method. On undulating terrain formed by the lava that once flowed down from nearby Mount Fuji, Aokigahara, the 'Sea of Trees', is a dense forest in which every year about a hundred people enter with no plan to return. Many Japanese believe it is haunted by restless *yūrei*. In recent times Japanese spiritualists have suggested that the suicides completed in the forest have permeated the trees themselves and curse those who enter from escaping. Rich deposits of magnetic iron in the volcanic soil have reportedly caused compasses to malfunction and the porous lava rock absorbs sound, presenting physical and psychological challenges for lost visitors. The gigantic *sugi* trees, the 'old men of the forest', have witnessed much sorrow in the silence.

One tree folk tale stands out. It comes from an isolated area of north-west Wales, later abandoned, known as Nant Gwrtheyrn. On her wedding day bride Meinir and groom Rhys play a game of hide-and-seek in the woods. Meinir proves so good at hiding that she is never found, and Rhys is consumed by life-long heartbreak and near-madness believing that his bride ran away. When he is elderly a mighty storm hits the north-west coast and splits open an enormous oak tree, revealing inside a skeleton wearing a wedding dress. One day she was there and the next she wasn't. It was like she had disappeared into the tree, eaten by the forest.

My preoccupation with these stories was around the sense of genetic oblivion, taking a cauterising iron to one's own branch of a family tree. Maybe it was why I kept going back to Country Park in Cleethorpes to search for the specific one. The tree was, after all, the last living thing to see him alive.

On the top deck of the Thames Clipper I watched as Dad bent down to re-tie his trainers and the young woman was winched from the swirling water. Cheers and applause surrounded her on all sides, but with her expression one of horrifying exposure and the crowd so numerous and enveloping, it felt closer to a jeer. We were of course next to Tower Hill, site of public executions for nearly 400 years, the other end of London to the Tyburn Tree, and this public rescue was its opposite number, a collective death spectacle. She looked perfectly normal; no outward clue to seize upon, no pathology to be presumptuously parsed. That is the limit of Durkheim's altruistic and egoistic categorisation. They are as many 'reasons' for suicide as there are suicides.

It's the not knowing why. It's the groom searching for his bride when her secrets were all dust and bones inside a hollow.

The past year I'd convinced myself I had been grieving, but I had never really got past this point. It was during the long airless summer of 2021 when I decided I needed to talk specifically about the act itself.

Beckie, from the charity Rethink, became my suicide bereavement worker. She was comfortingly unshockable, with a south London accent and a thoughtful frankness. Weekly on Zoom I talked myself to exhaustion. I told her about the yellow stickers, the organised documents, and his thrill that day on the Thames. Beckie quickly spotted that it could all be boiled down to the most obvious and plaintive. The only thing I needed to know. Did he mean to?

'I can't bear the thought of the few minutes before. The

sureness of what he was about to do. Did that continue for the few seconds ... after ...?' I told Beckie.

By now I had the pathology report. I told Beckie those details that didn't quite add up, those details that made Mum have hope that something else had happened, they all still gnawed at me. All that science that had been done to his poor injured body and yet it resisted the definitive. I thought once I had looked up phrases like 'dorsal lividity' and the structure of the human jaw, it would give me that. There was no peace to be found because it didn't answer the fundamental questions. Did he change his mind? Did he try to free himself?

It felt like a betrayal, almost as if I hoped he wanted and embraced death. I hope it wasn't just an impulse that another day or new medication could have changed. The thought otherwise of his last moments of panic and torment is too horrific.

'So believe that. You can be sorrowful about the choice and also hope that he wanted that choice completely,' Beckie said composedly, as if she hadn't just spoken the most miraculous sentence I had ever heard.

'You will never know. So give yourself a story you can live with.'

Beckie encouraged me to create my own ending, because I cannot ever know. It is as likely as not that he died suddenly and felt no pain. Is it as likely as not that he changed his mind – yes, this is a hard one to contemplate – but if so the story can be that his will and spirit were alive at the end and his death was therefore a tragic misadventure. Whichever one I pick I can take comfort from the gift of giving myself certainty. More important, Beckie said, is to come up with a better abiding image, one where he was happy, fill it with colours and ambient sound and smells and close my eyes and be there with him whenever I needed to. Make the five senses come alive in processions of tender portraits.

The seconds around his death were a vanishingly short timespan of his overall time on earth, so why should they be the seconds I keep? I hope it was lovely, like falling into a welcome blackness. I hope his brain flooded with the chemicals of euphoria and he went on his way in a bath of serotonin. The world was sparkling and the forest was beautiful and the next one even more.

Sin-eaters and sanctuary, faith and phantasms

In 2010 the parish of Ratlinghope, Shropshire raised the money needed to restore the neglected burial plot of one Richard Munslow, its occupant since 1901. It was a belated acknowledgement that many in his line of work were spurned in life. Munslow was Britain's last sin-eater.

In European folk tradition a sin-eater was a hired individual, most often a man, who by consuming food and drink in the presence of a corpse would ritually take on any sins that the deceased had committed in life. The dead would thereby be absolved and ascend to the next realm unencumbered. The first record of sin-eating comes from antiquary and early folklorist John Aubrey, who in the 1680s recorded an old custom in rural Herefordshire wherein 'a long, lean, ugly, lamentable Raskel' would be passed a crust of bread and a cup of beer over a newly deceased corpse 'which he was to drinke up, and sixpence in money, in consideration whereof he took upon him (ipso facto) all the Sinnes of the Defunct, and freed him (or her) from walking after they were dead'.

The meagre meal was part of the payment, giving a hint as to the type of person who would undertake such a job. When a man has nothing, what else is there to pawn but his immortal soul? This was a time when life was precarious; deaths from injury, childbirth or disease were sudden, preventing many from atoning for sins before their hourglass ran out. The sin-eater offered a posthumous solution. But the desperation that would drive a person tacitly of Christian belief to offer himself as scapegoat meant that those forced to take on the occupation were reviled by the same individuals who partook of their services. A magic act that saved others might seem heroic; but no, sin-eaters were shunned to such an extent they were forbidden to look any God-fearing person in the eye. On completion of his duties, a sin-eater was run out of one Welsh parish under a shower of sticks and stones. In his book *Funeral Customs*, Bertram S. Puckle describes a funeral that took place near Llanwenog, Cardiganshire in 1825, after which the 'tainted' cup and plate used by the sin-eater were purposefully burnt.

Of course, sin-eating is not held up by scripture, and most often had to be performed clandestinely. Any Anglican priest that let this pagan custom play out did so with a blind eye. Reticence to record instances of heresy is probably why we have scant first-hand sources. The few we do have show that in Wales and the Welsh–English borderlands called the Marches the practice was fairly common up until the end of the nineteenth century. Many villages had a sin-eater on retainer, usually a homeless itinerant figure, ready to be called up as soon after the last breath as was practical and banished just as quickly.

I read everything I could find on sin-eaters, looking for something but not entirely sure what. Those Bavarian corpse-cakes, served on the breast of the dead, that I'd found revolting back in autumn seemed now by comparison a ritual of humility. Dutch *doed-koecks*, 'dead-cakes' too, marked with the initials of the deceased and eaten in honour of them, a custom that travelled with émigrés to America and came to endure in funerals in old New York. Tlazoltéotl, the Aztec goddess of vice, filth and purification and patroness of adulterers, was invoked at the end of a devotee's life to hear their confession. Tradition says that she would then cleanse the soul by eating its 'filth'. Chicken is still served at Chinese funerals as it is believed to help the soul fly up to the next world. Humility, honour, cleansing, releasing: none of these quite fit with the sin-eater's degradation and self-imperilment. A ritual foisted upon him for no more a crime than being poor. It was so unjust. How could this practice, performed in front of and adjacent to Christianised culture, have allowed such despicable transactions to occur?

My sensitivity wasn't coincidental. Over the past year lighter, even happy, memories were becoming accessible to me; thinking about Dad pruning the roses or telling me I had a single evening to eat an eight-pack of yoghurts didn't immediately hobble me. But there was one always-unwelcome reminiscence, and I got smacked in the face by it whenever I walked past the church near Mum and Dad's house. His interaction with our local Anglican church in the final years of his life is a matter I can't focus on too long without a veil of red descending.

A few years after the first episode Dad had been acting weird again and I decided I needed to take pre-emptive action. I didn't yet understand that when someone is at the limits of what they can bear there is almost nothing anyone can do. But like many loved ones of the suicidal I felt compelled to try.

Churches have intimidated me since I was a kid, so rather than walk the few minutes round the corner I telephoned. I wasn't expecting the vicar himself to pick up.

I introduced myself and told him that my father was one of his ... congregants (this was an area of language I was unsure of. 'Flock' seemed silly. The word that first occurred, tellingly, was 'patient'). I described him: Rod, mid-fifties, medium build, close-cut greying hair, glasses that he often wore on his forehead, often in a navy fleece and on a bike. He may appear distressed.

'He's been coming to you a lot recently, often several times in the same day.'

The other end of the line remained silent.

'I'm not sure if you would be aware but my dad has had some health difficulties. A few years ago he had a nervous breakdown. He had been very depressed for some time and this ended up in an episode of psychosis.'

Still nothing.

'One of his delusions was that he had committed a terrible crime, and that the police were going to take him away. By the time we realised his state of mind he was already planning to end his life. And looking back one of the major changes in his personality beforehand was a sudden ramping up in his visits to your church.'

I described the crucifixes hidden around his bedroom, the Bibles, some partially filled-in forms I found for some sort of residential study camp. I recalled how confused I was to hear him talk about forgiveness, absolution, the cleansing of his sins.

'I've no doubt the work you do is incredibly comforting for a great many people. But, you see, in my dad's specific case, an increase in visits to you is one of the few indicators we have that things aren't quite right.'

I said I was emailing some details, phone numbers for myself, Mum, Dad's GP and his private therapist, and asked that if Dad was seen often and/or in distress please could he contact one of us straight away?

It certainly didn't feel like the sort of request that would prompt immediate impassioned defensiveness. He didn't see what any of this had to do with him, he said. I moved my voice up an octave, the way women do when we wish to de-escalate a situation, return the tone to lightness. My words ran away with me.

'It's obviously not your intention at all, I completely understand that, but the thing is, when Dad is unwell he gets the obsessive thought that he's committed a crime and – please – can you see how, if a person tends towards suicidal thoughts, that having several conversations about sinfulness being forgiven after death could be harmful? Even if he's got that message out of his own head – I'm obviously not suggesting that you have encouraged him in *any* way – that a conclusion could be made by a very ill person to take an act that can't be undone.'

'What are you talking about, you silly girl?' A haughty half-laugh.

A brief and heated volley of words followed. I wanted to cry. The only interaction I have ever had asking for help from a religious authority, it seemed like such a meagre request. Though I wouldn't have thought of it like that, I too was his parishioner seeking help. How could the man on the other end of the phone fail to understand that in this case the offer of 'forgiveness' was only confirming the existence of a 'sin', legitimising the false beliefs and taking Dad further and further from reality? I held it enough together to make my utter disregard for that man and the total failure of his mission completely known. Then I hung up.

A long time has passed since that conversation and I wonder now if scouring ancient folklore for meaning in sorrow and suffering is a self-conscious kick against the system in which I nominally grew up. The Church has had many guises, one of which is helping people, but others too which preserve and prop up divisions in society; while folklore, in its purest form, can cut through that with its intimacy and specificity. It has taken me several years to admit that Dad's embrace of religion made me uncomfortable, that I was judging him. This year I've been floundering too and seeking consolation, and I have come to know how singular that is. Solace is something every person is permitted to find on their own terms. I owe him an apology for that judgement. I owe Dad an apology, but not the vicar, one of the most uncharitable and compassionless people I have ever encountered.

In a quiet moment once I asked Dad why he suddenly felt he needed to go to that church so often when it hadn't been his habit in my lifetime. He said, 'I need to go to church, it is my last chance. The police are coming for me at four o'clock today.' I said I'd spoken with the vicar here and that I hadn't found him very kind. Why there? Why him? He looked genuinely perplexed and all he could say is that he went to church when he was at school. The school he stopped attending after his father died.

Recently I stumbled across a YouTube interview with a person actively experiencing symptoms of their schizophrenia. The interviewer asks the young woman, 'Where in the room can you see the hallucinations now?' and her face fixes and with lucidity she explains why she must decline to answer that. If she answered truthfully, she says, the first thing the interviewer would do would be to look in that direction, causing the real-life images in the room to collide distressingly with the not-real images, which she is so desperately trying to confirm as not real. It gives them a legitimacy that is harmful.

This is why I am not going to divulge details of the delusions of my dad, the crime he felt he'd committed or was being set up to have committed. Even though he is no longer here he deserves that respect. He especially deserved not to have this confusion confirmed by a figure of authority, forged in childhood, to whom he went for help.

It might be presumed that living the cursed life of a sin-eater would lead a man to take last refuge in the Church. Go to confession, buy an indulgence, anything that the clergy prescribed for one's sins to be absolved. Unfortunately, sin-eaters knew that coming into contact with Church authorities could mean certain exile, imprisonment or even execution.

Sin-eating, perilously close to the Catholic sacrament of Eucharist, was highly illegal.

The idea that some people are beyond redemption is contemptible, and yet that is how sin-eaters died. The only way out, to secure a place in the afterlife, might be to find a sin-eater for himself. Until then he was the walking dead, having already committed spiritual suicide. How many of these pariahs turned eventually to the physical act? We do not know because their stories have been forgotten, their motivations are obscured, and often our suppositions about them are wrong.

Richard Munslow is a rare exception. We know he was not poor. He did not become the last of his kind through economic need. He was a successful farmer who owned a fair amount of land. But this could not protect his family from a whooping cough epidemic in 1870. Munslow buried all four of his children – three in the same week. It is speculated that this tragedy drove him to the sin-eating trade, not through lack of alternative but as an expression of grief, a sacrifice of self to deliver his beloved children to an eternity of peace and rest.

It's 2.40am and I am thinking again how everyone I love will die. I turn to my sleeping husband. I watch his chest in the darkness until I'm certain I have seen it rise and fall, hover my hand over his nose to feel the confirmatory current of air. I think about how I couldn't bear him going first. To hold his hand as I slip away into whatever does or doesn't await is the only way I can hold the concept in my head without screaming at intervals throughout the day. I direct a question to the ceiling: *But if I have already gone, who will hold his hand when it's his time?* The selfishness of willing myself to die first, of leaving him to die alone. With the giddy mania of lack of sleep I scroll through the options. I nearly wake him up to say I have decided: we will knock back a syringe of fentanyl each and leap from a hot air balloon together over Everest, aged 100. Between now and then we must commit to alienating all of our friends and family, perhaps through joining a cult or getting involved in a pyramid scheme, so that our exit will cause minimum sadness and optimally vague relief.

Death, and the neurotic contemplation thereof, has been my constant companion for as long as I can remember. There rarely passes a day when I don't think about it. To the surprise of no one I also have generalised anxiety disorder.

Anxiety has had its thumb-screws on me since I was a kid. It often feels like three different syndromes. The first is a cannibalism of my thoughts. Minor inconveniences become stultifying impediments. A bone-melting terror visits me in crowds or pleasant social situations with equal predictability. A moment's drop in vigilance will bring disaster. I am never going to be better, I am sabotaging my own happiness: these agitated thoughts fire a feedback loop until the reactor core reaches meltdown, Chernobyling radioactive panic into the air. Memories of a full panic attack, while blessedly rare for me, are as indelible as the crescent moons I find in my palms after each one; the mouthless scream, the spirited flailing of a trapped animal and the pre-verbal insistence within some cavity deep inside that something is very, very wrong.

The fear of having another panic attack is the number-one reason for my having another panic attack, an irony that I can appreciate is not without humour when I heard it reflected in an old Hungarian folk tale:

On the night before her wedding a girl goes down to the cellar to fetch wine. She sees the large stone that her mother uses to press cabbages and is struck with a vision of disaster:

she is happily wed and blessed with a beautiful infant son, who grows up and is playing in the cellar when the big stone falls on him and crushes him to death. The girl is so devastated at the thought that she breaks down crying on the cellar floor. On hearing her daughter's cries the girl's mother rushes down, and when she hears the reason she too begins to wail. In turn so too does the father. When the groom enters the cellar and finds out that the entire family of his betrothed is crying about the death of a hypothetical child, he storms out, swearing that he will only go through with the marriage if he finds bigger fools than her. But every person he meets has foolish ways of their own. So the groom marries the girl, and they live happily ever after.

The second constituent of the disorder is the physical manifestations, and this is harder to see the funny side. The palpitations, hot flushes, haywire temperature regulation and occasional fainting are particularly hard to bear because their occurrence is often completely separate from the content of my thoughts. Before it happens I can be perfectly calm and at ease. Afterwards the drain of adrenaline can knock all the energy out of me, issuing a period of listlessness and demotivation which can last days.

The third head of the anxiety Cerberus, however, is the cognitive, and is one I have never felt equipped to deal with.

I can trace its onset back to childhood. One day, aged five or six, I was sitting on the sofa watching cartoons when I noted with curiosity that the television set was changing size. It swelled up and filled the living room alcove entirely, metres wide, and then shrunk down to the size of a matchbox. It returned to normal and my attention returned to *Pingu*. From time to time there were other strange happenings. When brushing my teeth the fingers holding the toothbrush twisted and distorted as if they were made of rubber and then began briefly to melt. Now and again I had the sense that inside my head time had slowed down; moving objects in my fields of vision seemed to be at a lag accompanied by a sort of whirring throb like when the blades of a helicopter are switched off and continue to rotate, progressively slowing.

It was many years later that I found what I suffered with had a name: Alice in Wonderland syndrome. I say I suffered, but actually I quite enjoyed it. The instances were rare and after about the age of seven stopped altogether, but I never found these perceptual distortions frightening, merely quirky and interesting.

The depersonalisation and derealisation of my twenties I enjoyed less. These are forms of dissociation; depersonalisation is the sensation of detachment from your own body and reality, and derealisation is the perception of distortion or unreality in the external world. If this sounds impossible to imagine, there are excellent depersonalisation and derealisation simulators on YouTube. They demonstrate some of the typical presentations: the fish-eye-lens visual effect, the sense of being on a film set where everything is too bright and too loud, spatial disorientation and a warping of noises, with a deep reverberant throb that is what I imagine it is like to be inside a cello inside a municipal swimming pool.

During these periods I try to avoid looking at my hands due to the powerful feeling that they do not belong to me. More troubling is the inability to speak in my own voice. During extended periods of derealisation, when I haven't been able to safely hide somewhere private, I have the sense of having to 'act' like myself without the necessary script. And unlike my adventures in Wonderland, these perceptual quirks, when combined, strike a cold terror of 'losing my mind'. I'm back there, that night in 2011. Dad is up front making jokes with the police escort while I am in the metal box of the riot van speculating between sobs on my own latent psychosis.

Oliver Sacks, the British physician whose accounts of the neurological conditions of his patients resulted in several best-selling books, believed abnormalities in perception are much more complex than the binary of 'sane' and 'insane', and function beyond the level of the individual affected. In *Hallucinations* (2012) Sacks considers to what extent 'percepts arising in the absence of any external reality' have informed human art, folklore and religion:

> Did Lilliputian hallucinations (which are not uncommon) give rise to the elves, imps, leprechauns and fairies in our folklore? Do the terrifying hallucinations of the nightmare, being ridden and suffocated by a malign presence, play a part in generating our concepts of demons and witches or malignant aliens? … Why has every culture known to us sought and found hallucinogenic drugs and used them, first and foremost, for sacramental purposes?

In Wonderland, Alice consumes substances and experiences changes in size, temporal distortions, talking animals and disembodied voices in a series of vignettes that possess the coding of folk tales. Like me, Lewis Carroll suffered from migraines; experts now believe that everything temporarily going a bit funhouse mirror could be considered part of migraine aura. (Though in retrofitting an origin for that particular author's hallucinatory iconography, let's not throw the opium out with the bathwater.)

It works both ways: the onset and content of hallucinations can be informed directly by the folklore and cultural beliefs to which a person has been exposed from youth. A 2017 research paper produced by the University of Botswana found a prevalence of psychiatric patients presenting with hallucinations involving a Thokolosi, a small hairy goblin-like creature of Zulu and Xhosa superstition. Children are warned not to sleep on the floor otherwise the Thokolosi may bite off their toes. While exposure to such stories in childhood probably did not alter the likelihood that a person would later experience a psychiatric condition, the potent imagery may have shaped the form of any such hallucinations that did arise. The specificity could reasonably be said to have been inherited, demonstrating again that travel through family trees is not always through 'blood' or DNA, but through stories.

It is an interesting notion to place next to the more problematic one to which lately I kept returning; that of 'bad blood'. With the judgement, pseudo-science and social-Darwinist implications of that phrase, it is uncomfortable for me to admit that its fixation has been the subject of more than one of my panic attacks. Is it only a matter of time until I too lose touch with reality?

There is no single gene that causes psychosis, rather a number of different genes that may, in the presence of other environmental factors, increase the likelihood of developing some traits of psychiatric illness. Plenty of people born with these genetic markers may never develop any. There is no definitive way to prevent the onset (aside perhaps from avoiding hallucinogens; a recent study demonstrated a fivefold link between cannabis use and a primary psychotic episode). Impairment in regulation of emotions, say in the interpretation of a slightly raised heart rate as reason to panic, may prefigure derealisation and depersonalisation. In the genetically predisposed this dissociation can switch on the delusionary thinking that kicks off many psychotic episodes. I couldn't help but think: if it was inevitable should I just give up now?

'Do you think about suicide?'

'Well, yes, pretty constantly, I guess.'

The fine July sun spot-lit the dancing dust motes in the room. I shifted in the pleather chair. 'And after I said that to the GP she sent me to you. So that's "why I'm here", I suppose.'

'Yep, that'll do it!' The psychiatrist was neither the nodding avuncular nor the glacial statement-necklace type I'd anticipated, but a warm-eyed man in his mid-forties, ideally placed between my age and that of my dad.

I told him of my frustration that there had been no space for nuance in a ten-minute phone consultation. Had I been permitted I would have given what I felt was crucial context. That I was aware what 'suicidal ideation' was and in my case that it was only partially applicable.

I exhaled. I suddenly now had the time, and the attention, of a clinician who appeared deeply interested in what I had to say. A luxury psych eval!

He asked questions to clarify exactly what I meant to convey, an active listening that was a first in my healthcare-accessing career. Over the next hour I had the space to finally talk things through. How I remembered being incredulous when I learnt people didn't think about death all the time, as I had done from childhood ('Yeah, me too!' he replied), and perhaps that was the reason those photos of my parents before I was born captivated me so much. How, though I did not contemplate the carrying out of the act itself, the notion of non-existence was simply a fantasy of sublime rest ('an opt-out, a pause on the noise'). How recently the foremost thought on my mind was my mum dying. It was inevitable, as was the death of my husband, my brother and all my friends. And the only way to avoid this devastation, to never be ambushed by this type of grief again, the only feasible insurance policy available to me was to make it so that I go—

'That you go first.'

'Yes.'

He nodded. That he found that conclusion not a statement of intent or any sort of plan to end my life but in the spirit it was meant, as both perfectly logical but simultaneously out of the question, is the most strikingly humane moment I have ever experienced in a doctor's office.

I didn't need him to assess whether or not I was depressed. I could tell him I wasn't, because I have been only once, years ago, before a slow recovery whose necessary amnesiac quality means I can no longer fully access it. The exhausting impasse of perpetual blandness did eventually recede and I know now that I never had quite what Dad had, that grey vacuum with its never-ending hunger. The faculty that allows me to type these words is the very absence of depression. My mind's disequilibrium has always been in the direction of too much rather than too little.

'You sound like you know your mind very well.'

Well, hmm. These philosophical wranglings had been entertaining to the both of us, but there was something I had been gearing up to broach. Something I hadn't told anyone.

Over the past few weeks something unusual had been happening, outside my biography of occasional enhanced reality. On a few occasions I had been talking to someone when I became aware that their eyes had moved position to the centre of their face, so it briefly looked as though they had three eyes. Or else their eyes would quickly flip sides, so that they looked like a collage. It had happened with Michael, my auntie and the receptionist at the acupuncture clinic. Each time I was both terrified and determined not to think about it.

The psychiatrist was unfazed. 'You're not cracking up,' he explained. 'This isn't like your father – you had a few kooky visual tricks because this is extreme anxiety which isn't being afforded an outlet by your stressful attempts to keep your emotions reined in under perfectionist self-scrutiny.

'What I suspect you are, in fact, is very, very angry.'

I was. I was apoplectic at the world. Spitting angry at the cruelty and injustice of what I had to bear. And seething with the unfairness of my having likely been a completely different person without this primordial death obsession, neuroticism and the anxiety around health I had lived with for the past decade.

Knowing the assessment was nearing its end I brought up the concept of 'bad blood'. I still had to frame it like a gag: was madness contagious, did he think, like divorce?

The response I got was circumspect, not the firm line that I assumed medicine would have. In fact it was far closer to philosophy.

'If there was any genetic predisposition to inhabiting certain states of sensory experience, would it matter? What exactly would you do about it?'

Considering this involved admitting that I had been holding myself to a higher standard. That I simply couldn't 'go mad' involved a prejudice I didn't realise I had been holding. If this something hereditary had an environmental trigger of the peaks in stress I had experienced over the past ten years then I had also to consider the others. Because love is also an environmental factor. A safe, healthy, happy childhood of encouragement and education were also the building blocks my parents gave me. My plastic brain was moulded by their care in early life, its physical changes encoded by their love.

Will this be enough to override what might be waiting for me? Who can say. What would drive a person mad is wondering who they could have been had the circumstances been different.

As Sacks finds in his patients, plenty of people don't find hallucinations or other sensory misalignments troubling. Charles Bonnet syndrome, a disorder of visual hallucinations exclusively experienced by the blind and visually impaired, for example, can involve whimsical parades of tiny people or vivid and complex patterns or landscapes that are entertaining or even awe-inspiring. Many cultures regard hallucinations as a heightened state of consciousness, and are often actively sought through ritual, sensory denial or pharmacological substances. It is modern medicine that is most insistent such experiences are something to be treated. Often, Sacks insists, hallucinations are harmless.

Since my talk with the psychiatrist I have had no more instances of enhanced reality. The vagaries of derealisation are still with me but I am much better sitting in the feeling knowing it is temporary and not necessarily a sign of my unspooling reason. And if it is my inheritance in some way, then I chose it as much as I chose to have Dad's small hands and feet and vocal tics, and as much as he did, and that is not bad blood but family blood. The shared blood of ordinary human frailty.

Folk narratives of labour and resistance

To my darling wife Marie,

Just a few lines to say I am o.k., fit and well, only sea-sick the one day. I am eating well, the weather has been good up til now. I think we shall be about six weeks. I have been doing some washing tonight, there is plenty of hot water to go at. We have a nice crew, the skipper is o.k.

Give my love to the kids. Is Rod looking after the garden for me?

Well my dear I will close for now, you know I am not much good at letter writing. Goodnight darling, all my love

John

P.S. Happy birthday darling on the 22nd

P.S. Sorry about the paper, this is all I have got.

I miss you.

What I like best about the letters between my grandfather, John, on his last few postings with the deep-sea trawler the *Northern Queen* in 1970, and my grandma, Marie, in a bungalow in Humberston with four kids, is the simple unadorned sweetness, apparently undamped after 19 years of marriage. A number of times he expresses how much he misses and loves her only to do so again a few lines later, as if he cannot concentrate for pining. John and Marie are caring parents but this isn't one of those marriages where the kids have been allowed to monopolise all attention; they still have it down bad for each other. I am sitting with a shoebox of letters on the floor of Auntie Ros's living room grinning. It is no less true for being hackneyed: there is something preposterously romantic about being separated by the sea.

For both of them there is always space on the page for sentimentality between the exchange of humdrum domestic details. However, these scraps of ordinary life I find to be almost equally endearing. After John reports being 'a bit fed up' after a mechanical problem that had the crew stranded near the Soviet Union for several weeks, Marie buoys him with fragments of family life: the chocolate the kids got her for her birthday, arrangements for her sister's upcoming wedding and assurances that Rod was indeed keeping up with garden maintenance as much as he could, though it had been too wet recently.

As their separation drags on, however, the outside world begins to encroach. Details leak into their correspondence that hint at economic pressures. There's been talk of a coal strike, says Marie, and she hasn't yet received his final pay cheque from the bread factory – 'but not to worry'. Always an optimistic tone before signing off. I turn over to what I assume is the last letter in the bundle, only to find instead a notification from the Grimsby Fishermen's Dependents Fund, informing Marie that her widow's pension will be £2 per week and a further £1 for each child.

After some months of muddling through with her brood of grief-shook kids Marie couldn't ignore it any longer. Her only son, who'd never once cried after he'd been told his father would not be coming back, had grown so listless and withdrawn that Marie took him to the family doctor. Dr Crowley had been the one to show up on the night they'd received the terrible news to deliver a sedative to the widow, a prophylactic for the dam-break of womanly wailing that would no doubt otherwise have inconvenienced the neighbours. Now, however, Dr Crowley had an uncharacteristic caution. On examining the 14-year-old boy, a lad from the well-mannered but hardly affluent rank that has long been fodder for the manual industries and the armed forces, Dr Crowley could see that a referral to a psychiatrist could well be required, and he was prepared to make it; however, it was his opinion that it may do more harm than good in the long run.

'Treatment from a psychiatrist would go on his record, Mrs Heenan. He won't be able to get a job.'

It is no slight on Marie that she listened to him – a doctor's advice was simply taken. She left with a prescription for one of the earlier tricyclic antidepressants. At least Dr Crowley could be relied on as a free and easy dispensary. Still, she dished out the large white tablets once daily herself, afraid of the consequences if she handed over the bottle to her sullen boy. Auntie Sarah believes that Dad almost certainly didn't always take them, and imagines his compliance petered out eventually. And that was all the 'treatment' he received.

Health is a class issue. What it means to have 'good health' has over the past couple of centuries drifted semantically towards what that means for the productive components of capitalism. The social machine expects productive labour in return for the fruits it purports to supply: work hard and reap. We are told that there will be dire personal and systemic repercussions if we don't go all out. But if danger and drudgery breaks your body, or if workload, burnout or employment precarity collapses your mind and spirit, your value rapidly plummets. If health is so vital to the smooth running of the modern economic model you might assume it would be a priority above all else, wouldn't you?

Dad was working as normal the day before he killed himself.

It is almost too on the nose how words that we use to describe qualities of being – 'strength', 'depression', 'recovery', 'bounce back', even 'health' itself – have all been co-opted to describe the state of global economies. As if together workers function in service of this great mechanical body, this lurching and ever-hungry homunculus so complex a contraption it is beyond any one person's understanding, except to know that if it tumbles over we'll likely never get it up again.

As markets sought to recover from the 2008 world economic crash the UK saw one of the most brutal applications of austerity politics. One of the key findings from the far-reaching *Dying from Inequality* report compiled by the charity Samaritans in 2017 was the extent to which these measures have disproportionately contributed to the suicides of people in the lowest socio-economic bracket, and particularly older men. I still recall the first time I read a news report about a vulnerable man with complex mental and physical illness who had been cut off from welfare benefits, left with zero income, who specifically referenced the Department for Work and Pensions in his suicide note. There have been others since.

Communicated to the British public as the only viable hope for recovery in recession, austerity gave a premise for continued underinvestment in the National Health Service.

Reforms such as the 2012 Health and Social Care Act fragmented health services and created access deserts in rural and traditionally deprived areas. In places like Lincolnshire funding became stretched as mental health services were skeletonised. Patients with mild mental illness were able to access medication and cheap therapeutics such as cognitive behavioural therapy, and patients in extreme crisis and at risk to themselves and others were admitted to facilities on secure holds. But if you were in between, severely depressed and experiencing delusions like Dad, you were both too sick and not sick enough for intervention.

My father's last consultation with his GP was a telephone appointment, during which he, a man in the throes of psychosis and with little to no capacity for acting in his greater interest, was told that contact details for local mental health services would be forwarded to his mobile phone. Dad didn't use a mobile phone.

Dr Crowley's patrician woodenness may not have got him far today but he did at least have one thing in his favour: constancy. The sheer skirting-board permanence of the now implausible concept of the 'family doctor'. Mum and I never really knew whether Dad was taking his medication as instructed. If he had stopped picking up his prescriptions, how easily might that fact have been missed between a changing roster of doctors limited to ten-minute appointments months apart? Given his history of severe mental ill health, following a distinct pattern with progressively shorter intervals, the most pronounced of which ended with attempts on his life, I am appalled that this was the sum total of the care he received from his GP. My mother was left to cope alone with a severely ill man intent on taking his own life.

The welfare state has always had to see off ideological assaults but there is a newer missile. Concomitant with the reduction in resources has been the individualisation of mental health. 'Self-improvement' is an expression of our ancient impulse to know ourselves and has a long history, extending back to the wisdom traditions of Marcus Aurelius' treatise on suffering to the teachings of Laozi, founder of Taoism, on accepting the will of the universe. 'Wellness', however, is a relatively recent concept. In *Natural Causes* Barbara Ehrenreich interprets wellness as the fantasy that with some concentration we can 'cheat' illness. And because wellness usually depends on nutrition, access to nature and being time-rich enough for mindful recuperation, we have invented for ourselves another social division. We had to invent 'wellness' so we don't have to talk about class.

Self-care concepts are politically expedient to avoid confronting that despair is disproportionately experienced by those living under adverse material conditions. Individualising healthcare tells us access to the medical system is for the truly deserving, not for those suffering a failure of willpower and resilience. Our bodies aren't made to work forever, so when we strive to overwork and to optimise ourselves, who or what are we doing it for?

I fell for it! The entire year I had persevered with the idea that with enough focus and forest breathing I could cure my grief and my death anxiety. That is about as ridiculous, and offensive, I now realise, as my concept of 'bad blood'.

When identity is bound up with work, what happens when a person can no longer complete his job, when the body commodity becomes obsolete through age? Dad's working life started at 14 and at his death he was five months from retiring. I had cautiously hoped it would bring him some peace but Mum sensed how much the prospect troubled him. In 2020, when everything was thrown up in the air, he was given a glimpse into what it would be like. Placed on furlough from the leisure centre he was suddenly no longer a working man. All that lay ahead was rootlessness and an expanse of time.

In *Suicide* (1897) Durkheim popularised a term to outline the social cause of suicide: anomie. Anomie is a sort of societal derealisation and purposelessness arising from a rapid change in cultural values. While crises arising from a perceived absence of meaning aren't peculiar to older men there is much to suggest that this demographic are at particular risk of the anomie of the broken social contract. Men may be more likely to base the majority of their social lives around work colleagues. They may have inherited ideas of the breadwinner, a strong provider, whose time at work may have meant they were less present for their children with whom they have a poorer relationship as a result. They may feel alienated from the family unit and, without a workplace, experience a literal placelessness. They may have forgone hobbies and leisure and as a result, come retirement age, they do not know who they are and what it is they enjoy.

Folklore deals with the notion of ageing, redundancy and decrepitude in a number of ways. Geronticide or senicide has its own designation, Aarne–Thompson–Uther type 981. D.L. Ashliman's *Folktexts* records a grim custom, which originated in Germany and Poland. It was said that Roma travellers would set their camp in the marshlands near Chodzież, where they would drown the elderly who had slowed down the journey. As they pushed them alive under the water they would chant this verse:

> Duck under, duck under;
> The world is misery for you!

It is entirely possible that this rumour arose due to the millennia-old favourite pastime of racist othering, coding heathens as cruel and gruesome. Regardless, accounts of groups relieved of the burden of the elderly are plentiful in antiquity. Writing in the fourth century AD, Festus records older men first being disenfranchised as citizens, by having their right to vote taken away. Then, as they no longer provided a service to Roman democracy, younger men suggested that the elders over the age of 60 be thrown off a bridge into the River Tiber.

These are examples of elder homicide, but there are legends of the elderly taking their own lives in service to a community. An influential translation of the Old Icelandic epic *Gautreks* saga introduced to seventeenth-century Sweden the supposed existence of *ättestupa*, or the 'suicide precipice'. These were sites of supposed ritual senicide during Nordic prehistory at which older people who had become a burden leapt to their deaths. In his opus *The History of Sweden*, historian Anders Fryxell described the practice like this:

> Close by this farm there was a very high perpendicular rock, such that it was certain whoever should cast himself from the top would never reach the bottom alive. Here ... ancestors had always put an end to their own lives, as soon as they became very old, that their children might be saved from maintaining them, and that they themselves come to Odin and be freed from the pains and sufferings which accompany old age and a straw-death.

The legend captured the imaginations of learned men in Europe, newly fascinated by stories of the Norsemen and intrigued by the supposed belief they held that a suicide death was noble and could mean the soul be 'fared to Valhalla'. However, though *ättestupa* is a name by which several cliffs in Sweden and Norway are still known, the practice of ritual senicide at the sites is now generally accepted to have been legend.

Historically factual or not, what most of these tales have in common is the pressure of poverty. There is no tradition of a king or cleric tumbling off a cliff edge or pushing his weighted grandad into the sea.

Occasionally there is a happy ending that requires no one to die. Ashliman reports many variations found in story-telling traditions in Macedonia, Serbia and Romania where the order of geronticide is given but the old person is hidden and is spared. Then later he or she comes out with a nugget of wisdom that somehow saves the people from disaster, and everyone finally sees the value of old age and hard-won experience.

The act of suicide became decriminalised in England in 1961 but in 2020 was still illegal and punishable by custodial sentences in up to 20 countries. The majority of suicides, 77 per cent, occur in nations with lower-income populations. The World Health Organization estimates that one million people take their lives worldwide each year. Every day in the UK 18 people are lost to suicide, 12 of whom are men. In the USA suicide research gets funded about as much as smallpox. The Church of England only mandated that full funeral services be permissible for victims of suicide in 2015.

Sometimes it is worth taking all the miserable statistics together for the true impact. It should come as a punch to the gut.

I don't know whether to count Dad as one of the hidden 'excess deaths' of the Covid pandemic. His was a complex case involving psychological, physical, cultural and economic factors to which no one reason can be ascribed. However, given that there was a 29 per cent increase in NHS referrals for a first episode of psychosis during the first and second lockdowns and an estimated 53 million extra cases of major depressive disorder reported globally in 2020 alone, a second wave of suicidal behaviour is sure to follow.

While much of the work of suicide prevention is structural there is plenty on a more everyday scale that needs addressing. Calling out insensitivity is work we can all do.

I once had a manager who commuted by train. On several occasions she would have to leave work early, complaining about travel chaos and the delays she would have to suffer 'because some genius decided to jump on the tracks'. With mock astonishment she would marvel that 'rush hour is obviously the perfect time to jump in front of a train'. It wasn't just the failure of imagination, that the stranger she was tutting at was in a crisis so profound that it can hardly be conceptualised by those of us fortunate enough to never experience it – it was that she didn't appear in any way embarrassed to have said such a thing out loud. On these occasions I was immobilised by repulsion, but also by being junior and one day likely in need of a reference, so I didn't speak up. I hate myself for that. I will never let such a noxious lack of compassion go by unchecked again.

Ignoring what we know to be wrong is not a neutral act. The language of dismissiveness, derision or disinterest denies dignity to the suffering. The many ways in which we socially isolate people who act erratically in public or hold delusional beliefs label them as alien or dangerous. We are disgraced by the persistence in a misogyny that insists correct masculinity precludes men from experiencing powerful emotions, as if male lyricists, philosophers and storytellers have not been expanding our comprehension of the depths of love, grief, hope and despair since the beginning of language. We risk further tragedy when we ignore that those bereaved by suicide might need more support, or more nuanced support, from employers, and this should be considered an absolute duty of safeguarding.

This is what I am thinking about as I prepare to go back to work. Any grievers reading will consider my full calendar year of furlough when my dad died as a blessing, and I don't disagree, though 'lucky' to have had this happen during a pandemic is stretching it a bit. However, it has presented some unforeseen challenges. Primarily, I have got weird. I don't know how to be around people, how to answer the casual question 'How are you?' with a not-100-per-cent probability that I won't start crying, and the hot flushes of my anxiety disorder mean I turn up everywhere with my hair stuck like wet pondweed to my face. In terms of processing, not having had to interact with the world has meant in many ways I have kicked the can down the road. One unanticipated ordeal of the extraordinary length of the interval has been having to divulge the worst thing that has ever happened to me repeatedly to various managers and HR people that I have never met.

A few weeks ago Beckie, my suicide bereavement worker, set me as homework a written plan of survival for my return to work. Copying it here it now sounds impossibly sad: care less; complete whatever work is set without complaint; don't contribute more than necessary; don't have opinions; be kind but quiet to colleagues; calibrate withdrawal so as to seem as boring as possible but imperceptible enough to disinvite enquiry. It was not meant as a pity party, but simply how I needed to reconfigure the work part of my life, the artificial but necessary part, so as to limit as far as possible any surprises.

Roused by resentment of a system whose exploitation of its most powerless is not a symptom but a feature, and my own feelings of anxiety and pointlessness about work, I went looking for stories of resistance and collective action. Pitchforks and guillotines get to the point, but stories of a fairer world are ultimately the greatest agitator.

In Europe the model for moral parables is of course Aesop. When you discover that Aesop was a former slave many of his animal allegories of right and wrong take on deeper political meanings. Perhaps most blatantly in 'The Wolf and the Dog'. A wild wolf marvels at the dog being so well fed. Yes, it is marvellous, agrees the dog, and all he has to do for it is wear this collar and answer to a master! That the wolf decides he is better off as he is is plenty subversive.

Workers' Tales, a fantastic collection edited by children's author Michael Rosen, presents the revolutionary potential of fairy stories and fables and shows how their recognisable tropes and structures were utilised by the progenitors of the labour movement. Rosen identifies how the familiarity of traditional stories cut through the intellectualism to reach ordinary working people. Thus Tom Hickathrift, a character in East Anglian folklore similar to Jack the Giant Killer, defeats the ogre, naturally, but the real corollary is a celebration of the communitarian and redistributive: 'The ground that the giant kept by force for himself, Tom gave part to the poor for their common land, and part he turned into good wheat-land to keep himself and his old mother.' In this context hearing a familiar legend such as the exploits of Robin Hood might prompt an audience, without any persuasion necessary, to ponder the class dynamics and recall that the word 'outlaw' was simply a person who had run away from serfdom.

To me, this is why folklore and ritual around death feels particularly reflective of ordinary people. Dying is our last act on earth and entrusting its formalities to kin speaks to our hopes for immortality: to be remembered not as people who worked but as people who loved.

It's funny to me that in our relationship I brushed up so hard against Dad's fondness for tradition, from 'many happy returns' right through to wedding traditions to which I turned up my nose, and now I come to defend tradition as revolutionary. I thought with no small snobbery he was unhealthily fixated with the past. His wistfulness revealed so much more.

Back in the garden the sun had started to drop but my skin was tight and warm. As a kid I was pale and easily flustered by the heat and much preferred to spend the summer holidays reading book after book in my cool bedroom. Lewis had his stash of pirated PlayStation 2 games. Nothing could have enraged Dad more. The idea of a wasted sunny day was the worst thing he could have imagined and he would yell as such up the stairs.

'A day like this and you are inside reading! You'll miss the whole bloody summer!'

It was one of the differences in us that he could never get his head around.

'Well, I'm outside now, Dad,' I say, toasting my ice pop in the direction of the house. Now with everything reeking of his absence I didn't enjoy being in that house longer than I had to be.

We'd put Henry, Mum's new orange companion, on a lead to cautiously test him in the garden. A rescue of mysterious origin, Mum was terrified of his unpredictability, that he might just taste freedom and hit the dirt. Being so very small in stature I was more worried about the Cleethorpes seagulls that were clacking their considerable beaks, looking for easy pickings. So poor Henry had to suffer every cat's worst indignity, and was making sure his disdain was amply known.

'Come on, Henry,' I said, as Mum tugged on the lead, 'you're missing the bloody sunshine! A day like this!'

It occurred to me then that perhaps Dad's keenness to be in the garden, pottering, planting, twiddling with the radio in the shed, and to have us join him, was down to the house. To Dad the house and the thousands of hours he spent toiling away at it was both a curse and a crowning achievement, and being outside of it looking at its edifice held a nauseating and awesome power. That Lewis thought he built it himself was not completely wrong. He'd given it so much of his lifeblood that reserves eventually ran low.

Here's a thought that provokes similar mixed emotions in me. Like others of my generation and means I had largely come to terms with the idea that I would probably never own a house. Now, with savings, I might. If that comes to pass it will have taken the deaths of no fewer than six people to have become within my reach. Ultimately it was a matter of value.

If it sounds like I have a working-class chip on my shoulder you'd be underestimating. I am furious. I am furious that lockdown rules meant I didn't see my dad for the last seven months of his life, while those who set the rules granted themselves different ones. I am furious that Dad's physical ailments from a lifetime of labour forced him to consider his body as a commodity of depreciating value. I am furious that he didn't receive dedicated bereavement counselling in childhood which might have prevented some of the mental torture he would experience in adulthood. I am furious that with a Potemkin NHS we keep telling the vulnerable to 'just ask for help' knowing that is a cruel lie. I am furious that my trawlerman grandfather was compelled by economic circumstances to endanger his life for the profit of others. I am furious that Emma, my great-great-grandmother who died during her 20th pregnancy, was forced to put her body through such extreme strain through lack of privilege, lack of contraception access, lack of capital, lack of escape. I am furious that every passing Covid-death milestone conceals many preventable 'excess deaths', every one of them the direct result of decisions taken to serve administrative interests in the name of public safety. For all of them I want a great raucous feast day, a bacchanalia of dancing and dirges, piles of fruit, barrels of punch, garlands of peonies. Pilgrimages, devotional shrines, invocations to greater forces, purification rites, sacraments. An effigy to burn. I want to howl on ground consecrated not by the Church but by people who made their own meaning and to push it into the soil. I want to stand on that ground and recite their names.

One of its most well-known passages of the Icelandic book

of songs *Hávamál*, translated into English by H.A. Bellows in 1936, discusses the immortality of folk memory and the pointlessness of hoarding wealth when it is words and deeds that people will remember:

> Cattle die, and kinsmen die,
> And so one dies one's self;
> But a noble name will never die,
> If good renown one gets.

Do not misinterpret that 'noble name'; it is most definitely ordinary folk who are being addressed. The 1972 translation by Lee M. Hollander makes the value of a good name clear: 'fair fame will fade never'.

At his funeral Dad's work colleagues turned up in such numbers a speaker had to be rigged in the carpark. There was Sean, supportive as ever. Andy, who'd taken over the invitations for me, reaching out to people from Dad's working past and present. Nicola, who'd organised a whip-round for a new bike when Dad's was nicked.

The nickname they gave him, Super Rod, for that one particularly memorable rescue. The name embarrassed him because it was just something that needed doing, so he did it. It is the landowners, the plutocrats, the highborn, who get to have names in history, but these things alone don't grant one the right to a 'noble name'. A noble name has to be awarded. In nicknames, legends, songs, stories that commemorated the life a person lived and that their death happened. I thought this past year I was cherry-picking folk stories to tell me why this had happened and where he was now, for any type of solace or insight. Some did, a little. But coming to see many of these narratives as alternative histories, as a protest against systems of injustice, I found something else. Solidarity.

Something remarkable happened at Dad's funeral. It was by

no prior arrangement, there was no one taking charge or assigning positions. Simply the intuitive stagecraft of a community of people brought low by sorrow coming together to express their shared esteem. So loved was Dad by his work colleagues that they turned up in numbers far too great to fit the social distancing required by the chapel. Instead they lined the long concourse, spacing themselves out either side of the path to be taken by his coffin. My family and I walked behind it. And as we did they started clapping. One by one, each step of the way. It was a small and gentle gesture but its spontaneity is the most beautiful thing I have ever known, a group promise that his name will not be forgotten. Fair fame will fade never.

The men assemble at the top of the hill. In daylight they would have been able to see the whole of Lower Konz and the vine-latticed hills of the Rhineland beyond, but the light of the torches illuminates only the men's hands as they work. Huge quantities of straw, tithed by every family in the village, is bound to the great wheel, packed tight in the spaces between its spokes, as it is heaved into place. A signal is given and the torch lowered. *Woomph*. The wheel erupts against the night. The two strongest-limbed seize each end of the long axle and launch the flaming wheel over the precipice and down the long slope that ends at the banks of the Moselle. A great shout goes up from the multitude in the dark. All are anxious of it staying alight all the way down.

> If the fiery wheel was successfully conveyed to the bank of the river and extinguished in the water, the people looked for an abundant vintage that year, and the inhabitants of Konz had the right to exact a waggon-load of white wine from the surrounding vineyards … If they neglected to

perform the ceremony, the cattle would be attacked by giddiness and convulsions and would dance in their stalls.

Konz's night of the burning wheel is described in James Frazer's exhaustive work of comparative folklore, *The Golden Bough*, alongside many similar rituals from Ireland to northern Russia. It is a compelling and irresistible image, a community effort to harness the awesome power of the symbolic, and by guiding its path attempt to wrest control over the harvests that govern so much of their lives.

The influence of *The Golden Bough* on European art and thought was substantial, but nevertheless it continues to provoke the judgement that its project of drawing parallels between disparate mythological narratives and motifs serves only to homogenise them and advance the theory of some shared origin. Throughout, Frazer gestures to an unknown source to help demonstrate his point. In the matter of burning wheels being catapulted down hills at midsummer's end, a helpful 'medieval writer' allows Frazer to explain the custom of setting alight and 'trundling a wheel to mean that the sun, having now reached the highest point in the ecliptic, begins thenceforward to descend'. The wheel here is a sun god on his celestial path. It is the vanquish of the Oak King and the coming ascent of the Holly King. It is the ouroboros, the snake eating its own tail.

There is a danger to it, both the presumption to and levelling of significance, and throughout these four seasons I don't know if I've managed to resist it. That I haven't just plumbed the reservoir of alternative ways of looking at the world to furtively fill my own, so unexpectedly and cruelly empty. I've been desperate for stories and symbols to pack into the void.

It is the 26th day in August, again. Once an arbitrary point on the calendar and now it's most significant. An ordinary day has been overlaid with a different spoke on the wheel, of death and the potential for beginning. Those communities throughout the Celtic world chose sundown on *Samhain* as their new year because it made the most sense to the way they lived their lives, but that isn't true for me. This date is my new year now.

The day had inched round and now it was here and I had been caught unprepared. I didn't have anything planned. We should do something, shouldn't we, to mark it?

'Let's just go for a walk,' said Mum, firmly.

She was right. It was something to get through. An unremarkable route up the promenade and then a loop round the Boating Lake, Lewis and me either side of her, speaking of unremarkable things. Weatherworn, all, but we'd made it. One year. Appending meaning to everything is exhausting; sometimes it's enough just to survive the day.

I set out to examine the repeated bromide of grief culture, that of needing to experience each of the seasons without your dead person. Was it true? The currents of the past year had been undeniably seasonal, like an internal clock running within me, but largely unhitched from the natural flavour of the seasons. Autumn with its shock and disarray, subsiding to a winter of innervation, before the spring brought imbalance and derangement, and a summer powered on guilt and fury. One thing was different. Only a year ago death had seemed this obvious and immovable thing, as definitive as a full stop, but in holding death's hand through all four seasons it had seemed different, *weighed* different, in each. Death is a projection of ourselves, and nothing is less static than the pitching of our thoughts, emotions and memories.

Way back at the funeral when Dad's eldest sister told me about my great-great-grandmother Emma, who died during her 20th pregnancy aged only 38, I had been unable to comprehend the scale. Her young age, the many children that did not survive, and knowing in her bones that nothing could be assumed and that she could very well be about to leave her remaining children motherless. How could she have ever coped being steeped in so much death?

I think she survived because she had her own hard-won wisdom, but vitally also from being of a time and place that kept death so near and so familiar. It is a necessity that can be summed up in one last folk story, 'Death in a Nutshell'. The Story Museum in Oxford holds in its collection a version from traditional Norwegian folk stories, as retold by the Scottish traveller storyteller Duncan Williamson:

Once, in a cottage by the sea a mother lay dying, her son, grieving by her side. The son heard a noise on the path and looked out the window to see Death walking up to the cottage. He ran to the door, 'I won't let you take her!' he cried. He grabbed a big, thick stick and began beating Death. Again and again he struck Death down and with each blow, Death got smaller and smaller until he was so small the son could hold Death in his hand. He then grabbed half a walnut shell and pushed Death in. He took the other half of the walnut shell, bound the shell together with string and threw it out to sea.

His mother woke up feeling much better. 'I'm hungry,' she said. 'I'd like some chicken soup.' The son went into the back garden and cut off the head of a chicken but the head just popped back on. He did this time and time again but each time the same thing happened and he just could not kill the chicken. He picked out some carrots from the vegetable patch but each time the carrots just popped back into the ground. He went to the butcher but there was no meat. He went to the grocers but there was no food – nothing was dying! Finally the son returned to his mother and told her the story.

'Son, it's my time to go now,' she told him, kindly. 'You can't have life without Death. Now go out and release Death from the walnut shell.'

So the son combed the beach, found the walnut shell and opened it up. Death popped out, bowed to the sun and walked up to the cottage where the mother was waiting for him with open arms.

Death is not just inevitable but essential. The uncomfortable truth is that death stands at every fork along the way that resulted in the exact happenstance of you existing. The second child that only came along because the first died in infancy. The woman who died in childbirth, leading your great grand-father to seek another wife. Like the roots of a tree that thrives on the rot of biological matter. Snags and seeds are two spokes on the same wheel.

Our shared experience of 2020 was an unwelcome echo from times of ceremonial impoverishment. A parallel to those paupers denied funerals because of plague, or penury, or the spiritual sin of suicide. Death isn't always preventable, and grief is the tax we pay for love, but in preserving ritual ties, or developing our own, we can acknowledge it in a manner that is commensurate. Whether that is exhuming the body and parading it through the streets, washing it in the home in spiced oils, arranging a barkcloth cloak and pressing a lei of flowers into the hair, making memorials and undertaking pil-grimages or putting on widow's weeds and carrying a locket of hair, rites bodily and ethereal, people have found ways to bridge the divide and to keep death an intimate acquaintance, not because it is comfortable but because it is necessary.

If we want to reorient ourselves we must again become familiar with death. We have to set a feast for the ghost.

In their dual model of grief the theorists Stroebe and Schut talk about the loss-oriented and the restoration-oriented phases, and that the bereaved move in and out of intense grief so as to confront the reality of the loss bit by bit. We reorder the narrative of our experience into something we can live with, even if the process feels chaotic. Nature too can appear this way, but with time and sustenance the biosphere arrives at a place of supreme organisation. Eventually the restoration periods last longer. I am finding this to be true. Memories that I could go nowhere near at the beginning of this year are now becoming possible. I can now bear to look at my wedding photos and think about the day.

A man in skeleton makeup is pouring himself a pint from the barrel and my drunk friends are strewn about the teepee in carnival masks, giving each other tarot readings. The cards have got all over the floor: the Sun, the Hermit, the Wheel of Fortune, the Hanged Man. I pick up the Ten of Cups and wonder aloud when the band is starting.

'We're starting right now!' says the skeleton, over one shoulder.

I gather up the plumes of my dress and follow him to the barn just as the double bass begins to thump. Michael and I are too awkward for a first dance and so we had decided against it. But that means everyone is a little too reserved to step on tradition and kick things off.

Dad, glasses steamed up and tie askew, takes my hand and leads me to the centre of the floor. It really is a first. I can't even remember the last time he held my hand. I suppose I must have been very small. When he had extracted a splinter, or in the ambulance when I had a meningitis scare, perhaps. His fingernails, as ever, are bitten to the quick. Doing hands: for making, providing, repairing, but also for worrying at. Those heavy thoughts in his head that he carried alone for so long but, like tonight, whose weight could unpredictably lift. Here he is surprising me again, taking my hands as he begins to spin me around to the music.

'Come on, Hollie!'

The roaring fire and church candles flood the barn in

golden warmth, a world enclosed from the year's dark half dawning outside, as the zombies and skeletons with their trumpets and drums like a real-life *Danse Macabre* begin playing the jazz standards, and the floor fills up around us.

Dad had an infuriating habit of describing places that no longer existed and expecting me to know what he meant. I'd ask for directions and he'd say it was across from where Marks & Spencer used to be, or where Clifton bingo hall was before it was demolished. To anyone who didn't know him I will now describe my father in the same way. I will try to conjure an absence with words alone. That will never stop being sad. But my grandparents, John and Marie, died before my recollection, Emma and the others too, and these long-dead have become graspable to me, and not just on the night when the veil is at its thinnest. There is purpose and excitement in being able to do the same for Dad to whomever may wish to listen.

I can tell them about the skeleton band and that my first dance was not with my husband but my father, that his grin was as wide as the moon, that we spun like Catherine wheels until the candle wicks blurred. That he let go of my hands because the song was over, and how we stood there smiling at one another. It was only the briefest of lulls, because we knew there was another about to start.

SHRINE TREE

51°00'17.5"N 0°02'15.3"E
East Sussex, England

'SORRY OUR FIRST WEDDING ANNIVERSARY is being spent building a death shrine. You don't mind, do you?'

But Michael had already disappeared soundlessly into the trees. Tramping through the woods was never a big ask for him.

Stepping off the lane up into the verge had been like drawing a curtain. Half of the crisp afternoon light had stayed behind on the path. Witches Lane: an intimation of Sussex's past. Branches met in arches of all sizes, marking tunnels through the thicket. Moss-painted passages for combing the forest floor of its wild herbs, or for quick crouching escape.

Sounds above of groaning limbs and parched leaves twitching. Boot leather pressed into breadcrumb soil, a percussive crunch to the sloshing rhythm of the ghyll that ran just inside the treeline. One tuneless nightjar like radio interference, the slap of his wing-beats like wet sucking mud.

Skeins of ivy latticed every part of the ground, burying my feet up to the ankles like tidal water and making every step blind. Something sharp caught at my tights and extracted a bead of blood. I wiped it against the ribs of a fallen elm. The tree was hollowed from the inside and strung with spider webbing and knots of lichen, feeding life as it fell into a slow, sleeping burial.

Only a handful of times in the past century has the end of

British Summer Time fallen on Halloween night. I was lucky: an extra hour when the worlds of the living and the dead are at their closest.

Michael had located some good options but I was being fussy. I had it pictured. It would be stout and symmetrical like a kid's drawing. Not one of the showy pines towering in nearby Ashdown Forest but a stocky knobbled oak with limbs as wide as it was tall.

As the sun dipped we found it.

We set up the lights. A string of plastic skeletons that one year ago had lit up the wedding teepee. Inside the tent there had also been masks, kabuki theatre and woodland animals. I'd lifted them all from the discount bin after Halloween, like cleaning up on cut-price eggs after Easter. He had been pleased when I'd told him about it.

Ribbons of black and white wrapped three times around the thick trunk and, at its base, a scattering of hazelnuts. Whatever prophecy could be divined from where they fell I missed due to the sudden russeting of the evening sky. By phone light we placed the rest of the food, all circular to recall the infinite cycle: bread, apples, a chocolate Hobnob.

At some point, through the poetic alchemy of love and memory, a collection of irregular objects becomes a shrine. I enclosed my shrine with a ring of sand. It was from Cleethorpes beach, though of course sand comes from everywhere. Maybe this handful started out in cretaceous rock beds under Icelandic waters, was churned in by the tug of the North Sea and silted up on the banks of the Humber to be turned out into castles by a couple of sun-sticky kids while they bartered their dad for a Solero. Magical thinking, but nevertheless I added totem whelk shells and a blue plastic chip fork to will it so.

Next foamy brown ale poured out from a satisfying height

and with amusement: that in this particular watering of ancestor roots nothing else would suffice but John Smith's.

Rosemary for remembrance, nettle for sorrow, marigold the altar flower for the day of the dead. The leaves and petals lay at my feet like a wedding buttonhole disassembled.

And in the middle of the trunk my father's smiling face, captured while he was seated at the top table illuminated by candlelight. It mirrored the tealights dotted about, a startling effect that made the picture I'd affixed to the tree look like a window. As if he was inside peering out.

At the centre a pair of glasses, one arm splattered with matt white emulsion.

I stepped back then to see the effect. Twinkling lights and the muffle of falling incense ash against the pin-drop night.

When I had pressed 'print' I hadn't been sure. It felt like a pretension. But all together now it looked correct. It would confound anyone who might stumble across this little altar of mine, and I liked this cryptic eulogy. Halfway up the trunk, I placed the paper with his name in ogham, the runic tree language of the Celts, a language that runs from bottom to top, from root to sky:

Dusk settled then and for a moment the forest seemed a deep navy sea, storm-tossed and heaving, and this little illuminated scene the only lighthouse.

'He probably would have found this a bit daft.'

'It's not for him,' said Michael.

The wind stirred, filling me with something close to a thrill. Cailleach, the hag who brings winter, can transform herself into a deer. Earlier in the day we'd been stunned by a sudden flash of taupe across the path ahead and a bright white tail dashing into the woods.

When the candles were nearly out I picked up anything that couldn't be eaten by the forest and slipped the glasses into my coat pocket.

'We can stay as long as you want,' said Michael.

But the sun had set, and for people long ago that meant a new day, and this sunset specifically, a new year. This time last year he'd given me away and now the wheel had turned and it was time for me to do the same. We begin again. Everything begins with darkness, like a seed in the earth.

I slipped on my gloves as the forest exhaled us.

'Did I ever tell you about the time Dad punched a goose for swallowing my glove?'

'Not just ran off with it? Actually *ate* it?'

'Yes! Before Lewis was born, so I must have been two or so. It's how I learnt the words "cheeky" and "bastard".'

Over a field of dying wildflowers I conjured the stuff that would ward off that second death, at least until we reached the pub in the village. Woodsmoke in the air told us we weren't too many miles away and the bonfire in the beer garden had already been lit. The trail was nearly invisible in the gloom, but I knew the way out.

SELECTED BIBLIOGRAPHY

Autumn

Folklore and Mythology Electronic Texts, folk tales collected by D.L. Ashliman: https://sites.pitt.edu/~dash/folktexts.html.

'Cinderella' ('*Aschenputtel*'), Grimm, Jacob and Wilhelm, *Kinder- und Hausmärchen*, vol. 1, 7th edn (Verlag der Dieterichschen Buchhandlung, 1857): 119–26.

'Like Good Salt' from 'Venetian Popular Legends', *Cornhill Magazine* (July 1875): 80–83.

Ferdowsi, Abolqasem, *The Shahnameh: The Persian Book of Kings*, trans. Davis, Dick (Penguin Classics, 2016).

Murray, Sarah, *Making an Exit: From the Magnificent to the Macabre – How We Dignify the Dead* (Coptic, 2011).

Jung, C.G, *The Archetypes and the Collective Unconscious (Collected Works, vol. 9 part 1)*, trans. Hull R.F.C. (Routledge & Kegan Paul, 1968).

Dumézil, Georges, *The Stakes of the Warrior*, trans. Weeks, David; ed. Puhvel, Jaan (University of California Press, 1983).

Eson, Lawrence, 'Odin and Merlin: Threefold Death and the World Tree', *Western Folklore* 69(1) (2010): 85–107.

The Historical Library of Diodorus the Sicilian in Fifteen Books, to Which are Added the Fragments of Diodorus, 2 vols, trans. Booth, G. (W. McDowall, 1814): https://archive.org/details/bub_gb_agd-e LVNRMMC.

Doughty, Caitlin, *From Here to Eternity: Travelling the World to Find the Good Death* (Weidenfeld & Nicolson, 2017).

Lunde, Paul, *Ibn Fadlan and the Land of Darkness: Arab Travellers in the Far North* (Penguin Classics, 2011).

Beowulf: An Anglo-Saxon Epic Poem, trans. Hall, Lesslie (D.C. Heath & Co., 1892).

Kelly, John, *The Great Mortality: An Intimate History of the Black Death* (Fourth Estate, 2005).

Lysaght, Patricia, '*Caoineadh Os Cionn Coirp*: the lament for the dead in Ireland', *Folklore* 108 (1997): 65–82.

Bushnell Jr, D. I., *Native Cemeteries and Forms of Burial East of the Mississippi*. Smithsonian Institution. Bureau of American Ethnology. Bulletin 71. Washington (1920).

Harrington, C. and Sprowl, B., 'Family members' experiences with viewing in the wake of sudden death', *OMEGA – Journal of Death and Dying* 64(1) (2011): 65–82.

Chapple, A. and Ziebland, S., 'Viewing the body after bereavement due to a traumatic death: qualitative study in the UK', *British Medical Journal,* 30 April 2010.

H.J. Blackham, quoted in *Ethical Record, The Proceedings of the South Place Ethical Society* 106(7) (2001).

Buchan, James, 'Ayatollah Khomeini's funeral: the funeral of Ayatollah Khomeini was not a tragedy but a gruesome farce', *New Statesman*, 12 March 2009.

McVeigh, Tracy, 'Diana's death prompted big rise in suicide rate', *Observer*, 28 October 2000.

Winter

Codd, Daniel, 'Supernatural evil: necromancers, wisemen and toadmen', *Mysterious Cambridgeshire* (DB Publishing, 2010).

'The Lincoln Imp', BBC, 1 September 2005.

Balfour, M.C., 'Legends of the Cars', *Folklore* 2(2) (1891): 145–70.

Rudkin, E.H., 'Folklore of Lincolnshire: especially the low-lying areas of Lindsey', *Folklore* 66(4) (1955):385–400.

Hurst, James, 'The Scarlet Ibis', first published in *The Atlantic*, July 1960. Accessed from: https://www.theatlantic.com/magazine/archive/1960/07/the-scarlet-ibis/657805/.

Swanton, Michael, *The Dream of the Rood* (University of Exeter Press, 1987).

Russell, Claire, 'The Life Tree and the Death Tree', *Folklore* 92(1) (1981): 56–66.

Cook, Stanley Arthur, 'Tree-Worship', in Chisholm, Hugh (ed.), *Encyclopædia Britannica*, 11th edn (Cambridge University Press, 1911).

Wordsworth, William, 'Yew-Trees', *The Collected Poems of William Wordsworth* (Wordsworth Editions, 2005).

Blair, Robert, 'The Grave', *The Book of Georgian Verse*, ed. Braithwaite, William Stanley (Grant Richards, 1909).

Frazer, James George, *The Golden Bough: A Study in Magic and Religion* (Macmillan & Co., 1890).

Schillace, Brandy, *Death's Summer Coat: What the History of Death and Dying Teaches Us About Life and Living* (Elliott & Thompson, 2015).

Chainey, Dee Dee, and Winsham, Willow, *Treasury of Folklore: Woodlands and Forests: Wild Gods, World Trees and Werewolves* (Batsford, 2021).

Lee, M.R., 'The yew tree (*Taxus baccata*) in mythology and medicine', *Journal of the Royal College of Physicians of Edinburgh* 28(4) (1998): 569–75.

Grambo, Ronald, 'Ritual crying in folk tradition', *Anthropos* 66(5/6) (1971): 938–45.

Carey, Frances, *The Tree: Meaning and Myth* (British Museum, 2012).

Silber, Mark, DeWolf, Jr, Gordon, 'Yews in fiction and fact', *Arnoldia* 30(4) (1970): 139–47.

Miller, S. I., and Schoenfeld, L., 'Grief in the Navajo: psychodynamics and culture', *International Journal of Social Psychiatry*, 19(3–4) (1973): 187–91.

Bowlby, John, *Attachment and Loss* (Basic Books, 1969–82).

Stroebe, M. and Schut, H., 'The dual process model of coping with bereavement: rationale and description', *Death Studies* 23(3) (1999): 197–224.

Humphrey, Sheryl, *The Haunted Garden: Death and Transfiguration in the Folklore of Plants* (Lulu.com, 2012).

Frazer, J.G., *The Belief in Immortality and the Worship of the Dead*, (Macmillan, 1913): https://www.giffordlectures.org/lectures/belief-immortality-and-worship-dead.

Boss, Pauline, *Ambiguous Loss: Learning to Live with Unresolved Grief* (Harvard University Press, 1999).

Werner, E.T.C., *Myths and Legends of China* (G.G. Harrap & Co., 1922)

Sharma, Arvind, *Sati: Historical and Phenomenological Essays* (Motilal Banarsidass, 2001).

Folklore and Mythology Electronic Texts, Folk tales collected by D.L. Ashliman: https://sites.pitt.edu/~dash/folktexts.html.

'Wooden Johannes' ('*Von einem hölzern Johannas*', Kirchhof, Hans Wilhelm, *Wendunmuth* 1, ed. Österley, Hermann (H. Laupp, 1869): 388–9.

Boyle, P.J., Z. Feng and G.M. Raab, 'Does widowhood increase mortality risk?: testing for selection effects by comparing causes of spousal death', *Epidemiology* 22(1) (2011): 1–5: https://journals. lww.com/epidem/Fulltext/2011/01000/Does_ Widowhood_Increase_Mortality_Risk___Testing.1.aspx.

Spring

Chainey, Dee Dee, and Willow Winsham, *Treasury of Folklore – Seas and Rivers: Sirens, Selkies and Ghost Ships* (Batsford, 2021).

Living on Earth podcast, 'Unraveling the Myths and Mysteries of the Tides', 5 May 2017.

Aldersey-Williams, Hugh, 'On the Irresistible Pull of Tidal Metaphors: The Language of Love and Death Deep Beneath the Sea', *Literary Hub*, 20 September 2016: https://lithub.com/on-the-irresistible-pull-of-tidal-metaphors/.

Rees, W.D., 'The Hallucinations of Widowhood', *British Medical Journal* 4(5778) (1971): 39–41.

Ratcliffe, M., 'Sensed Presence Without Sensory Qualities: A Phenomenological Study of Bereavement Hallucinations', *Phenomenology of the Cognitive Sciences* 20 (2021): 601–616.

Datson, S.L., and S.J. Marwit, 'Personality constructs and perceived presence of deceased loved ones', *Death Studies* 21(2) (1997): 131–46.

Freud, Sigmund, 'Mourning and melancholia', in Strachey, J. (ed. and trans.), *The Standard Edition of the Complete Psychological Works of Sigmund Freud*, vol. 14 (Hogarth Press, 1953).

Grimby, A., 'Bereavement among elderly people: grief reactions, post-bereavement hallucinations and quality of life', *Acta Psychiatrica Scandinavica* 87(1) (1993): 72–80.

Ratcliffe, Matthew, 'Grief and phantom limbs: a phenomenological comparison', *New Yearbook for Phenomenology and Phenomenological Philosophy* 17 (2019): 1–24.

Isaacs, Jennifer, *Australian Dreaming: 40,000 Years of Aboriginal History*, (New Holland, 1979).

Klass, Dennis, Phyllis R. Silverman and Steven Nickman, *Continuing Bonds: New Understanding of Grief* (Routledge, 1996).

Levinovitz, Alan, *Natural: The Seductive Myth of Nature's Goodness* (Profile Books, 2020).

Folklore and Mythology Electronic Texts, folk tales collected by D.L. Ashliman: https://sites.pitt.edu/~dash/folktexts.html.

The Brothers Grimm, 'The Burial Shirt' ('*Das Totenhemdchen*'), *Kinder- und Hausmärchen*, vol. 2, 7th edn (Verlag der Dieterichschen Buchhandlung, 1857): 120.

'A West African Tale', in Courlander, Harold, and George Herzog, *The Cow-Tail Switch, and Other West African Stories* (Henry Holt & Co., 1947).

Goldie, Peter, *The Mess Inside: Narrative, Emotion, and the Mind* (Oxford University Press, 2012).

Archive of the Royal Naval Patrol Service, maintained by the Royal Naval Patrol Service Association: http://www.rnpsa.co.uk/cms/index.php.

Meurger, Michel, and Claude Gagnon, 'Lake monster traditions: a cross-cultural analysis', (Fortean Tomes, 1988).

Iwasaka, Michiko, *Ghosts and the Japanese: Cultural Experience in Japanese Death Legends* (Utah State University Press, 1994).

Parry, Richard Lloyd, *Ghosts of the Tsunami: Death and Life in Japan* (Jonathan Cape, 2017).

Spinney, Laura, 'Epigenetics, the misunderstood science that could shed new light on ageing', *Guardian*, 10 October 2021.

Summer

Stengel, E., *Suicide and Attempted Suicide* (Penguin, 1969).

Humphrey, Nicholas, 'The lure of death: suicide and human evolution', *Philosophical Transactions of the Royal Society* 373(1754) (2018): 1–7.

Clauss-Ehlers, Caroline, *Encyclopedia of Cross-Cultural School Psychology* (Springer, 2010).

Asala, Joanne, *Polish Folklore and Myth* (Penfield Press, 2001).

Philips, Charles, and Michael Kerrigan, (eds), *Forests of the Vampire: Slavic Myth* (Time-Life, 1999).

Pilkington, Ace, and Pilkington, Olga (eds), *Fairy Tales of the Russians and Other Slavs* (Forest Tsar Press, 2009).

Pérez Cuervo, Maria J., 'Purgatory in Spanish folklore: the night of the ánimas', FolkloreThursday.com, 15 September 2016.

World Health Organization fact sheet on global suicide statistics, published 17 June 2021: https://www.who.int/news-room/fact-sheets/detail/suicide.

Pickering, W.S.F., and Walford, G., *Durkheim's Suicide: A Century of Research and Debate* (Routledge, 2000).

Lönnrot, Elias, *The Kalevala: An Epic Poem After Oral Tradition* (Oxford University Press, 2009).

Pridmore, Saxby, Jamshid Ahmadi and Zainab abd Majeed, 'Suicide in Old Norse and Finnish Folk Stories', *Australasian Psychiatry* 19(4) (2011): 321–4.

Billington, Sandra, 'The Midsummer Solstice as It Was, or Was Not, Observed in Pagan Germany, Scandinavia and Anglo-Saxon England', *Folklore* 119(1) (2008): 41–57.

Foucault, Michel, *Madness and Civilization: A History of Insanity in the Age of Reason*, trans. Howard, Richard (Tavistock Publications, 1967).

Luhrmann, T.M., Padmavati, R., Tharoor, H. and Osei, A., 'Differences in Voice-Hearing Experiences of People with Psychosis in the U.S.A., India and Ghana: Interview-Based Study', *British Journal of Psychiatry* 206(1) (2015): 41–4.

Evans, Zteve T., 'British legends: the madness of Merlin (part 1)', or FolkloreThursday.com, 24 January 2019.

Geoffrey of Monmouth, '*Vita Merlini*', trans. John Jay Parry, *University of Illinois Studies in Language and Literature* 10(3) (1925): https://www.sacred-texts.com/neu/eng/vm/index.htm.

Alighieri, Dante, *Inferno*, trans. Kirkpatrick, Robin (Penguin Classics, 2006).

Gatrell, V.A.C., *The Hanging Tree: Execution and the English People, 1770–1868* (Oxford University Press, 1994).

Hollander, Lee M. (ed.), *The Poetic Edda* (University of Texas Press, 1988)

'Last "sin-eater" celebrated with church service', BBC News, 19 September 2010.

Sedgwick, Icy, 'Inviting sin-eaters to a funeral: fact or folklore?', IcySedgwick.com, 22 February 2020.

'The Stone in the Cellar', in Virág, Zalka Csenge, 'Anxiety folktales (a #FolkloreThursday special)', The Multicolored Diary blog, 8 August 2019.

Sacks, Oliver, *Hallucinations* (Picador, 2012).

Opondo, Philip R., Keneilwe Molebatsi, Anthony Olashore, James Ayugi, Ari Ho-Foster and David Ndetei, 'Mythical and Supernatural Creatures in Psychiatric Symptomatology: Thokolosi in Southern Africa', *International Journal of Culture and Mental Health* 11(3) (2018): 248–54.

MacNeill, Máire, *The Festival of Lughnasa: A Study of the Survival of the Celtic Festival of the Beginning of Harvest* (Oxford University Press, 1962).

Samaritans, 'Dying from Inequality: Socioeconomic Disadvantage and Suicidal Behaviour' (2017): https://media.samaritans.org/documents/Socioeconomic_disadvantage_and_suicidal_behaviour_-_Full.pdf.

Folklore and Mythology Electronic Texts, Folk tales collected by D.L. Ashliman: https://sites.pitt.edu/~dash/folktexts.html.

'Duck Under, Duck Under' ('*Duuk ünner, duuk ünner*') Schütze, Johann Friedrich *Holsteinisches Idiotikon: Ein beitrag zur Volkssittengeschichte*, (Heinrich Ludwig Villaume, 1800): 267.

Fryxell, Anders, *The History of Sweden, Volume 1* (Bibliolife, 2008).

Pidd, Helen, 'Psychosis cases rise in England as pandemic hits mental health', *Guardian*, 17 October 2021: https://www.theguardian.com/society/2021/oct/18/psychosis-cases-soar-in-england-as-pandemic-hits-mental-health.

'Global prevalence and burden of depressive and anxiety disorders in 204 countries and territories in 2020 due to the COVID-19 pandemic', *The Lancet* 398(10312) (2021): 1700–1712: https://www.thelancet.com/journals/lancet/article/PIIS0140-6736(21)02143-7/fulltext.

Rosen, Michael (ed.), *Workers' Tales: Socialist Fairy Tales, Fables, and Allegories from Great Britain*, (Princeton University Press, 2018).

'Tom Hickathrift', ed. Jacobs, Joseph (1894): 65–70.

'Death in a Nutshell', 1001 Stories Collection, Story Museum, Oxford: https://www.storymuseum.org.uk/1001-stories/death-in-a-nutshell.

Tales

Quirino, Carlos, García, Mauro and García, Maria Luisa (trans.), *Boxer Codex: A Modern Spanish Transcription and English Translation of 16th-Century Exploration Accounts of East and Southeast Asia and the Pacific* (Vibal Foundation, 2016).

The Aswang Project, collating myths and legends of the Philippines: https://www.aswangproject.com/

Sabanpan-Yu, Hope, 'The practice of waking the dead in the Philippines', *Philippine Quarterly of Culture & Society* 37(4) (2009): 231–8.

Yanagihara, Hanya, 'A real-life enchanted forest', *New York Times*, 17 May 2018.

Drott, Edward R., *Buddhism and the Transformation of Old Age in Medieval Japan* (University of Hawai'i Press, 2016).

The Kojiki: An Account of Ancient Matters, ed. Yasumaro, Ō no; trans. Heldt, Gustav (Columbia University Press, 2014).

Beckwith, Martha Warren, *Hawaiian Mythology* (University of Hawai'i Press, 1982).

Smith, Robert, *Hiking Oahu, the Capital Isle* (Wilderness Press, 1980).

Kamakau, Samuel Manaiakalani, *Ka Po'e Kahiko: The People of Old*, ed. Barrère, Dorothy B.; trans. Pukui, Mary Kawena (Bishop Museum Press, 1964).

Green, Laura C. and Martha Warren Beckwith, 'Hawaiian customs and beliefs relating to sickness and death', *American Anthropologist* 28(1) (1926): 176–208.

Thrum, Thomas G., *Hawaiian Folk Tales* (A.C. McClurg & Co., 1907).

'Ka'ena Point Natural Reserve' brochure, State of Hawai'i Department of Land and Natural Resources, Division of Forestry and Wildlife, June 2005.

Thomas, Dylan, *Under Milk Wood: A Play for Voices* (J.M. Dent & Sons, 1962).

Thomas, Dylan, 'Light Breaks Where No Sun Shines', 'And Death Shall Have No Dominion', 'The force that through the green fuse drives the flower', 'Poem in October', *The Collected Poems of Dylan Thomas* (New Directions, 2010).

Thomas, Dylan, *A Child's Christmas in Wales* (Orion Children's Books, 2014).

Clarke, Gillian, 'Y Fflam', *Collected Poems* (Carcanet Press, 1997).

Story of Viviane and Merlin, *Vulgate and Post-Vulgate Arthuriad*, *c.* 1230–40.

Heard, Peter, 'The bleeding yews', Nevern Church, St Brynach website: https://www.nevern-church.org.uk/the-bleeding-yews/

Ogham generator, https://ogham.co/

FURTHER READING

Funeral rituals and memorial

Arnold, Catharine, *Necropolis: London and Its Dead* (Simon & Schuster, 2006).

Davies, Douglas J., *Death, Ritual and Belief: The Rhetoric of Funeral Rites* (Continuum, 2002).

Doughty, Caitlin, *From Here to Eternity: Travelling the World to Find the Good Death* (Weidenfeld & Nicolson, 2017).

Kaliff, Anders and Terje Oestigaard, *Cremations, Corpses and Cannibalism: Comparative Cosmologies and Centuries of Cosmic Consumptions* (Cambridge Scholars, 2007).

Murray, Sarah, *Making an Exit: From the Magnificent to the Macabre – How We Dignify the Dead* (Coptic, 2011).

Murray Parkes, Colin, Pittu Laungani and William Young, *Death and Bereavement Across Cultures* (Routledge, 1997).

Puckle, Bertram S., *Funeral Customs: Their Origin and Development* (T. Werner Laurie, 1926).

The Good Funeral Guide: https://www.goodfuneralguide.co.uk/

The Merry Cemetery: https://www.atlasobscura.com/places/merry-cemetery.

The Order of the Good Death: https://www.orderofthegooddeath.com/

Death contemplation and dead bodies

Ars Moriendi; printed by William Caxton, Google e-book: http://bav. bodleian.ox.ac.uk/news/ars-moriendi-the-art-of-dying.

Barley, Nigel, *Dancing on the Grave: Encounters with Death* (John Murray, 1995).

Campbell, Hayley, *All the Living and the Dead: A Personal Investigation into the Death Trade* (Raven Books, 2022).

Connerton, Paul, *The Spirit of Mourning: History, Memory and the Body* (Cambridge University Press, 2011).

Davies, Douglas J., *A Brief History of Death* (Blackwell, 2005).

Laqueur, Thomas W., *The Work of the Dead: A Cultural History of Mortal Remains* (Princeton University Press, 2015).

Mims, Cedric, *When We Die: What Becomes of the Body After Death* (Robinson, 1998).

Mitford, Jessica, *The American Way of Death Revisited* (Virago, 2000).

Shelley, Mary, *Frankenstein; or, The Modern Prometheus* (Lackington, Hughes, Harding, Mavor, & Jones, 1818).

Troyer, John, *Technologies of the Human Corpse* (MIT Press, 2020).

Grief, bereavement and suicide

Adichie, Chimamanda Ngozi, *Notes on Grief* (Fourth Estate, 2021).

Alvarez, Al, *The Savage God: A Study of Suicide* (Bloomsbury, 2002).

Bell, Poorna, *Chase the Rainbow* (Simon & Schuster, 2017).

Boss, Pauline, *Ambiguous Loss: Learning to Live with Unresolved Grief* (Harvard University Press, 1999).

Didion, Joan, *The Year of Magical Thinking* (Fourth Estate, 2005).

Durkheim, Émile, *On Suicide*, trans. Buss, Robin (Penguin, 2006).

Erlbruch, Wolf, *Duck, Death and the Tulip* (Bounce!, 2008).

Lewis, C.S., *A Grief Observed* (Faber & Faber, 2014).

O'Rourke, Meghan, 'Good grief: is there a better way to be bereaved?' *New Yorker*, 1 February 2010.

Vann, David, *Legend of a Suicide* (Penguin, 2009).

Williams, Mark, *Cry of Pain: Understanding Suicide and the Suicidal Mind* (Piatkus, 2014).

Wix, Katy, *Delicacy: A Memoir About Cake and Death* (Headline, 2021).

Podcasts: *Griefcast, Dead Parent Club, Good Mourning, Terrible, Thanks for Asking, The Happiness Lab, Man Talk, How Do You Cope? … With Elis and John*.

Folklore and storytelling

Baring-Gould, S., *Curious Myths of the Middle Ages* (Rivingtons, 1866).

Chainey, Dee Dee and Willow Winsham, *Treasury of Folklore – Seas and Rivers: Sirens, Selkies and Ghost Ships* (Batsford, 2021).

Chainey, Dee Dee and Willow Winsham, *Treasury of Folklore – Woodlands and Forests: Wild Gods, World Trees and Werewolves* (Batsford, 2021).

Dawood, N.J. (ed.), *Tales from the Thousand and One Nights* (Penguin Classics, 1973).

Dorson, Richard M., *Folklore: Selected Essays* (Indiana University Press, 1972).

Folklore, Myths, and Legends of Britain (Reader's Digest Association, 1977).

Frazer, James George, *The Golden Bough: A Study in Magic and Religion* (Macmillan & Co., 1890).

Graves, Robert, *The White Goddess: A Historical Grammar of Poetic Myth* (Faber & Faber, 1948).

Hartland, E.S., *English Fairy and Other Folk Tales* (W. Scott, 1890).

Hazlitt, W. Carew, *Faiths and Folklore of the British Isles: A Descriptive and Historical Dictionary of the Superstitions, Beliefs and Popular Customs of England, Scotland, Wales, and Ireland, from Norman Times to the End of the Nineteenth Century, with Classical and Foreign Analogues* (Reeves and Turner, 1905).

Hollander, Lee M. (ed.), *The Poetic Edda* (University of Texas Press, 1988).

Lönnrot, Elias, *The Kalevala: An Epic Poem After Oral Tradition* (Oxford University Press, 2009).

Manning-Sanders, Ruth, *Festivals* (William Heinemann, 1972).

Ovid, *Metamorphoses*, trans. Mary M. Innes (Penguin Classics, 1955).

Pálsson, Hermann and Paul Edwards (trans. and eds) *Gautrek's Saga and Other Medieval Tales* (University of London Press, 1968).

Virág, Zalka Csenge, The Multicolored Diary: http://multicoloreddiary.blogspot.com/

1001 Stories Collection, The Story Museum, Oxford: https://www.storymuseum.org.uk/1001-stories.

British Library Listening Project, a collection of oral history: https://sounds.bl.uk/Oral-history/The-Listening-Project.

Twitter: @folkhorrormagpi @FolkloreThurs @folk_horror @Library Folklore @HooklandGuide.

Instagram: @folkhorrormagpie @fantastic_folk @folktaleweek @folkwayschannel @thefolkarchive @helleborezine @weird_walk @museum_of_british_folklore @museum_of_witchcraft_and_magic @nationalfolklorecollection.

Nature and tree worship

Adams, Max, *The Wisdom of Trees: A Miscellany* (Head of Zeus, 2014)

Baker, Margaret, *Discovering the Folklore of Plants* (Shire Publications, 1996).

Cook, Stanley Arthur, 'Tree-Worship', in Chisholm, Hugh (ed.), *Encyclopædia Britannica*, 11th edn (Cambridge University Press, 1911).

Humphrey, Sheryl, *The Haunted Garden: Death and Transfiguration in the Folklore of Plants* (Lulu.com, 2012).

Lehner, Johanna and Ernst, *Folklore and Symbolism of Flowers, Plants and Trees* (Dover Publications, 2003).

Long Litt Woon, *The Way Through the Woods: Of Mushrooms and Mourning*, trans. Haveland, Barbara (Scribe, 2019).

Sheldrake, Merlin, *Entangled Life: How Fungi Make Our Worlds, Change Our Minds and Shape Our Futures* (The Bodley Head, 2020).

SIGNPOSTS

In the UK

Samaritans, providing listening and support to anyone in need: https://www.samaritans.org/
  24-hour helpline: 116 123

Shout 24-hour text service: text SHOUT to 85258

Campaign Against Living Miserably: https://www.thecalmzone.net/
  Helpline 0800 58 58 58 and web-chat for men struggling with suicidal thoughts

Papyrus under-35s helpline: 0800 068 4141 https://www.papyrus-uk.org/

Rethink Mental Illness, support and counselling: https://www.rethink.org/

Mind, mental health resources and support: https://www.mind.org.uk/

Survivors of Bereavement by Suicide, community-led support groups: https://uksobs.org/

Suicide & Co, support and low-cost counselling after suicide bereavement: https://www.suicideandco.org/

Winston's Wish, support for children and young people bereaved by suicide: https://www.winstonswish.org/

National Suicide Prevention Alliance, a collaboration between several organisations to reduce the suicide rate in the UK: https://nspa.org.uk/

Zero Suicide Alliance, providing individual and workplace training in suicide prevention https://www.zerosuicidealliance.com/

Cruse Bereavement Support, for anyone experiencing bereavement and grief: https://www.cruse.org.uk/

In the USA and Canada

988 Suicide & Crisis Lifeline, 24-hour helpline for people in suicidal crisis available anywhere by dialling 988: https://988lifeline.org/

The Veterans Crisis Line, crisis support for military veterans and their families: https://www.veteranscrisisline.net/
Textline: 838255

The Trevor Project, 24-hour webchat for LGBTQ+ youth in crisis: https://www.thetrevorproject.org/

Trans Lifeline, crisis intervention resources for the transgender community: https://translifeline.org/

SAVE, grief support for suicide survivors in USA: https://save.org/

Talk Suicide Canada, toll-free national helpline for people who experiencing suicidal thoughts: 1-833-456-4566
https://talksuicide.ca/

Canadian Association for Suicide Prevention, awareness around suicide and support in English and French: https://suicideprevention.ca/

Children's Grief Foundation of Canada, providing support to grieving children: https://childrensgrieffoundation.org/

In Australia and New Zealand

Lifeline Australia, listening and support for people experiencing crisis: https://www.lifeline.org.au/
Helpline: 13 11 14

Beyond Blue, supporting mental health and suicide prevention: https://www.beyondblue.org.au/

Life Matters New Zealand, suicide bereavement support and postvention: https://www.lifematters.org.nz/

ACKNOWLEDGEMENTS

So many people have worked in ordinary and extraordinary ways to get this book into print, and foremost among them is my literary agent – and folk community grandee – Joanna Swainson. Joanna snatched my submission from the brink of obscurity, guided it on its way with sensitivity and wisdom, and got me through more than one crisis of confidence. For supporting *her*, I am also indebted to the Hardman & Swainson family: Caroline, Hannah, Nicole, and particularly Thérèse Coen and Hana Murrell for international rights.

Thank you to all at Rider and the wider Ebury team, and to so many across Penguin Random House for all their time and work on my behalf. I am especially thankful to Bianca Bexton for commissioning this peculiar idea for a book and for course-setting with invaluable guidance and instinct. Holly Whitaker carved my colossus of a first draft into the shapely form you are holding now and turbo-thrusted the whole ship (with a keen editorial eye for my tendency toward mixed metaphors). Thank you also to Olivia Morris for reassurance and encouragement.

My gratitude to Alice Brett for choosing the frankly intimidating occupation of copy-editing and performing it with sniper-like precision, as well as the proofreader Zoë Jellicoe for catching all my misteaks.

Everyone in the communications team worked tirelessly on this project. I am particularly grateful for the Campaign Lead Morgana Chess, Katie Cregg from Publicity and Jessica Cselko from Marketing, who listened to my ideas and piloted the campaign with the utmost respect and sensitivity. A huge thank you also to the assistants and interns behind the scenes, who do so much easily overlooked but vital work.

I also wish to give my appreciation to Jess Anderson in Editorial, Phil Spencer in Production, Aslan Byrne, Rachel Myers and Antony De Rienzo in Sales, Ashleigh James in Audio, Vanessa Milton and Nathalie Coupland in Legal, Brendan Murphy in Finance, Alicia Ofori in Contracts, and all of their talented and motivated teams.

I knew right from the beginning that *The Bleeding Tree* should be beautiful. The illustrations and cover design supplied by Sindre Pettersen surpassed all expectations. They are cryptic and dreamlike and full of runic meaning, exactly what I hoped this book could be. Thank you, Sindre, for agreeing to illustrate, I feel extraordinarily fortunate to have had you involved.

The essay that would become this book was published in the Canadian magazine *Folklore for Resistance* in March 2021. I am deeply indebted to its editors, Becka Nathan and Julie Yerex, for allowing me the space to explore these ideas at a time when I was still in thrall to them. Their important work around decolonisation, reconciliation and anticapitalism through the lens of folklore and ancestry continues to inspire.

For research help I would like to give thanks to the Royal Naval Patrol Service Association museum and archives; Kory Penney at the Maritime History Archive at the Memorial University of Newfoundland, Canada; and Anna Murphy of the Local History Library in Grimsby, UK. Thank you also to the staff of the British Library and to Amy McMullen at the British Museum for all the ILL requests. Thank you to Estelle

Asselin at the Connective Space, and to Heath Hands. Thank you to Louise Coggle-Smith at Co-op Funeralcare. I was delighted to discover the Heenan Footsteps website – 'on the trail of Heenans worldwide' – and its carefully maintained records were such a big help. Thank you to its diligent authors for introducing me to a family tree more vast and more colourful than I ever knew. I hope my small addition to the canon is sufficient.

People I have met in the folk horror spaces on- and off-line have gifted me countless diversions and rabbit holes. Thank you especially to anyone who follows me at @folkhorrormagpie.

Completing a book like this requires a whole network of personal support, which I am fortunate to have had in abundance.

I am so very grateful for my suicide bereavement counsellor, Rebecca McKenzie, and the support team at Rethink Camden. My gratitude to David Thorne for early intervention, and with whom many of the ideas that would put me on course to conceive this book were first discussed (among other less comprehensible noises). Thank you especially to Dr Chenduraan Kailayapillai at St Pancras Hospital mental health service for listening and for getting me back on track.

At the big place with the columns a huge thank you to Amanda Gregory for all the help and representation (join a union!), a massive *tak min kære ven* to Ashley Kelleher for mutual support in the trenches (January–June inclusive), much appreciation to Jim Hamill for the last-minute fact-checking, and my continuing gratitude to Corinne Stritter for her kindness and the stress buckets.

Many thanks to Marty and Gabriella for the neighbourly company, to Merlin Trotter, all the chip shops in Cleethorpes, Hawker's Kitchen on Caledonian Road, and Olivia Rodrigo for *Sour*.

My gratitude to Dad's colleagues, including Nicola, Rick, Mark, Sarah and especially Andy Carr, who was the first person to make me laugh after it happened, whose generosity of spirit and deed is unmatched, and who puts on a cracking mobile disco at a very reasonable price point: call for rates. Sean Jacklin, are you tired of hearing me say it? Well, here it is in print: thank you, thank you, thank you. I'll stop when you stop.

Thank you to all the dead, my unknowable antecedents who became a little more knowable.

Much love and thanks to Cathy and Ray Starling for having such ironclad belief in me, and for providing a quiet space to write when I was going a bit crackers. I continue to appreciate that I won the in-law lottery.

Awkward hugs to Peter Burgess for doing the big read. It is an enormous time debt owed and I'm not sure I can convey my gratitude: there are vanishingly few people I would trust with unfinished words. Thank you particularly for accepting that any errors are yours and that I bear no responsibility for them. Pint soon?

Masses of appreciation to Tom Gibbs and Isabel Abril Fernandez for cheerleading throughout and for a restorative weekend in Canterbury that helped me more than they know.

Wonderful Richelle Freeman: though our friendship may forever remain hemispherically-challenged I know I can always rely on the constancy of your empathy and insight. And for my camera roll to be full of pictures of Lil from slightly different angles. Thank you.

Thank you to Carly Vickers and Charlie Dwyer for unwavering support in the group chat. Hello and welcome to baby Vickers: I hope you are enjoying the world so far.

To Dad's sisters, Ros, Sarah and Judith, for loving him and for keeping the precious stories. Auntie Sarah: for being so generous with your time and for so many anecdotes that didn't make it to the book, from the poignant to the hilarious. Thank you, Auntie Ros, for filling in so much and for sharing all the photos. I also want to thank my cousin Adele Marie Heenan for her diligence and understanding.

To Lewis: I intentionally misremembered minor details knowing it would incense you because this is funny to me. Thank you for letting me say what I needed to, for being my talented, kind and funny brother as well as my very good friend. Sorry about your trainers. Isabella: thank you for taking care of him, answering all my translation queries, and for enlivening my weather-beaten little family with your contagious warmth.

Mum, thank you for your inspirational fortitude and keeping me afloat with your love. I am inconceivably lucky to have you as a mother.

The lion's share of my gratitude has to go to my husband Michael, the only person who I let take care of me and really the only person who knows how. Especially when I don't. Thank you for never letting go even when I was barely tethered to the world.

The final acknowledgement is of course the only one I can't give directly. Forgive me. I love you.

ABOUT THE AUTHOR

HOLLIE STARLING IS A WRITER and folklorist from the North East of England whose essays have appeared in *Folklore for Resistance*, *Horrified* magazine, the journal of *The London Horror Society* and *Lincolnshire Strange Delights*. Hollie currently works in the libraries of a national museum. She runs the page Folk Horror Magpie (@folkhorrormagpie) on social media.